“Has there been a more urgent time for cultivating the prophetic imagination in our teaching and learning spaces? Has the need for courage that emboldens us to better understand and accompany those we teach been greater? How deeply do we long to channel the kind of hope that attunes our students for the good amid the ‘roar and tumult’ of these days and calls forth their gifts to grow it? If your pedagogical vocation, or even your weary soul, needs a shot of any of these, the wisdom curated here is sure to deliver.”

—Maureen O’Connell, PhD

“At a time when colleges and universities are under extraordinary political pressure to be silent rather than prophetic, this volume makes the case for why and how the religious commitments of the institutions and faculty often compel prophetic education. Experienced and pedagogically thoughtful faculty share ways of teaching that help students see and face suffering and injustice, find their voices, and be active agents of hope in the world.”

—Thomas M. Landy, director, Rev. Michael C. McFarland, S.J. Center for Religion, Ethics and Culture, College of the Holy Cross, and founder of Collegium, a colloquy on faith and intellectual life

“Right now, the academy needs this book to reinforce the enduring principles of Catholic social teaching and to give colleagues renewed license to anchor their pedagogy and leadership in these convictions. It reads like a conversation among colleagues, wrestling with how to translate the prophetic into the teachable. *Beneath the Roar and Tumult* is not just a tool kit for good practice. Its publication is, in fact, a compelling example of the prophetic imagination in action.”

—Donna M. Carroll, president, Association of Catholic Colleges and Universities

Beneath the Roar and Tumult

Promoting Radical Hospitality and Belonging in College Classrooms

Edited by
Rachel Wheeler and Karen E. Eifler

LITURGICAL PRESS
ACADEMIC

Collegeville, Minnesota
litpress.org

Cover image courtesy of Getty Images.

Scripture quotations are taken from the New Revised Standard Version Updated Edition. Copyright © 2021 National Council of Churches of Christ in the United States of America. Used by permission. All rights reserved worldwide.

"Protesters" by Denise Levertov, from *Evening Train*, copyright © 1992 by Denise Levertov. Reprinted by permission of New Directions Publishing Corp.

Library of Congress Cataloging-in-Publication Data

Names: Wheeler, Rachel editor | Eifler, Karen E. editor
Title: Beneath the roar and tumult : promoting radical hospitality and belonging in college classrooms / edited by Rachel Wheeler and Karen E. Eifler.
Description: Collegeville, Minnesota : Liturgical Press Academic, [2025] | Includes bibliographical references. | Summary: "Beneath the Roar and Tumult is a collection of essays from faculty in Catholic higher education who offer strategies that embolden students to utilize a prophetic lens to see the world as it is and to creatively imagine a better way forward"—Provided by publisher.
Identifiers: LCCN 2025021504 (print) | LCCN 2025021505 (ebook) | ISBN 9780814689592 trade paperback | ISBN 9780814689608 epub | ISBN 9798400802300 pdf
Subjects: LCSH: Catholic universities and colleges | Social justice—Religious aspects—Catholic Church
Classification: LCC LC487 .B46 2025 (print) | LCC LC487 (ebook)
LC record available at https://lccn.loc.gov/2025021504
LC ebook record available at https://lccn.loc.gov/2025021505

Contents

Part II: The Epicenter

Welcoming who and what have been excluded as we cultivate hospitality

Preface

The Catholic intellectual tradition has many treasures. Two of them are especially vital to contemporary Catholic education: sacramental imagination and prophetic imagination. The first draws from the sense that beauty (and all materiality) expresses something important about the Creator. Sacramentally, beauty draws us to contemplation of order, purpose, and meaning—human needs that, if unmet, create susceptibilities to injustice, harm, and trauma. Our human creativity as beauty-makers functions sacramentally to share with others a sense of how the elements of our world express something fundamental and grace-filled. Even those without a religious sensibility can participate in this process when focusing on connecting with others and deepening their experience. Practical exercises for honing students' sacramental imaginations were provided in this book's companion, *Becoming Beholders.*

This book points us to the second vital treasure for Catholic education today: the prophetic imagination. A key role in the vocation of teaching at Catholic colleges and universities is to help students hone their instruments of sense perception, equipping them to see all that their eyes can see and hear all that their ears can hear. Seeing may be believing, but it is also often the case that believing is seeing. That is, the imaginative lens one dons to observe any phenomenon will determine what one perceives. The sacramental and prophetic imaginations may be conceived of as a Möbius strip; each exists in ongoing tension with the other. Our neverending task is not only to seek out and celebrate the sacred, but also to reflect on it—to question and look again, and to perceive all that can be perceived. This can be difficult and even painful when what we discern is unsettling. Given the challenges of the twenty-first century, college students and those who work with them have a heightened sensitivity to injustice. Learning during the COVID-19 pandemic and racial reckoning in the United States meant coming to terms with countless disparities in equity and access. In addition, concurrent climate crises compromise our hope for a human-friendly future. Many of us have become the protesters of which Denise Levertov's poem speaks, which inspired the title of this book:

> **Protesters**
> Living on the rim
> of the raging cauldron, disasters
>
> witnessed but
> not suffered in the flesh.
>
> The choice: to speak
> or not to speak.
> We spoke.
>
> Those of whom we spoke
> had not that choice.
>
> At every epicenter, beneath
> roar and tumult,
>
> enforced:
> their silence.

Poets such as Denise Levertov evoke the trauma of severed relationships among humans, between humans and the rest of creation, and between humans and our Creator. They also evoke the beauty of restoration and inspire their readers to take up the hard but satisfying work of realizing that restoration. In "Protesters," Levertov describes the vulnerable position of those of us who contribute to and read a book like this: witnesses of trauma who are only indirectly affected by it. "On the rim," she names this position, we have a decision to make: to speak or not to speak of these disasters of the past two centuries. She reminds us that most of those who endured these disasters did not have the choice we have now. What will we do with our power to speak?

The Role of Prophets

These are days of roar and tumult. The painful realities of our time have shaped the students who show up in college classrooms, led by teachers who are themselves part of a tectonic shift in the profession of higher education. Public confidence in the worth of a college degree is low, exacerbated by soaring costs and a rapidly changing workforce. Catholic higher education is not immune to any of these challenges; the landscape of Catholic higher education often appears to be hopelessly corporatized, with students and their parents treated as customers whose demands must be assuaged. Relying on vulnerable, contingent faculty simply to try to keep an institution's doors open seems counter to precepts of Catholic social teaching.

Prophetic imagination may be blossoming already in the consciousness of young people for whom recognition of injustice has become normative. Ready to call out wrong when they detect it and eager to expect their peers and elders to act with mature responsibility, our students (and we ourselves) may too easily mischaracterize the "other" as beyond redemption. Prophetic imagination is a useful concept for harmonizing the imbalance emerging in our time between righteous indignation and self-righteous contempt, between honest accountability and cancel culture. What might be lacking in young people's approaches is a vision of hope that the biblical prophetic imagination provides.

Biblical prophetic imagination is premised on commitments to care for the orphan, widow, and stranger. In the Israelites' patriarchal society, the orphan and widow were particularly vulnerable, and the community was supposed to exercise radical kinship by taking up the part of a lost father or husband. The stranger or the exile was also to be specially cared for because the biblical peoples were meant to remain mindful that they themselves had been strangers among foreigners when enslaved, a part of their foundational history. Because of their own history of trauma, they were to embody radical hospitality to all who lived among them. Empathy undergirds this biblical commitment. Biblical prophets repeatedly called on the Israelite communities to fulfill this commitment.

For the biblical peoples, prophetic imagination exposed unjust power relations and described how insecurity often leads to selfishness, and points out how securing one's own safety often compromises others' well-being. Today, these concerns persist in our human societies, which are prone to habits of entitlement and complacency. Indeed, they may even be exacerbated by our addictive technologies, which make some of our lives easier and yet also enable us to more readily ignore the destruction they cause elsewhere. Prophets of today continue to call out misogyny, racism, and class and social inequities; they criticize the culture and prod us to consider the implications of our unjust actions and invent possibilities for establishing justice.

The Möbius strip of sacramental and prophetic imaginations contains what biblical theologian Walter Brueggeman describes as the *denouncing* activity of identifying and calling out injustice, coupled with the *announcing* activity of hope, joy, and freedom as justice is enacted. As a consequence, prophets not only lament but they also hope. Their hope is an act of imagination based on reason and logic. They discern connections between current actions and future consequences, and they call people's attention to these connections, empowering them through a commitment to the vulnerable. Prophets provide beautiful visions of a world restored, of relationships between the human and more-than-human members of Earth's community, at ease with and enjoying one another through the human commitment to social justice. The biblical prophet, Isaiah, proclaims, for instance:

> If you offer your food to the hungry
>   and satisfy the needs of the afflicted,
> then your light shall rise in the darkness
>   and your gloom be like the noonday.
> The LORD will guide you. (Isa 58:10-11)

The Role of Creativity in Prophetic Imagination

Prophets are often artists. On the one hand, they exhort us to envision future scenarios in which climate change and social inequality have devastated human cultures and people's bioregional homes. On the other hand, they may also envision what's possible if justice is restored, capitalizing on the essential need to imagine something first to make it possible. When partnering sacramental and prophetic imagination, the artist creates a powerful connection between the past and present, and the present and the future, using creativity and art to generate the energy needed to establish justice and transform blighted landscapes, internal and external.

From our tenuous position of safety, we can now give prophetic voice to naming and lamenting disasters, in solidarity with others, and co-imagine abundant futures for those most in need of such a vision, wresting us away from lives of complacency. Our acknowledging the enforced silence of the oppressed may erupt in not only the "roar and tumult" of the world in which we are now immersed, but also in the future to which this roar and tumult leads. Levertov asks us: Will we be complicit in enforcing the silence of the oppressed, or will we contribute to what may from our limited vantage point look chaotic and unformed but is really gesturing toward a more just and abundant future for humans and the more-than-humans?

While this moment calls for educators whose prophetic imagination can evoke their students' acknowledgment of pain and suffering amid hope and meaningful action, use of generative artificial intelligence (AI) tools may compromise their and our capacity for imaginative thinking and dreaming. For some, it may feel liberating to have access to tools that will slash their teaching preparation time and help them evaluate work more fairly and quickly. More expansively, prophetic creativity may also prompt educators' imaginations to go further in designing class activities to more fully engage our distracted, jaded students. When used as a tool to bolster, and not supplant, our creativity as educators, generative AI may create spaces for educators to answer the profound questions we need to address: What is education? What is learning? What skills and dispositions do students most need to meet the challenges of their lifetimes? How might learning these new tools alongside students contribute to deeper collaboration in the classroom?

Suggestions for Exploring This Book

These moments of roar and tumult demand the muscularity of Christian hope. Declaring 2025 to be a Jubilee Year focused on hope, Pope Francis noted, "Even when many around us have succumbed to disillusionment, those who are inspired by hope . . . are able to get through the darkest of nights." He linked our need to hope with the practice of patience, suggesting that without hope and patience, we lack "the courage to make decisions that commit us for a lifetime."[1] Ultimately, this volume is one of muscular hope.

1. Pope Francis, "General Audience," May 8, 2024, https://www.vatican.va/content/francesco/en/audiences/2024/documents/20240508-udienza-generale.html.

We have used elements of Levertov's poem to form the three sections in this book. Part I, "On the Rim," offers essays in which the authors look on from a place where disasters are witnessed but not suffered directly by themselves or their students. That place offers enough critical distance to elicit deep, often unsettling, critical conversations with and among learners. In Part II, "The Epicenter," you will be immersed in conversation with colleagues from fields as disparate as communication studies and community nursing who describe how they go about cultivating spaces of authentic belonging. These spaces of silence nurture students and colleagues to be ready to speak and act in ways that deeply matter. Essays in Part III, "The Choice: To Speak or Not to Speak," describe pedagogies that form learners into ethical decision-makers, prepared to engage their prophetic imaginations to discern and ultimately take positive actions to reform some part of their world.

Of course, most of these essays could be at home in any of the three sections, as the sacred work of educating—whether from the Latin *educare* ("to nourish") or *educere* ("to draw forth")—minds, hearts, and hands tends to defy impulses to silo approaches and tools. All three parts offer pieces in which authors tap the deep wellsprings of their various institutions' founding charisms and engage explicitly with the broader mission of Catholic higher education, often reimagining venerable contemplative practices to help their students and colleagues form habits of mind and heart that sustain the unceasing work of healing the world. All three parts offer insights into community-based learning that honors the wisdom and genuine needs of partners outside the academy. In each part you will encounter educators who are honest about their own journeys to re-vision their roles to teach from a stance of vulnerability and humility.

This book emerged at the request of alumni of Collegium, a national colloquy on faith and intellectual life that helps faculty of all disciplines at Catholic colleges and universities understand their crucial role in integrating their institutions' founding missions—including the fullness of the Catholic imagination—across the curriculum. While its companion book *Becoming Beholders* supports infusing the sacramental aspect of Catholic imagination into college teaching, recent Collegium alumni noted the absence of similar help for cultivating students' abilities to identify the world's brokenness and envision sustainable constructive responses: the work of the prophetic imagination. A call went out to Collegium's three thousand alumni, and this book is the result.

Each essay in this volume is written by a teacher or team of teachers recognized by their institutions for their consummate skills at meeting the needs of the students in their classrooms, students who are very different from those of a generation ago. Although each author writes from within a particular discipline, every essay contains strategies and ways of leaning into one's teaching vocation that work in multiple contexts. You may start with a piece from your own field, and that will certainly bear rich fruit. We also suggest you read a piece from someone whose discipline seems far removed from yours, and ask yourself as you encounter their ideas, "How might I tweak this for my own unique context?" This book lends itself well to faculty reading groups, with participants creating a warp and weft of ideas that, taken together, produce a tapestry of inspired teaching. This can be especially robust when accompanied by even the simplest refreshments.

All essays here are self-contained, but you may find yourself inspired to do some digging into the documents of your own institution. For instance, several authors draw on the charisms of their schools' founding orders; what are the essential principles of your institution's founding order or body? You may be inspired to retrieve the documents from your own now-distant new faculty orientation. In other pieces, authors writing from disparate fields reimagine institutional rituals and traditions in ways that may catalyze your own thinking about revitalizing practices at your institution to tackle the daunting challenges of our present moment. That sort of translation—making the venerable practices and languages of institutions' founding bodies accessible to a generation for whom those might be altogether new—embodies the intentional, active inclusion this volume intends to foster.

We have the luxury to choose to speak for those who have not had that choice, whether people or more-than-human inhabitants of our shared planet. We hope that this book offers you ideas to employ your distinct voice, and the voices of your colleagues and students, to contribute to the healing of a world that is both bruised and blessed. Any problem worth tackling will require the wisdom of all the disciplines in the academy. Honing our senses to perceive a myriad of severed relationships and taking meaningful actions to repair them embody the prophetic teacher's sincere welcome to all entrusted to their care. Young people today consistently express a yearning to feel they truly belong. That is one of the unheralded joys of a college classroom: nourishing a space of mutual recognition, love, and respect. We trust the imaginative work of our colleagues represented in this volume will provide you with more of what you need to listen, see, reflect, and accompany our students in this vocation we share.

Rachel Wheeler
Karen E. Eifler
June 2025

PART I

ON THE RIM

Engaging in critical conversations from places where disasters are witnessed, not suffered

RE-UN-DIScover Heuristic

Pedagogical Practices for Imagination and Generative Action

Elizabeth Keenan
Southern Connecticut State University

College students are coming of age during a time of global unrest fueled by the pursuit of political and economic power that disproportionately harms marginalized groups of people through war, violence, famine, forced migration, racism, and poverty. Public leaders spark a sense of urgency with catastrophic language that distorts what is happening, conflating options into good/bad, right/wrong binaries. The demand for profit and followers propels news outlets and social media to cover these events in dramatic, epic ways.

Many young adults feel overwhelmed, powerless, and paralyzed in the face of these immense forces. It is heartbreaking, yet not surprising, that numerous young adults are experiencing depression, anxiety, and other forms of mental health distress. They wonder what they can possibly do to "make a difference" in the world. They also face continued adverse impacts of the coronavirus and rapidly increasing costs of higher education, housing, and other living expenses.[1]

1. American College Health Association, "American College Health Association—National College Health Assessment III: Undergraduate Student Reference Group Executive Summary Spring 2024" (Silver Spring, MD: American College Health Association, 2024).

I came of age in the late 1960s and the 1970s, during the initial implementation of Vatican II and at the height of the Civil Rights Movement, as part of the last wave of middle-class children who could expect to have economic success greater than their parents'. As a white Catholic social work instructor with twenty-plus years of experience, what role can I play to cultivate hope for college students during these challenging times?

My experiences as a Catholic social worker and instructor provide me with a broad understanding of the power of communal action in relation to oppressive forces. I have deep roots in the Benedictine communal tradition of Catholicism, first as a student, and then as an oblate (a layperson who commits to living according to the Rule of St. Benedict).[2] Several professors taught me about Catholic social teaching, including the preferential option for the poor and the pursuit of peace and economic justice for the common good.[3] I also have fifteen years' experience of community organizing with an interfaith, multiracial, nonpartisan, grassroots organization, whose members come together to imagine and work toward what they yearn for. I see higher education as a place both to critique the harmful impacts of dominant culture and institutions and to spark hope and imagination for how things could be otherwise. I pay it forward by providing students with the knowledge and experience to learn how to create the world they want to live in. I reflect on the strategies and aims that Jesus modeled to ground my decisions.

The Power of Imagination

Christian sacred texts present a God incarnate; as a human, Jesus challenged existing religious and political leaders by questioning their integrity and ways of using authority.[4] Jesus did not transform these larger oppressive political and religious structures; rather, he engaged in loving,

2. Timothy Fry, ed., *RB 1980: The Rule of St. Benedict in English* (Collegeville, MN: Liturgical Press, 1981).

3. David J. O'Brien and Thomas A. Shannon, eds., *Catholic Social Thought: Encyclicals and Documents from Pope Leo XIII to Pope Francis*, 3rd rev. ed. (Maryknoll, NY: Orbis, 2019).

4. Jon Sobrino, *Jesus in Latin America* (Maryknoll, NY: Orbis, 1982).

liberating encounters that, like yeast, awaken new life and possibility.[5] A prophetic imagination functions like yeast by bringing life to those who are despairing and binding them into a community with ingredients of recognition, love, and respect. Imagination can also function like a kaleidoscope by taking existing oppressive ingredients and transforming them into a new image, a new creation. Experiencing the power of collective resistance, healing, and resilience creates new images of seeing, making sense of, and dismantling oppression. Through intentional course design, I cultivate students' imaginations through a critical consciousness to read the power dynamics of the world as it is in tandem with strategies and tools from my research and their experience to move toward their imaginings of a world as it could be.

Social work students and students pursuing other professional degrees in education, nursing, public health, and related fields need this scaffolded learning to understand *how* to imagine and achieve the impacts they desire. Students seeking these degrees typically want to help others in the ways *they* have been helped, or in ways they *wished* they had been helped, from a sense of *solidarity* with those who have similar struggles. Although social work students want to have an impact, most do not initially know how to go about it. Pedagogical scaffolding hones their ability to read power as patterns across smaller actions and larger institutional and structural systems, and then to act in ways that are productive, *not* oppressive.[6]

The RE UN DIScover heuristic described in this essay provides scaffolding for students to cultivate the ability to listen with compassion and read a situation with a critical consciousness to imagine everyday, small-scale transformations toward flourishing.[7,8]

5. Mary A. Wagner, *The Sacred World of the Christian: Sensed in Faith* (Collegeville, MN: Liturgical Press, 1993).

6. adrienne maree brown, *Emergent Strategy: Shaping Change, Changing Worlds* (Chico, CA: AK Press, 2017).

7. Elizabeth K. Keenan, "RE/UN/DIScover Heuristic: Working with Clinical Practice Impingements in Dehumanizing Times," *Clinical Social Work Journal* 52 (2024): 253–64, https://doi.org/10.1007/s10615-023-00872-4.

8. Elizabeth K. Keenan, "In the Meantime: RE/UN/DIScover Heuristic for Small-Scale Antioppressive Action within Systems and Organizations," *Social Work* 68, no. 4 (October 2023): 321–30, https://doi.org/10.1093/sw/swad026.

RE-UN-DIScover Heuristic

The RE-UN-DIScover heuristic (see figure 1) is a set of three practices that work in a dialogic manner in changeable order—REcover practices support the openness to "listen with the ear of your heart,"[9] UNcover practices reveal an alternative consciousness through critical frameworks, and DIScover practices imagine the world as it could be with the hope promised by a liberating God.

Figure 1

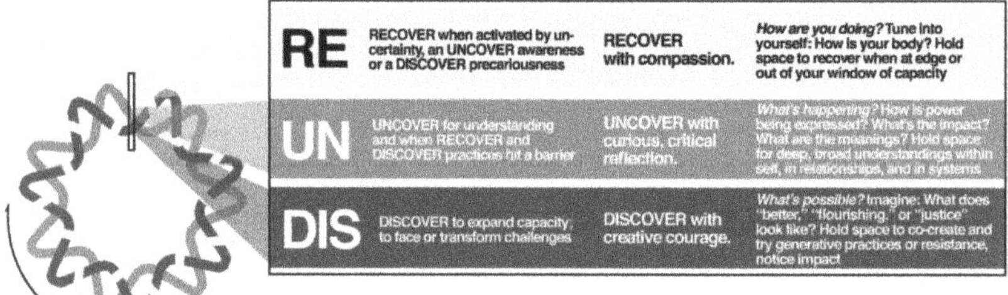

REcover practices facilitate students' ability to listen and respond well in the moment by helping them cope with feeling overly stirred up or depleted. Research from interpersonal neurobiology supports the use of practices to bring one's body back into an optimal range of arousal so that one can listen deeply and fully engage with others.[10] These breathing, grounding, and movement practices quiet the mind, strengthen focus, and cultivate awareness of the interconnectedness of life among oneself, other beings, and God. Contemplative practices from various religious and spiritual traditions cultivate awareness and attention to the present moment, including prayer, meditation, yoga, and mindfulness.[11] A range

9. See Benedict, *Rule*, Prologue.

10. Daniel J. Siegel, *The Developing Mind: How Relationships and the Brain Interact to Shape Who We Are*, 3rd ed. (New York: Guilford Press, 2020).

11. Center for Contemplative Mind in Society, "Body of Practices," accessed August 9, 2024, https://www.contemplativelife.org/body-of-practice#all.

of other practices can also be experienced as contemplative if one brings an intention to have a contemplative experience. Regular practice fosters the ability to be nonjudgmentally present in the moment, aware of one's likes and dislikes without being driven into action by them.

Developing an initial critical consciousness and imagining specific decisions for the common good can feel destabilizing, resulting in paralysis, avoidance, and emotional distress, especially for those who are in advantaged positions. Institutional and systemic critiques can spark cognitive dissonance because a collective perspective runs counter to the individual emphasis of the dominant US culture. Feelings of guilt, shame, or denial can also arise from these critiques of dominant consciousness when students become aware of how they have personally benefited from government and economic policies. REcover practices create a space of grace, respect, and potential for mutual listening and learning. When used over time, REcover practices strengthen students' spirit and "power to sustain more complex and enriching tensions . . . and the magnanimity of concern to provide conditions that enable others to increase in stature."[12]

UNcover practices use curious reflection, from a critical theory lens, "reading" how power is moving to illuminate a critical consciousness of a situation. Since students often view power as negative, offering various frameworks about how power moves can open up their curiosity and understanding to see that "history is made up of struggle, contradiction, resistance."[13] For example, Archbishop Oscar Romero used the gospel as an interpretative frame to reveal dominant narratives and structures and to lift up an alternative consciousness of a God biased towards those who are oppressed.[14] He illuminated counternarratives and engaged in active resistance to accompany those experiencing oppression and communicate collective dignity and hope. In his homilies, Romero showed people how

12. Bernard M. Loomer, "S-I-Z-E is the Measure," in *Religious Experience and Process Theology: The Pastoral Implications of a Major Modern Movement*, ed. H. J. Cargas and B. Lee (Mahwah, NJ: Paulist Press, 1976), 70.

13. Elizabeth Alexander, "Poet Elizabeth Alexander Celebrates the Power of a People's Voice," *Washington Post Magazine*, September 15, 2016, https://www.washingtonpost.com/lifestyle/magazine/poet-elizabeth-alexander-celebrates-the-power-of-a-peoples-voice/2016/09/14/065121a2-64ac-11e6-96c0-37533479f3f5_story.html.

14. CatholicIreland.net, "Oscar Romero—The Preacher," last modified November 30, 1999, https://www.catholicireland.net/oscar-romero-the-preacher/.

to see the world through the lens of the gospel by including the events of the week.[15] He believed that "the task of someone who really reflects on the word of God is to illuminate the signs of the times with the word of God; so that history and the present day have a sense of unity with God and they may move towards God."[16]

UNcover practices help students read the signs of our current times. Specific prompts help UNcover this multifaceted understanding of a situation, including: How are people treating one another, with what forms of power? Who has been impacted; who is invisible, blamed, exploited, marginalized? What are the various messages, assumptions, and beliefs influencing this situation? How are systemic and organizational factors affecting these circumstances? (see figure 2).

Figure 2

RE-UN-DIScover Heuristic Practices

REcover with Compassion

- Tune into your whole self: ongoing awareness of your level of arousal
- Use various practices when needed while UN- and DIScovering
- Seek to remain present with your whole self and those you are with
- Hold space for your feelings of confusion, overwhelm, anger, or despair

UNcover with Curious, Critical Reflection

- How are people treating one another, with what forms of power?
- Who has been impacted; who is invisible, blamed, exploited, marginalized?
- What are the various messages, assumptions, and beliefs influencing this situation?
- How are systemic and organizational factors affecting these circumstances?
- Who else wants to work for change?

DIScover with Creative Courage

- Create space to listen to the hopes and desires for this situation
- Imagine what "justice" or "equity" or "flourishing" looks like
- Using UNcover understandings and capacities, what's possible in this situation?
- Create possible actions using group members' talents; choose a viable option
- Hold space for hesitancy, not-knowing, urges to fix, and the anxiety of newness
- Put choice into action, notice impact; learn in relationship
- Use experimental mindset to regroup, redesign, and continue with additional actions

15. Martin Maier, "Archbishop Oscar Romero and Liberation Theology," The Archbishop Romero Trust, accessed August 9, 2024, http://www.romerotrust.org.uk/sites/default/files/MartinMaier1500words.pdf.

16. Maier, "Romero," 4.

DIScover practices use a transformative lens to courageously imagine what's responsive in a specific situation to generate possible actions for social change. In this way, "history is not punctuated with a period but rather with continuing ellipses. And history favors the bold colon, punctuation that makes us look ever forward into the yet-to-be."[17]

DIScover practices focus on "what's possible" because social workers believe in the capacity of human beings to "act in the world as an intentional, creative, meaning-making being, whose actions are shaped and constrained but never fully determined by life circumstances."[18] Students have a yearning for a "better world," yet they need models and examples of transformative change processes to spark their imagination about what justice, equity, or thriving looks like and how to get there from their current situation. DIScover practices embrace creative use of disciplinary methods; social work, for example, draws on case studies, experiential activities, videos, interviews, and community engagement.

DIScover practices cultivate imagination by engaging in a slow, deliberate pace to disrupt the urge to replicate dominant actions or to become "co-opted into the culture of the day."[19] These brainstorming prompts open up possibilities (e.g., "What does inclusion look like? Who is doing what?"), then tack back and forth between ideals and current realities to shape imagined ideas into concrete actions of what they do to create with other people in specific situations. Prompts at this point in the learning illuminate individual and status quo tendencies and invite collective courageous thinking, including: "You don't have to do this alone; who else cares about this issue?," "What do you need to take action?," and "What if you helped pave the way by trying this out?!"

To start, I co-create a receptive environment through shared agreements of how we will learn together. I briefly provide students with an overview of the heuristic and neurobiology research about optimal, hyper, and hypo zones of arousal to help them understand their bodily reactions when learning about themselves within historical and current

17. Alexander, "Poet."

18. Janet L. Finn and Maxine Jacobson, "Just Practice," *Journal of Social Work Education* 39, no. 1 (2003): 71, https://doi.org/10.1080/10437797.2003.10779119.

19. Walter Brueggemann, *The Prophetic Imagination: 40th Anniversary Edition* (Minneapolis: Fortress Press, 2018), 125.

oppressions.[20] Over the first four classes I provide students with REcover practices to sit with the uncertainty of not knowing and hold the urge to fix or seek "the right answer" so we can DIScover possibilities together. The practices are extending the exhalation while breathing (inhaling for four counts and exhaling for six counts); touching the palm, arm, or thigh with the opposite arm; imagining a loved one or pet next to or behind you offering support; and grounding with STOP: Stop, Take a breath, Observe your emotions and reactions, Proceed. I encourage students to try each of these and to use the one(s) they find useful. In week five I introduce WAIT/Q: "Why am I talking/quiet?" to increase awareness of their verbal participation and encourage a rhythm of listening and talking in small and large group discussion. As the course proceeds, I introduce group REcover practices when I sense a flatness in the room to increase energy and decrease hypoarousal. These activities can include projecting a brightly colored image, playing lively music, reshuffling where students sit, reassigning small group membership, and standing while sequentially sharing responses to a prompt with three other people in a six- to ten-minute time frame.

Each course has frameworks to inform how we "read" a situation to illuminate forms of oppression across ecological levels. Students reflect on their experiences and understandings of power using course frameworks that expand those understandings. We then engage in critical curiosity to UNcover how power is operating within specific practice settings, listening for both productive and oppressive dynamics (see figure 2). When students feel an urge to fix or have "the right" response in practice seminar classes, REcover practices can hold space to DIScover several possible responses.

I often ask, "What else?" or suggest, "Let's build on that," to expand the range of options. Throughout, I am listening to how course materials and interactions are experienced by various students who bring diverse understandings and histories. My REcover practices experiencing compassion and grace help me listen more with the "ear of my heart" to students who are not yet seeing at a group level alongside students who experience discrimination, stigma, and structural barriers. I continue to

20. Siegel, *Developing Mind*, 342.

DIScover ways to model not knowing alongside the knowing for which I am responsible as an instructor.

RE-UN-DIS-cover in Action

What follows is a portable example of how I use the RE-UN-DIScover heuristic to promote student engagement with a prophetic imagination for use in a range of courses, especially courses toward various professional degrees.

This example is from a graduate course on diversity, oppression, and anti-oppression. Students take the course early in the Master of Social Work (MSW) program to learn theories and research about how structural inequality is perpetuated with diverse social groups; the negative effects on individual and collective well-being; and the forms of resistance, social change, and community cultural wealth that are simultaneously exerting collective power. After creating group agreements for learning; introducing the heuristic; and discussing some initial critical theory frameworks about power, racism, and resistance, an experiential activity occurs in the fourth week to begin to UNcover the impacts of policies and laws on everyday experiences.

StarPower[21] is an activity that uses trading rounds, chips of varying points, and small group decision-making to simulate how socioeconomic classes and inequality are perpetuated. Students are told that the winners will be the three students who earn the most points. Following an initial trading round, students are divided into three small groups (low, middle, and affluent classes) based on their individual total points. Students then must decide which individuals get additional points within their group. In the final round, the group with the highest number of points can create the rules for the last trading round; those in groups with fewer points can suggest rules to the other group. The final round can elicit disengagement, anger, apathy, group bonding, and sometimes joy within the low class group.

I facilitate a short debrief to UNcover students' feelings and reactions at the end of the activity. During the subsequent week, students write a reflection paper describing what they noticed about the actions of self

21. Simulation Training Systems, "StarPower," accessed August 9, 2024, https://www.simulationtrainingsystems.com/corporate/products/starpower.

and others and UNcover potential meanings using their beginning critical consciousness and course frameworks. In their papers, some students make connections between structural socioeconomic inequality and the activity, while other students make connections between their actions and how people in low, middle, and affluent classes think and act.

In the next class, I engage students in further UNcovering the themes that surfaced (e.g., how some acted during the activity, how some interpreted the actions of others, how some collapsed into helplessness). I use prompts with a curious tone to invite further reflection on the various ways power was used, and how those prompts connect with students' emotions and reactions, as well as how the students' actions connect with structural patterns of low, middle, and affluent classes. I refer to specific students' actions and comments during the activity to wonder with them about why they chose to act that way or about the impact of their actions on others. I move from the general and abstract to the concrete and specific language characteristic of prophetic imagination.[22]

Students often talk about the inevitability of inequality, and the room can feel heavy with helplessness and despair. At that point, I shift into a DIScover practice by pointing out that there were opportunities throughout the activity for them to act in ways that had them all "winning," i.e., earning enough points for a living wage. I move them back into their three groups (low, middle, and affluent classes) to DIScover what they could have done differently to resist or share power from that social position. This DIScover practice helps them see how resistance is "outside the box" of the rules of the "game" we participate in, how resistance becomes possible if done in groups, and how our desires for individual "wins" often keep us reinforcing the status quo. I plant seeds of imagination—bringing a critical consciousness to bear on structural inequality and within that, the possibility for it to be otherwise at an everyday interaction level.

In the next several weeks, students continue to UNcover the ways that oppressive power negatively impacts groups as we focus on immigration, gender, sexuality, religion, and intersectionality. Students learn about past and current anti-oppressive actions to inform their desires for a more just world. They often experience anger when they see the oppressive structural patterns across social groups. Consistent with pro-

22. Brueggemann, *Prophetic Imagination*, 121.

phetic imagination, I honor their emotions and UNcover the grief and woe underneath the anger. I'm mindful that many students in the class are living in the continued oppressive conditions, so I hold the tension between honoring the injustice and lifting up the resistance that groups have always engaged in to fuel their hope. This hope is anchored in class discussion addressing specific details of how a more just law or policy came to be enacted, or how a group created an alternative affirming space for counter-storytelling.[23] These DIScover practices offer models for concrete social change, painting possibilities of how they can contribute to collective action. Students, however, often remain stuck with an individual lens, having difficulty imagining how they can impact larger systems.

Reflecting on their stuckness, I thought back on how *I* developed the ability to read a situation through a power analysis lens. I had instructors and community organizers who shared stories that used this critical consciousness, along with informal and formal power moves that oppressed groups used to "work the system" or create equity. I realized that I need to model, to narrate how power is operating, and to share more examples of what's possible so they can get a foothold into possibilities. Students need context and familiarity with what has been done before, including "show and tell" stories as the soil from which seeds of other possibilities can emerge. At the same time, I also know that prophetic imagination often requires actions that have not yet been realized. I try to hold the tension—not unduly constraining while sufficiently scaffolding.

In the final weeks of the course, I lean more on these DIScover practices that encourage students to imagine the world as it could be in different social work practice settings. One way is through a guest speaker with follow-up DIScover work. For example, I invited an MSW alum to come speak on her work with transgender children and adolescents. She UNcovered the mental health distress that transgender youth often experience when families, schools, and community groups fail to protect youth from bullying and microaggressions. She shared the trainings she provides to counter that, along with her individual and group work with transgender youth to support and affirm their gender journeys.

23. Daniel G. Solórzano and Tara J. Yosso, "Critical Race Methodology: Counter-Storytelling as an Analytical Framework for Education Research," *Qualitative Inquiry* 8, no. 1 (2002): 23–44, https://doi.org/10.1177/107780040200800103.

In the next class I have students work in small groups to DIScover what they could do as a school social worker to create a greater sense of inclusion for transgender youth. I encourage them to think about their own high school experiences, identifying actions that created affirming spaces for transgender youth and/or others who experienced exclusion or stigma. I then have them imagine what they could do in a social work role now, encouraging small group conversation to share and imagine together.

I have found that some students can become blocked during these conversations. Some will say, "I didn't have that in my high school, so I don't know," or, after a leadership idea is shared, others say, "That's not me, I couldn't do that." In response, I scaffold the DIScover practices by having them remember that they do not need to do this alone and will likely be more impactful if they work with others. I ask them to identify the various staff and student groups in high schools and invite them to think about which staff or student groups might have an interest in working together. We also explore how they could invite transgender youth to be part of the work to make sure that those who are impacted are included but not expected to do all the labor. I then have them consider that a school social worker can be a *facilitator* of a small group that imagines strategies and organizes the specific actions together.

Throughout this process, students often voice woe or despair (e.g., "the bullying still happens," when recounting a story of how those who bullied did not face significant consequences from school administrators). Prophetic imagination gives voice to the woe, so I honor that reality while holding out an "and"—that countercultures can simultaneously exist which affirm the dignity of the members, and that providing alternative spaces within the school for transgender youth and others to gather keeps the counterculture alive in that school. I leave them with the experience of how to imagine *within* despair to preserve the hope that a prophetic imagination can bear fruit in their practice.

Conclusion

The RE-UN-DIScover heuristic is a pedagogical tool that scaffolds the cultivation of the prophetic imagination with students. Students learn about the heuristic, learn and practice REcover practices, and are introduced to theoretical frameworks to inform their critical consciousness as they UNcover the power dynamics of dominant cultural and structural oppression. Engaging the prophetic imagination, the instructor acknowledges the woe and despair as students see patterns of human cruelty, and intentionally pairs this learning with collective countercultural actions that resist injustices, create alternative narratives, and offer spaces for collective healing and well-being. DIScover practices initially focus on these past and current actions and then shift to student-generated ideas by drawing on their experiences or the settings they can act within. The heuristic's changeable order allows for instructors to pause for group REcover, circle back to UNcover power patterns or understandings, or lean into imagining a world as it could be. REcover and reflection practices support instructors' efforts to listen to students and others experiencing injustice with a compassionate heart, to reflect on the despair that students share, and to circle back again and again to the promise of a liberating God.

Social Suffering and the Scholarship of Bearing Witness

Kathleen M. Gallagher-Brau
St. Mary's University

> "*And what is as important as knowledge*?" asked the mind.
> "*Caring*," answered the heart.[1]

Israel, Palestine, Ukraine. Election vitriol. Wildfires and natural disasters. Gun violence and fentanyl. It is hard enough living in a world that is fractured by hurt, let alone teaching about it with sensitivity and hope. How do we encounter and interpret suffering on an unprecedented scale? And how do we do so from a Catholic faith perspective that not only inspires hope, but also presents the possibility of redemption and healing? In a world filled with collective hurt, how do we cultivate the seeds of individual and structural healing?

The essay that follows recounts the evolution of a course on social suffering, the questions this course sought to answer, and the additional ones it raised. Takeaways include a conceptual and spiritual road map for navigating the study of collective suffering and sample assignments that support this exploration. Of paramount concern is the manner in which scholarship can be transformative for communities and researchers alike

1. Flavia Weedn, *Living Life Fully*, accessed December 15, 2024, https://livinglifefully.com/caring.htm.

when linked to the suffering of Christ and approached as a form of witness. The crafting and teaching of this class also raised questions about our responsibilities as educators at Catholic institutions and the spiritual silo-ing that compromises these goals; as such, this chapter is also a meditation on vocational identity and an invitation to restore its pursuit.

The section that follows traces the origins of the course *Social Suffering and the Scholarship of Bearing Witness* and its development over time, beginning with the vocational journey in which it is embedded, student concerns that shaped it, and a pandemic that demanded its revision, all animated by an overarching desire to integrate Catholic spirituality more intentionally into coursework.

Vocational Journeys: Genesis and Evolution of the Class

Even though I had never heard the term "social suffering" prior to a graduate seminar on the topic, I was already familiar with its manifestations and effects. My circuitous route into graduate school included stops at Mother Teresa's Missionaries of Charity motherhouse in Calcutta, a stint with UNICEF, and long stretches in Nepal, much of it marked by violent conflict. Most of my time was spent in the company of squatters, internally displaced people, and enslaved populations (and later ex-slaves) that make up the communities in which I work and conduct research as a social anthropologist.[2] These experiences translate into research and writing about marginalized communities and crafting coursework that attends to the needs of the less fortunate.

Teaching a course on social suffering was a natural extension of this vocational journey and one that seemed to resonate with the interests of my students, most of whom were enrolled in a master's degree program in International Relations at St. Mary's University, San Antonio, Texas, where I was an associate professor. The first four iterations of the class, then entitled *Varieties of Human Suffering*, looked at collective experiences of hardship and the social, political, and economic factors that

2. The technical term for this type of slavery is bonded labor, a form of enslavement whereby a person's labor is used as loan repayment for previous debts incurred. These debts may be of recent origin, or inherited and longstanding, trapping households in servitude for generations.

give rise to deep poverty, disease, genocide, and other atrocities such as human trafficking.[3]

Across different versions and diverse students, class discussion often circled back to our responsibilities as scholars and practitioners in ameliorating the suffering of others in pragmatic solidarity with the oppressed. My students were hungry for such exchanges, and they wanted course content and projects that married theory with practice, particularly in the protection of vulnerable populations and uplifting of the poor. Whether they knew it or not, they were framing their vocational aspirations according to Catholic social teaching, which became a touchstone. They were also yearning for opportunities to assimilate what they had witnessed as soldiers or aid workers, including God's presence in turmoil and anguish. My students were trying to reimagine the world not as it was, but as it could be, a sacramental vision I nurtured and also sought. Three decades spent working with, writing about, and living amid the prophetic had left me weary, especially when these experiences were marked by violence and human rights abuses.

I tried to modestly address these inclinations with each revision of the class, but these efforts often felt ad hoc, and I was pulled towards integrating a Catholic faith perspective into class in a more robust fashion rather than as afterthought.[4] Although there were opportunities around campus for students and faculty to explore their faith life, to my knowledge few of them were built into syllabi of classes that were not designated vehicles of faith formation, a point to which I'll later return. Graduate education in particular lacked outlets for spiritual exploration. I was disheartened with what felt like a lack of Catholicism within the classroom, most pointedly in my own courses.

Not only did my students' growing desire for more transformative and spiritual approaches to the study of collective suffering coalesce with my own, it also coincided with the pandemic. Previous concerns about how

3. *Varieties of Human Suffering* is based on a life-changing class by the same name that I took at Harvard University during my doctoral studies. The class was taught by one of my mentors, Arthur Kleinman.

4. The notion of faith as afterthought is inspired by Archbishop J. Michael Miller, CSB, *Five Essential Marks of Catholic Schools*, accessed February 15, 2025, https://catholiceducation.org/en/education/five-essential-marks-of-catholic-schools.html.

we approach shared suffering took on a new urgency as students lost loved ones, jobs, and their sense of security in an uncertain global landscape. My students were confronting social suffering on an unprecedented scale as I was preparing to teach another class on the topic. I felt the weight of this responsibility, especially because of their despair, and did my best to reconfigure previous versions of the class to accommodate both the brokenness my students might be experiencing and the space for the possibility of hope and healing.

Course Overview and Conceptual and Spiritual Road Map

Social Suffering and the Scholarship of Bearing Witness debuted in the spring of 2021.[5] In addition to previously mentioned course components analyzing different types of suffering and the commingling of forces that give rise to collective hurt, the revised course included sections devoted to the notion of witness and transformation through redemptive suffering. Student learning outcomes for the class were delineated as follows:

1. To understand the concept of social suffering and structural violence, and how structural inequity is produced and maintained
2. To become sensitive to the different forms of collective trauma, and the pain of silence that often accompanies it
3. To examine the different types of witness and storytelling that can break the silence of collective suffering, and to be aware of the potential ethical dilemmas and politics of representation when bearing witness
4. To explore witness in praxis and develop an appreciation for its building blocks, including kinship, compassion, and empathy
5. To deepen our understanding of the interrelationship between suffering, witness, and transformation

5. This revision of the course was supported in part by the Edward and Linda Speed Catholic Studies Faculty Development and Research Grant, Center for Catholic Studies, St. Mary's University.

These goals were nurtured by several course touchstones and queries, including the nature of encounter and presence, the role of mercy, the importance of silence and contemplation, and the interrelationship among woundedness, connection, and transformation. How do we gaze at the world? Do we see the hurt of others and listen to its plaintiveness? Can we sit in the presence of suffering, including our own, with mercy? Are there spaces of silence in our lives in which to ponder the sacredness of these encounters? How do these connections invite personal and collective transformation, whereby woundedness also contains the seeds of healing?

This class was an attempt to integrate the rigors of critical analysis with spiritual exploration. Readings and assignments (described later) reflected this intent. Selections included works by Elie Wiesel and his student Ariel Burger. The concepts of social suffering and structural violence were elucidated by Arthur Kleinman and Paul Farmer. Interludes on the sacramental and prophetic were drawn from Matthew Eggemeier. Writings by Susan Sontag and Carolyn Forché explored the importance and challenge of witness. The work of Father Gregory Boyle was instrumental when striving to approach our encounters with others in the spirit of radical kinship, a perspective supported by *Fratelli Tutti,* Pope Francis' encyclical on social friendship. A key reading for entering the heart of redemptive suffering was *Salvifici Doloris,* Pope John Paul II's apostolic letter on the Christian meaning of human suffering. Woundedness and compassion were illuminated by Henri Nouwen, while reflections by Thich Nhat Hanh and Jack Kornfield espoused the virtues of stillness and contemplation.[6]

Social Suffering, Witness, and Compassion

Within this conceptual and spiritual road map, three major shifts were made when guiding students towards transformative engagement with

6. Specific readings referenced in this paragraph include, in order of appearance: *Night* (Wiesel), *Witness Lessons from Elie Wiesel's Classroom* (Burger), *Social Suffering* (Kleinman, Das, and Lock), *Pathologies of Power* (Farmer), *A Sacramental-Prophetic Vision: Christian Spirituality in a Suffering World* (Eggemeier), *On Photography* (Sontag), *Against Forgetting: Twentieth-Century Poetry of Witness* (Forché), *Barking to the Choir: The Power of Radical Kinship* (Boyle), *The Wounded Healer* (Nouwen), *Living Buddha* (Hanh), and *A Path With Heart* (Kornfield).

suffering. These movements included (1) the shift from critical analysis to scholarship as witness; (2) the shift from secular to faith-filled witness; and (3) the shift from transformative scholarship and witness to healing through redemptive suffering.

Several concepts proved integral in accommodating these transitions, beginning with social suffering and witness. Social suffering refers to hardship or trauma that is collective and transpersonal in both its experience and the manner of its production. To elaborate, social suffering "brings into a single space an assemblage of human problems that have their origins and consequences in the devastating injuries that social force can inflict on human experience."[7] Familiar examples include genocide, gendered violence, and racism. While the term underscores the communal aspects of suffering in both the generation and experience of hurt, the framework is similarly attentive to the phenomenology of pain and trauma or its lived experience, and the interrelationship between the two. Flexible in scale and multidimensional, a social suffering paradigm benefits from the critical analysis of structural frameworks but is not confined to them. Pain, as many of us know, is highly subjective even when its origins lie in larger systemic forces. A social suffering analysis of collective pain and trauma additionally "brings a stubbornly moral orientation to social analysis."[8]

Witness was also pivotal in the analysis of collective hurt and was approached from both a theological and secular perspective. At its simplest, witness verifies what one has seen or heard. From a New Testament perspective this entails keeping the story and message of Jesus alive in both word and "nonverbal testimony" by living in accordance with the teachings of Christ and manifesting the experience of God's goodness.[9] Nonreligious witness, sometimes called moral witness, conveys the direct experience of or deep acquaintance with harm and the responsibility to shape history as "special agents of collective memory."[10] As stated by

7. Arthur Kleinman, Veena Das, and Margaret Lock, *Social Suffering* (Berkeley: University of California Press, 1997), ix.

8. Kleinman et al., *Social Suffering*, xxi.

9. Donald G. Miller, "Some Observations on The New Testament Concept of 'Witness,'" *The Ashbury Theological Journal* 43, no. 1 (1988): 67.

10. Alex Danchev, "Our Brothers' Keeper: Moral Witness," *Sage Journals* 40, issue 3–4 (August 2015): 191–94.

Forché when explaining the power of poetry as witness, it "is not only a record of experience but an exhortation and a plea against despair. . . . a call for strength."[11]

Most importantly, social suffering and witness are relational and urge students to be as well. When collective pain is referred to as suffering, it underscores the experience of hurt, in addition to the hurt itself. Not every student will experience racism or misogyny, but everyone can relate to the experience of suffering and perhaps be less judgmental in its appraisal and less distant in feeling its effects. This engagement forms the basis for a pedagogy of witness, an approach that emphasizes proximity to suffering, empathy for those who endure it, and commitment to meaningful action. In this way, the course kindled a sacramental mindset, transforming the classroom into a space of critical inquiry and moral reflection, preparing students to act as agents of change in their communities and professions.

The transformative potential of witness is magnified when contemplated in terms of the qualities that characterize bearing witness from a Christian perspective, such as humility, mercy, openheartedness, and radical kinship. Radical kinship, according to Father Gregory Boyle, is the awareness that we belong to one another. If we take to heart the gospel of inclusion and nonviolence, then no member of our human family should be on the margins, let alone outside the circle of our love.[12] It is an entreaty reminiscent of Mother Teresa's: "The problem with our world is that we draw the circle of family too small."[13] When kinship is radical, it not only invites students to feel others' pain (empathy) and cultivate a desire to ameliorate it (compassion), it also enjoins students to see godliness in others, connected as we are in kinship with Christ.

Finally, the practice of compassion served as inspiration and moral compass throughout the course, particularly its beautiful rendering by Henri Nouwen, Donald McNeill, and Douglas Morrison:

11. Carolyn Forché, *Against Forgetting: Twentieth-Century Poetry of Witness* (New York: W. W. Norton, 1993), 32.

12. Gregory Boyle, *Barking to the Choir* (New York: Simon & Schuster, 2017), 2.

13. Jeannie Ewing, "10 Most Beautiful Mother Teresa Quotes on the Family," accessed November 10, 2024, https://www.coraevans.com/blog/article/10-most-beautiful-mother-teresa-quotes-on-the-family.

> Compassion asks us to go where it hurts, to enter into places of pain, to share in brokenness, fear, confusion, and anguish. Compassion challenges us to cry out with those in misery, to mourn with those who are lonely, to weep with those in tears. Compassion requires us to be weak with the weak, vulnerable with the vulnerable, and powerless with the powerless.[14]

As for the compatibility of these varied approaches, Parker Palmer is instructive: "The mind's vision excludes the heart, but the heart's vision can include the mind."[15] I was striving to widen the gaze of my students, to open up their hearts as well as their minds so that they might see differently, including the suffering of others.

Sample Assignments and Teaching Takeaways

The class culminated in a final capstone project in which students were asked to provide voice and visibility to a suffering community by bearing witness to their pain from a Catholic faith perspective. This is accomplished through a series of smaller assignments, several of which are shared below.[16]

At the beginning of the semester, students were configured into groups according to shared interests and compatible strengths; each group was then tasked with identifying a community in distress. Past examples include young girls at higher risk for human trafficking in the Democratic Republic of the Congo and the plight of Afghani refugees in the United States.[17] Students were encouraged to choose groups whose pain

14. Henri J. M. Nouwen, Donald P. McNeill, and Douglas A. Morrison, *Compassion—A Reflection on the Christian Life* (New York: Image, 2006), 4.

15. Parker Palmer, *To Know as We Are Known: Education as Spiritual Journey* (San Francisco: HarperOne, 1993), xxiv.

16. I often rotate assignments between versions of the class; for this chapter, I've included those that worked best across classes.

17. These examples are drawn from student contributions by Lusa Tshibangu (trafficking in the Democratic Republic of the Congo) and Divina Akuma (Afghani refugees in the United States). Both went on to present their work at the National Fulbright Conference (2022) for a panel we put together entitled "Social Suffering and Bearing Witness to Marginalized Communities in a Post-Pandemic World."

and needs are usually underrepresented in the public domain, or not acknowledged at all.

Students then critically analyzed the plight of their community through the lens of social suffering. This entailed identifying both larger structural forces that contribute to collective suffering, as well as individual responses that shape its experience. For the previously mentioned group of Afghani refugees, larger structural forces include how the pandemic shut down asylum proceedings in an already clogged legal system; examples of individual effects include the trauma of war that propelled them into refugee status and the ongoing distress of living in legal limbo in a foreign land.

As previously mentioned, several conceptual shifts were made when guiding students towards more transformative engagements with suffering. The first shift (from critical analysis to scholarship as witness) was initiated by having students share examples of witness that personally resonated with them. Past examples include sculptures that capture loss, murals depicting missing Indigenous women, and protest poems. Some of these contributions were discovered through travel and personal experience, and others were created by the students themselves. The assignment encouraged students to explore how and why different representations create connection and empathy, fostering a more intimate relationship to communities in duress and a heightened sensitivity to how to convey their pain. This exercise also started a conversation revisited during their final project: Who or what demands visibility and voice, and to what end?

The second shift (from secular to faith-filled witness), involved breaking down witness into constituent parts such as empathy, compassion, and radical kinship. Empathy exercises can be done individually or as a group. An example of the former includes fasting for a day. An example of the latter is role-playing. When examining human trafficking in central Africa, for instance, assigned roles include girls at risk for trafficking, border agents, and middlemen. During this enactment, students explore transpersonal aspects of human suffering, specifically how the conflicting interests of varied stakeholders shape the experience, production, and interpretation of pain.

For their final project, student groups were asked to reconfigure their critical analysis into a form of witness highlighting real-world problems and providing suggestions for their amelioration. Students began by analyzing the needs of communities in pain from a social suffering perspective. Students then bore witness through their representation of collective suffering and the creative adaptation of research findings to a specific audience and upliftment objective. In the case of human trafficking in the Democratic Republic of the Congo, the target audience could be a nongovernmental organization involved in the rehabilitation of trafficked children, while the proposed intervention might be training border agents how to recognize potential victims and identify middlemen during border crossings. This is a different enterprise than conventional scholarship and invited discussion about the intellectual viability of research that is purpose-driven and considerations to link scholarly analysis to practical interventions.

The third and final shift (from transformative scholarship and witness to healing through redemptive suffering) was the hardest of all.

Redemptive Suffering and Woundedness

From a Catholic perspective, encounters with suffering not only offer guidelines for its amelioration but also present opportunities for redemption. Redemptive suffering refers to suffering that is offered up for the sanctity of others (and ourselves) by uniting it with the suffering of Christ. We are not the source of grace, but its co-redeemers: Redemptive suffering cooperates with the transcendence of the Passion, allowing us to align our suffering and that of others with the absolute love and mercy of Christ—not just any Christ, but the suffering Christ on the cross. We are transfigured and restored to grace by inviting Jesus into our encounters with suffering. In this light, suffering not only contains the seeds of healing in the present but also of hope eternal. Woundedness invites the possibility of healing when incorporated into the Mystical Body of Christ.

This was the most challenging portion of the class to teach or, more accurately, facilitate. I was attempting to convey one of the deepest mysteries of Catholic faith life in four months to a diverse community of students during a pandemic. Despite my initial zeal, I struggled when crafting the class and in its teaching. The heart of my dilemma lay in the very factors motivating its revision: Was the latest version of *Social Suffering* so deeply Catholic that it might prove inaccessible or even off-putting to non-Catholics and nonpracticing Catholics?

The class also took me out of my intellectual comfort zone, where boundaries were determined by expertise and learning outcomes were predictable. Theology can be taught, but faith cannot be circumscribed. This teaching experience was more open-ended, an act of faith in which the ultimate goal, transformation through redemptive suffering, was not mine to give, which was the whole point. I came to appreciate the words of C. S. Lewis, who intellectualized the problem of suffering but "was never fool enough to suppose myself qualified" to teach about bearing pain except to say that "courage helps much more than knowledge . . . and the least tincture of the love of God more than all."[18]

Though I couldn't guarantee transformation and healing, I took solace in the possibility that I could create the conditions of their emergence through contemplation and praxis. This involved deciphering how to ask the right questions. Reflection questions such as the ones below were key components of spiritual exploration:

> Part of bearing witness to others' pain and suffering is coming to terms with our own. By transforming our own pain, we are better positioned to transform that of others; each small act of individual transformation collectively contributes to structural healing. Our suffering becomes transcendent and redemptive.
>
> Think about some of the pain in your life. How might these individual traumas inform your perception of others, including the openness of your heart and your ability to listen?
>
> I'm not sure I can explain the mysteries of transcendence and redemptive suffering. I only know that they exist, and that I experience them from a Catholic faith perspective through the person of Jesus and the crucifixion and resurrection.
>
> Consider the ways that faith life lends meaning to suffering. How do these insights transform personal suffering and brokenness into healing and wholeness such that your pain becomes a source of witness and transformation in the world?

18. C. S. Lewis, *The Problem of Pain* (San Francisco: HarperOne, 2015), xii.

For their part, most of the challenges students had with redemptive suffering were not doctrinal, but personal, and deeply intertwined with feelings of exclusion. The students who struggled most with the possibility of individual and structural healing were those who felt excluded from the Catholic Church, or hurt and condemned by it, an unsettling realization in a class aspiring towards radical kinship. Interestingly, students who struggled least and appeared to intuitively understand (and accept) the mystery of woundedness and transformation were those who had grown up in proximity to suffering, including several from marginalized communities and less developed countries.

Overall, student response to the class was extremely positive, including in ways unanticipated. Students appreciated the vocational undercurrent to the class, as it invited them to think about scholarship and work in terms of purpose, impact, and alignment with their spiritual values and faith life. Many of these same students later offered assistance with extracurricular projects in which I was engaged, such as the provision of an expert witness for an asylum case, and when I established a nonprofit with graduate students; *Social Suffering* created a community of witnesses that outlasted the class.

As for me, this teaching engagement was both disconcerting and rewarding, as I attempted to guide myself and my students through new teaching and learning territory. The open-ended nature of class outcomes summoned a posture of humility and detachment. One of the key aspects of witness is meeting others where they are, not where we want them to be. As much as I wanted my students to encounter the wonder, grace, and healing incarnate in the suffering Christ, I had to meet them wherever they were in their faith journey, including in their woundedness.

Making space for faith-filled engagements in the classroom was often unsettling. There is an emotional weight that accompanies a course on suffering, on a knife's edge between woundedness and healing. In addition, I couldn't teach about transformation without attempting to exemplify its virtues. On those days when I wasn't feeling particularly transformed, my stumbling reminded me to tend to my own spiritual needs and to extend the same grace to myself that I championed with my students. The ramifications of such grace were especially important in a course seeking individual and structural healing: In the Ignatian spirit of *cura personalis* (care of the person), we awaken the spirit of loving service in others, including through the discernment of their unique gifts, when we ourselves understand how best to discover, care for, and use our own.[19]

I was, however haltingly, bearing witness by trying to practice what I was teaching. Along the way, I could feel the modest stirrings of transformation. These glimpses of healing were gifts as I confronted my own brokenness. In addition to pandemic-related struggles, including the loss of extended family members and the near loss of immediate ones, I was diagnosed with a life-changing autoimmune disease two years before the pandemic. It wasn't the deepest wound I carried, but the most recent, and one that eventually propelled me into disability as I was preparing to teach *Social Suffering* again in the spring of 2023.

Vocational Identity, Spiritual Silo-ing, and the Call to Witness

When recounting the genesis of *Social Suffering and the Scholarship of Bearing Witness,* one of the motivating factors behind its recrafting was a desire to integrate Catholic faith life in a more dedicated fashion into the learning experience. In so doing, I not only explored the recesses of redemptive suffering, but my vocational identity as well. More specifically, to what extent are we called to bear witness to Catholic faith life in the classroom, including by actively inviting Christ into this space? Put differently, are we educators at Catholic institutions, or Catholic educators, and what is at stake in this distinction? These are questions born of my own struggles and reflections on vocation and experiences to date on Catholic college campuses as both a faculty member and a student.

As educators at Catholic institutions, most of us are familiar with the unique charisms animating our campuses. These and other components of Catholic higher education are discussed at new faculty orientation, outlined in mission statements, invoked to potential donors, and dutifully cited in tenure applications. Many Catholic universities are fortunate enough to have Catholic study centers, in addition to campus ministry.

19. I was reminded of the importance of *cura personalis* during a conversation with Professor Richard Klonoski, a friend and teacher from my undergraduate days at the University of Scranton. Awakening loving service through *cura personalis* is from Tim Muldoon, *Care of the Person, Care of the Self*, accessed February 12, 2025, https://www.ignatianspirituality.com/care-of-the-person-care-of-the-self/.

Students are typically required to take at least two classes addressing different aspects of Catholic education and faith life.

Such efforts towards faith formation, though important and laudable, risk relegating spirituality to the margins rather than weaving it into the everyday fabric of campus life, including our teaching endeavors, which results in a kind of spiritual silo-ing. This type of segregation, moreover, runs the risk of spiritual complacency, whereby there might be less awareness of or motivation for the deeper integration of a Catholic faith perspective since aspects of it are already being managed around campus, shifting the responsibility to other actors and forums. This matter gets murkier still when played out during the complicated and contested times in which we teach, whereby the quest for inclusivity might eclipse the practice of Catholicism, or at least give it pause, as it did for me when reconfiguring *Social Suffering and the Scholarship of Bearing Witness,* begging the question: How do we embrace non-Catholic students without compromising the integrity of a Catholic faith perspective?

The lack of a more intentional integration of faith into the classroom may also be reflective of academia, a space in which we are largely defined by our expertise and overextended by the competing demands of research, teaching, and service. It is easy to see how intellect overtakes spirit under such conditions, leaving less time for spiritual development, whether in the classroom or individual faith lives. Sadly, it is not just a deepening of our faith life that may be in jeopardy, but our vocational calling as well, and with it, the full revelation of our gifts, a manifestation that Parker Palmer likens to dwelling with God.[20]

Centuries ago, the Catholic intellectual tradition (CIT) anticipated not only these dilemmas but also their resolution. The CIT suggests that a key component for navigating paradox and accommodating tension is an identity and corresponding practices firmly grounded in Christ. Our ability to embrace strangers, entertain opposing viewpoints, and attune to human suffering resides in our capacity to see Christ in others and model it ourselves, including as teachers, because we are actively cultivating this divine indwelling.

20. The full quote is "One dwells with God by being faithful to one's nature," from Parker Palmer, *Let Your Life Speak* (San Francisco: Jossey-Bass, 2000), 51.

These are discomfiting concerns and questions, suitably so for disquieting times. They are also opportunities to reexamine passion, purpose, and why we chose Catholic higher education in the first place, including how we tend to our spiritual life. For me, the interconnectedness between faith, teaching, and vocational identity found expression through a class on suffering and its interrelationship with witness, redemption, and transformation. The course was an attempt to inspire a sacramental mindset and plant the seeds of hope and healing during a time of profound despair and brokenness. I didn't anticipate that this shared faith journey might be a small act of witness. I also didn't realize that the transformation would be mutual and restorative.

Learning to Scale

Teaching Sustainability as a Spiritually Activated Community Practice

Christopher J. Cobb
Saint Mary's College

> Rather than a problem to be solved, the world is a joyful mystery to be contemplated with gladness and praise.
> Pope Francis, *Laudato Si'*, par. 12

The global scale of the climate crisis provokes a sense of helplessness in many students when they grasp its magnitude. Nothing they can do would seem to make a difference: solutions must lie with world leaders. This essay describes the pedagogies developed by a group of faculty at three Holy Cross institutions—Holy Cross College, Saint Mary's College, and the University of Notre Dame—teaching integrated courses to counter this sense of helplessness by grounding students in an experience of sustainability as a community practice to which each person's actions contribute materially, culturally, and spiritually. This grounding activates students' prophetic imaginations to evaluate their institutions' response to the climate crisis and envision strategies for response that scale up from their personal commitments.

Although young people in the United States tend to be more attuned to the climate crisis than their elders, they often confront this crisis with a profound sense of helplessness, anxiety, or even despair. With respect to the climate crisis, the prophetic imagination may have little difficulty in pointing out the failure of institutions. However, achieving a prophetic vision of a better world requires radical hope and deeper insight, because little in the predictive trends of climate science suggests that the climate will not keep getting worse for the flourishing of human civilization and the entire biosphere for the lifetime of all people now alive. It is this challenge of prophetic imagination that we[1] have sought to meet by developing integrated courses that approach sustainability as a community practice in light of the Holy Cross charism and Pope Francis's *Laudato Si'*.

Although Francis seeks to address everyone on the planet, we have found that his encyclical benefits from supplementation to address the needs of young people as they learn to face the challenges of the climate crisis. Francis asks his readers to respond to "the cry of the earth and the cry of the poor,"[2] but the attitudes toward this cry that he most seeks to engage are indifference, complacency, and self-regard, which he calls out as the prevailing attitudes among the global elite. In the prayer that closes *Laudato Si'*, Francis asks God to "Enlighten those who possess power and money / that they may avoid the sin of indifference."[3] As studies of young people's feelings about the climate crisis show, indifference is not prevalent among them.[4] Whether they come from families of wealth or not,

1. Although I am the sole author of this essay, in it I describe the fruits of collaborative work undertaken over the last decade with many colleagues, whom I gratefully acknowledge here: Sally Geislar (Saint Mary's), Michael Griffin (Holy Cross), Daniel Horan (Saint Mary's), Rachel Novick (formerly of Notre Dame), Margaret Pfeil (Notre Dame), Shawn Storer (Holy Cross), and Brother Lawrence Unfried, CSC (Holy Cross).

2. Pope Francis, *Laudato Si'*: Encyclical Letter on Care for Our Common Home, May 24, 2015, par. 49, https://www.vatican.va/content/francesco/en/encyclicals/documents/papa-francesco_20150524_enciclica-laudato-si.html.

3. Ibid., par. 246.

4. See these recent studies: Caroline Hickman et al., "Climate Anxiety in Children and Young People and Their Beliefs about Government Responses to Climate Change: A Global Survey," *Lancet Planet Health* 2021; 5: e863–73, https://www.thelancet.com/action/showPdf?pii=S2542-5196%2821%2900278-3; Isaiah Thomas, "Understanding Youths' Concerns about Climate Change: A Binational Qualitative Study of Ecological Burden and Resilience," *Child and Adolescent Psychiatry and Mental Health* 16 (December 31, 2022): 110, https://pmc.ncbi.nlm.nih.gov/articles/PMC9805369/; Alec Tyson, Brian Kennedy, and Cary Funk, "Gen Z, Millennials Stand Out for Climate Change Activism, Social Media Engagement with Issue," Pew Research Center, May 26, 2021, https://www.pewresearch.org/science

many feel powerless in the face of the political, economic, and cultural hegemony of fossil-fuel civilization. They live in a state of resignation, if not despair, about an apparently intractable problem.

Or is it a problem? In this essay's epigraph, Francis rejects any characterization of the world as a problem, seeing it rather as "a joyful mystery to be contemplated with gladness and praise," a perception that follows from the status of "nature as a magnificent book in which God speaks to us and grants us glimpses of his infinite beauty and goodness."[5] However appealing this perception might seem, it is not readily accessible to young people fearful about the climate crisis, acclimated to a hyper-scheduled lifestyle, and trained to accept technocratic social mechanics. For students to acquire the prophetic imagination that opens a vision of the world as joyful mystery, they must have opportunities to experience contemplation as a mode of renewal and to learn a mode of action that breaks with the logic of the technocratic paradigm. To incorporate these modes into an academic sustainability course, we employ a set of pedagogical practices that bring together several modes of experiential learning and open dialogue embodied in six integrated course elements: landscape tours, conversations with sustainability practitioners, group conversation, community-engaged learning, engagement with ecologically informed theology, and mindfulness practices.

The most distinctive feature of this course is its tri-campus character, bringing together students from three Holy Cross schools into a single learning community. Each class has a teacher(s) of record from its institution, but the three classes meet together. On Tuesday afternoons, we gather for two hours on one of the three campuses to examine a sustainability issue. This long class period enables us to take an in-depth and hands-on approach. Visiting sites where sustainability work is taking place, we look directly at what the institution is doing and why, and we talk to the people doing the sustainability work. The course's three units focus in turn on landscape, food systems, and energy systems. Because the three institutions operate on very different scales—Notre Dame is an R1 university with 13,000 students, Saint Mary's is a liberal arts college with

/2021/05/26/gen-z-millennials-stand-out-for-climate-change-activism-social-media-engagement-with-issue/.

5. Francis, *Laudato Si'*, par. 12.

1,600 students, and Holy Cross is a college of 500 students—each faces distinct sustainability opportunities and challenges. Encountering this diversity, students learn that sustainable designs must fit the community for which they are intended. This awareness of scale helps students to see that the scale of individual practice is also crucial: individuals can make changes that institutions struggle with, and vice versa.

Following the joint session, students meet for shorter sessions on Thursday on their home campuses. The content of these sessions differs: Holy Cross adds a field biology component, while Notre Dame and Saint Mary's add seminar discussions of theological readings on sustainability. Assignments for the course emphasize action, reflection, and dialogue. Each week, students submit two questions on the Tuesday readings and a short response paper on the Thursday readings. Students also volunteer with a community partner doing sustainability or social justice work; they write monthly reflections on this experience. To integrate the different parts of the course, students write a short reflective midterm essay on their development of contemplative awareness and do a final project in which they pursue the transformation of a habit in daily life to reduce their use of resources and reflect on that pursuit as a practice of contemplative awareness.

The remainder of this essay presents in-depth accounts of the course's six main pedagogical elements to show how we use them and to suggest how they might be applied elsewhere.

Landscape Tours

During the first unit, we walk the grounds of one campus each week to examine the management of its land and buildings, considering how the campus has been produced and maintained and the role that sustainability commitments have played (or not). By reading the landscape, we observe the history of the academic community's development and its handling of relationships with the biological communities and natural processes co-present with it. The signs we read include the placement of plants, management practices applied to them, provisions for outdoor activity, the built environment, and external sustainability features such as solar arrays, rain gardens, and green roofs. To prepare for the tours, students read about the history and mission of each institution, including the sponsoring congregation's charism. The readings examine the founding of each institution and major decision points which shaped the institution's relationship to place. Other readings present several models for sustainable relationships with landscape: the Association for the Advancement of Sustainability in Higher Education (AASHE) Sustainability Tracking, Assessment, and Rating System (STARS) program website; the website for the Berea College Farm; and the agrarian visions of Wendell Berry and Norman Wirzba.

These tours de-center the classroom and establish experiential learning as the method of the course. They also begin the process of developing students' prophetic imaginations by deepening their relationship to their institutions. When students start to read the physical campus landscape not as a static backdrop for their lives but as a dynamic habitat being continually produced and modified by and for the community, their sense of agency and purpose grows.

The sequence of tours foregrounds history while gradually introducing contemplative awareness. The first tour at Notre Dame, the oldest of the institutions, traverses the central campus to focus on the founding of the university, its relation to the Potawatomi people and their removal, the development of a campus aesthetic without regard for sustainability, and recent efforts to reintroduce sustainable practices. The tour at Saint Mary's moves to the margins of campus, where the material life of the campus is produced at sites such as the power plant and wellhouses, and where the college works out its relationship with the surrounding natural environment. We observe how the Sisters of the Holy Cross invite spiritual engagement with the landscape by maintaining scenic river overlooks, a nature trail, their cemetery, a remembrance garden filled with native wildflowers, and a labyrinth. The tour at Holy Cross focuses on the integration of the Brothers' charism into the campus design through its focus on neighborhood and the placement of religious art. It then leads the students into contemplative awareness of nature by including a ten-minute silent walk on a woodland trail that runs along a reclaimed railroad bed. The students find their awareness of the world around them growing on each tour, launching them into discovery of a new sense of value in their lives through contemplative awareness. One student's reflection captures well this change in awareness and value:

> Today, our generation is . . . consumed in quick bursts of unsustainable dopamine, such as social media. Our consumer culture is so

> damaging to our environment, [yet] with the many blessings we are provided, many individuals are still unsatisfied. We try to keep up with society's fast pace, thus sacrificing our mind, body, and sometimes soul—but "what purpose does our striving serve?" (Wirzba). I appreciated the times when we were directed to just observe our surroundings and find the beauty in the simple things, such as our environment. As we were introduced to the Hesburgh Memorial Grove, the first thing that I noticed was how simple it was; there were no elements that fascinated me. Now looking back, I understand that simplicity is its own beauty.

Touring three campuses gives the landscape unit variety and depth, but these qualities could be achieved similarly by looking sequentially at different parts of a single campus or by examining other significant landscapes. A school adjacent to a college town might explore the interplay between town and campus development, or conduct tours of nearby parks or environmental restoration projects. However a landscape tour is structured, key outcomes can be grounding the students in the history of their community, teaching them to read the landscape, and opening them to contemplative awareness.

Conversations with Sustainability Practitioners

The course's consideration of landscape includes engagement with people who manage that landscape. This element continues in the course's units on food and energy systems. In the food unit, the class meets with urban farmers, leaders of nonprofits providing food for people in need, dining hall sustainability officers, and student food waste management interns. In the energy unit, students meet with engineers who design and manage campus energy systems and with campus administrators who make institution-level decisions about sustainability initiatives. Class meetings continue to include tours, which now feature growing space, dining halls, campus buildings, and power plants. Key readings for the food unit include excerpts from the writings of Peter Maurin and Michael Pollan. We also examine the website of the Menus of Change program, which strongly informs Notre Dame Dining's approach to food. For the energy unit, we examine the websites of Oberlin College's Office of Sustainability and Aquinas College's Zero Waste program, considering them as models for how academic institutions can set up integrated sustainability initiatives, and we consider news articles on fossil-fuel divestment campaigns.

Through interaction with sustainability practitioners, students see how sustainability work is done and learn about the kinds of personal and institutional commitments that motivate it, which students greatly value. As one student wrote, "I always love it when we have guest speakers because they're all so passionate about sustainability and really show how important this issue is." Equally important, when students meet with people who work "behind the scenes" to make sure that community needs are met, those encounters "pull back the curtain," giving students a deeper appreciation for how the institution makes their educational experience possible, shifting their perspective from entitlement to gratitude even as they are developing a critical perspective on institutional commitments to sustainability by discovering the extent to which those commitments depend upon sustainability's potential to cut costs. Another student highlighted the tension she observed between ethical and financial priorities: "It was interesting to hear that *Laudato Si'* affected Notre Dame's carbon emission goals and thought process [about] expanding campus. What's most financially responsible in the short term is probably not what's most sustainable for the earth, so instead of it just being budget vs. ecology the fight became budget vs. ethics/our institutional identity as a leading Catholic University." Discovering how the built environment of their institutions is managed and that serious efforts are being made to move the institutions toward sustainability also gives students hope that change is possible and helps them conceptualize how sustainability work must be scaled to the community in which it happens. An institution with 13,000 students has access to certain approaches to sustainability unavailable to an institution with 1,600 students, but conversely the smaller institution can take approaches and change at a pace unavailable to the larger institution. Seeing sustainability being implemented on different scales helps students to see that implementing sustainability on the scale of one person in their own lives is also meaningful, that change is needed on every scale.

Meetings with sustainability practitioners focus closely on how they work—or do not work—with community members to enhance sustainability. We compare sustainability initiatives that involve all community members, such as composting post-consumer food waste in the dining hall or setting up energy conservation contests between residence halls, to initiatives that require no community engagement, such as using a grinder to make a food waste slurry to feed an anaerobic digester producing methane that powers a dairy farm, or installing motion sensors in classrooms to automatically turn off the lights when the room empties. These comparisons help students to learn the differences between the material, social, and cultural components of sustainability projects. The technocratic approach to sustainability prioritizes material components and includes social components mainly by analyzing the incentives needed to effect behavior modification. It does not treat beliefs and values as relevant or subject to change. The prophetic imagination recognizes, however, that the most durable and meaningful components of sustainability projects are cultural, because it is culture, and the religion from which culture flows, that guides humans in their relationship to the rest of creation and promotes or undermines the conditions for flourishing. When students recognize that cultural work is both possible and necessary, and that sustainability practitioners are doing it, energized and guided by their own spirituality, students learn to see how a better world can come into being. One student considered these possibilities in her reflection on our class meeting with the students who manage the Saint Mary's food waste program, which uses dining hall scraps to feed chickens at the campus's sustainable farm:

> Often the mundaneness of food takes away from any spiritual association we have with it. The idea of reinstating a certain spirituality into our food system is an idea that I saw running throughout Tuesday's class. There were a few moments in which [a student sustainability intern] considered the spiritual side of the work that they do on the farm. . . . [She] described the spiritual atmosphere on the farm in which the morning dew is coating the ground, when all is quiet (except for the hungry chickens), and the sun is rising. Although [she] described the process of feeding the chickens as "not a glamorous job" she nonetheless reflected on some of the spiritual moments that have come about in the process. Sustainable practices like composting need to be accepted into a dominant belief system in order for them to be implemented on a large scale. Perhaps from a Catholic theological perspective, the spirituality of things like food and composting can be better implemented into Catholic moral formation.

Group Conversation

Students bring their changed perceptions from the landscape tours and the conversations with sustainability practitioners to summative World Café conversations at the end of each unit.[6] These broadly participatory conversations lead the group toward shared conclusions. As the session begins, students and course faculty are invited to take seats in groups of five. The facilitator opens by posing a broad, significant question relating to the topic of the unit in connection to the readings students have done for class, which is a substantial excerpt from *Laudato Si'*. The groups discuss the question for 15 to 20 minutes. One student in each group then reports the group's responses, which the facilitator summarizes, collates, and integrates into a record of the whole conversation. After the students mix among themselves to form new groups, the facilitator poses a second question that builds on the first, initiating a second round of conversation. The pattern then repeats again to complete two hours of sustained conversation.

This format is empowering because it invites and supports participation from everyone on equal footing. In our tri-campus context, students can speak as experts about their home campus, do comparative analysis of the practices they've observed, and explore how *Laudato Si'*s vision for renewal might be applied in their community. Through this process, students participate in knowledge creation.

World Café sessions often lead students to significant integrative insights. For example, the final session of our fall 2024 class began with the question: "Using Pope Francis's lens of integral ecology, what is your assessment of the relationship between personal behavior and structural change in reducing consumption, and between the social and environmental dimensions of the climate crisis?" In my small group, the students responded to this prompt with a wide-ranging discussion that began from their insight—grounded in their study of campus energy systems—that purely technical solutions to sustainability problems tend to create new problems in the process of solving the original one, so that "technology can't do it alone. Cultural change is also needed." Cultural change, they

6. For more details about the World Café pedagogy, see https://theworldcafe.com/key-concepts-resources/world-cafe-method/.

saw, needed to begin not with sustainability problems but by addressing social malaise: polarization and messages of discouragement. Students named and challenged societal messages that "nothing we can do can make any difference" and, therefore, "why try?" Identifying this starting point for cultural change led to further conversation about how to help people to care. Students identified detachment and isolation as challenges to caring. Students saw that we need to construct ways to connect people to the harms of the climate crisis, which can activate passion and empathy. Care needs to go into designs to bring people to work together: "We need to get things done," they stressed, not just talk. They made the case for community action in solidarity as an integrated response to hopelessness and detachment and as a way to accomplish systemic sustainability goals. The students came away from this conversation with a thorough social analysis of how to carry out cultural sustainability work, which they had developed for themselves in light of their learning, social experience, and Catholic social teaching. They had learned to face the "Why bother?" question that had burdened their hearts from the start of the semester and find responses that can sustain them in the face of apparent social indifference to the climate crisis.

Community-Engaged Learning

While the World Café conversations empower students through participatory knowledge creation, the community-engaged learning component of the course empowers them through direct participation in sustainability and social justice. By assisting community organizations, students observe up close the skill and dedication that organizations bring to meeting community needs sustainably and participate in meeting those needs: they help create a more just, sustainable way of life. These experiences provide a rich basis for reflection, which students undertake in monthly journal entries. These reflections ask students to make connections between their experience working with the community partner and the fifth pedagogical element of the course, ecologically informed theological readings. One student's reflection on her work with a food recovery nonprofit reveals the synergy between active work for social justice and theological exploration:

> Each time I pack meals at Cultivate, I almost can't comprehend so many kids without regular access to healthy food, or sometimes food at all. I think part of the reason it's so hard to conceptualize is due to our lack of recognition of our interconnectedness with others and with the rest of Creation which has been a common theme we return to throughout the course. I am reminded of the guidelines in "Economic Justice for All" by the USCCB which mentioned that "human dignity can be realized and protected only in community" (para. 13). Organizations like Cultivate that work within their communities to support those members who struggle for basic human rights are further fostering community through their work. I think part of the problem with overconsumption is the lack of recognition for the rest of our community and those who might need the excess we end up wasting. . . . I wonder what our world would look like if we practiced the ecological humility Pfeil talks about. If we began to practice this self-sacrificing reduction in our "energy consumption as a form of loving self-gift in relation to the rest of God's creation" ("Liturgy and Ethics," 128), would we see a societal shift? If indeed we as individuals were successful in cultivating ecological humility as liturgical practice, we could inspire friends and family, and hopefully the eventual inspiration for society.

Making the connection between the practical work of community partners and ecotheology helps students recognize the spiritual aspect of their community-oriented sustainability work, creating solidarity with both the human and more-than-human communities.

Engagement with Ecologically Informed Theology

The ecotheology readings are, pedagogically speaking, the most traditional component of this class, but they do as much as the experiential pedagogies to help the students achieve a new vision of the world. These readings, with *Laudato Si'*, situate sustainability within an integral ecology that considers all of creation in relation to God. This context both changes the stakes in environmental harm, as ecotheology attends together to "the cry of the earth and the cry of the poor" and changes the meaning of sustainability work for the individual person, as students become able to see it as informing their relationship to the whole of creation and its Creator.

The theology readings move in parallel with the landscape, food, and energy units. The first theological unit might be called "Beyond Dominionism." It begins by showing how Christianity has been implicated in the climate crisis through reading Lynn White's seminal essay, "The Historic Roots of the Ecologic Crisis," which finds in Christianity's dominionist model of the human relationship to nature an important source for Western civilization's treatment of the natural world. Accompanying White is Willis Jenkins's essay, "After Lynn White: Religious Ethics and Environmental Problems," which surveys theologians' efforts to give sustained attention to the environment in response to White's critique. We then look closely at dominion, stewardship, and kinship models of humanity's relationship to the rest of creation through articles by Elizabeth Johnson and Daniel Horan. Horan's attention to *Imago Dei* as requiring action leads into theology of gender, drawing on Ivone Gebara's exploration of human participation with God in creation. Exploration of these theological issues strongly engages the students. Students from Christian backgrounds discover that the Church's teachings on creation care are not limited to benevolent dominionism, while nonreligious students discover that Christianity can have an ecological conscience. The introduction of human participation in creation seeds the ground for deeper examinations of social and personal action to come.

The second and third units move the conversation from consideration of humans' relationship to nature to the theology of social and ecological action. This movement begins with food, probing the implications of eating for economic and environmental justice. Elizabeth Groppe's "The Seed That Falls on Fertile Ground" introduces the Catholic agrarian tradition, while Norman Wirzba's "Eating in Exile" and selections from Robin Wall Kimmerer's *Braiding Sweetgrass* offer other perspectives on the theological ethics of eating. Margaret Pfeil's "Becoming *Synergoi*: Food Justice and Economic Cooperation" places food justice within a larger framework of cooperative economic practice guided by the principle of the universal destination of goods and Paul's call for Christians to be co-workers *(synergoi)* with God (see 1 Cor 3:7-9). The theological readings done in parallel with the energy unit intensify the focus on action. Excerpts from Sarah McFarland Taylor's *Green Sisters* provide practical examples of how American women religious have responded through collective action to the promptings of ecological theology, and another essay from Margaret Pfeil, "Liturgy and Ethics: The Liturgical Ascetism of Energy Conservation," helps students develop a root sense of liturgy "as *leitourgia*, the work of the People of God at the service of the world."[7] This action in community can be directed, Pfeil suggests, toward any action that seeks unity with God through care for creation.

Mindfulness Practices

To integrate the socially oriented work of community-engaged learning and the cognitively oriented work of theological reflection, the course focuses students' attention on the integral relationship between their mental and material practices. The contemplative aspect of the landscape tours provides a gentle introduction to mindfulness as attending to the intrinsic value of nature and non-human beings, which *Laudato Si'* emphasizes (par. 33). Students build on this introduction to contemplative engagement with nature in a midterm reflective essay. Its prompt asks students, "How has the first part of our course inspired thought on your part about reconciliation with the land, with God, and [with] creation? How has our course inspired you to progress mindfully toward what Pope Francis calls an 'integral ecology'?" Student reflections speak repeatedly of the reorientation of their vision. One student wrote: "It would be safe to say that prior to this class, I found myself to be very separated from the land. . . . Through this course and specifically the volunteer requirement, my perception of the land and how to coexist with it has completely shifted." Another stressed the course's intensification of her awareness of the value of community: "This class . . . has solidified my . . . belief about community. Without community, without connection there is no human being because being human and being alive does not exist without connection. . . . [B]eing alive is . . . acknowledging the land one is on and the food one is eating and all of the beauty and connectedness that comes from it." As they put the parts of the course together, students grow more mindful of the world around them.

With that growth in mindful awareness comes growth in capacity for mindful action. The students' final project, with which they are engaged

7. Pfeil, "Liturgy and Ethics," 134.

throughout the second half of the semester, takes them into more intentional mindfulness practice in the context of sustainability:

> Drawing on your experiences and new perspectives in the first half of the course, including your practice of contemplative awareness, students will identify, practice, and reflect on transforming their own habits in relation to some resource use in their daily lives. Students will select a specific aspect of a domain of sustainability. For instance, if you selected food, you might focus on reducing food waste. Or if you chose water, you might focus on reducing water use during showering. Over the course of five weeks, you will identify a way to measure your behavior, commit to some behavior change, track your progress, and reflect on the challenges and successes in pursuit of that goal. Essential in this reflection is the consideration of the role of equity, community, and larger structural changes needed to support these new practices.

The roots of this project lie in environmental psychology work on how long people have to apply themselves to make a sustainability practice habitual.[8] In the context of this course, we consider habit formation as an opportunity for mindful contemplation, which we discuss in a theological context as liturgical ascesis. During their college years, students are forming the habits that will guide their adult lives. It is a time of active lifestyle experimentation, but often that experimentation lacks intentionality or awareness of countercultural possibilities. This project invites students to make intentional changes to their behavior and introduces them to the rewards of incorporating mindfulness and contemplation into their daily lives. They often find that, although it may be inconvenient, "giving something up" makes their lives better because they gain a greater awareness of their relationship to the world around them, a deeper appreciation for that world, and a greater sense of purpose and agency in their own lives. When we discussed the projects in our last World Café, students repeatedly expressed that the project had value for them beyond its specific sustainability goals. "It's making my life better," one student said.

8. For the research that shaped this project, see Sally Geislar, "The New Norms of Food Waste at the Curb: Evidence-Based Policy Tools to Address Benefits and Barriers," *Waste Management* 68 (2017): 571–80.

"By doing this one small act, I've become more productive," said another. "Intentional habit formation led to mindfulness in a lot of other ways" was a third comment. Similar perspectives appear in students' papers:

> I am grateful for . . . this project because it has truly adjusted my way of thinking about sustainability in my own life. Prior to this course, I did not think much about wasteful habits and believed that I couldn't make a difference as one person anyway. This course has taught me that not acting sustainably hurts my relationship with God and I am grateful that I have been able to focus more on that aspect. Also, doing this project has inspired me to instill more sustainable practices in my life, which I hope to be successful in.

Pursuing a more sustainable lifestyle in the context of contemplative awareness and theological reflection makes sustainability more satisfying and meaningful and makes virtuous habit formation easier. Students' projects provide experiential confirmation of their cultural insights in the World Café conversations.

Concluding Thoughts

A one-semester course is not long enough for the students to undertake a full journey to *action in community* together. We see a need for a follow-up that has been met, to some extent, at Holy Cross, the smallest of our three institutions and thus the most responsive to student initiative. Students from the Holy Cross class have created student organizations and have worked with college administrators to implement sustainability and social justice measures on campus as a direct response to what they have learned in this class. More is needed at Notre Dame and Saint Mary's to create structures for follow-up to the class. Other frameworks for students to continue the work of the course into a second semester may emerge. Still, we have evidence that we are making a difference in awakening students' prophetic imaginations. One student began her midterm essay by stressing her renewed vision:

> Prior to this class, my pessimism toward the future of our earth was greater than my hope for its salvation. In our studies of *Laudato Si'* and other course materials, I have realized that many more people

> do care about the well-being of our environment. Real solutions already exist as well as communities that encourage their neighbors to live sustainably, while also working towards bettering the earth. This class has inspired me to continue to seek out solutions in my own life and for my community around me, while also understanding the intersectional nature of sustainability.

Another student concluded her final project paper with this reflection:

> Reflecting on my experience throughout this project and this course, I have found inspiration in community efforts and the idea of creating change on a local level that begins with our own personal initiatives, whether that be through limiting your shower time, limiting your food waste, or researching sustainable energy sources. Regardless of those who acknowledge it or not, global change begins with individual change and everyone's stewardship and charism matters.

Enabling students to achieve this kind of inspiration isn't the end of our work, by any means, but it is a promising and necessary beginning if we are to scale up to a flourishing world.

“What Moves the Human Heart”

Visual Art as a Catalyst for Healing, Hope, Imagination, and Justice

Rebecca Berrú Davis
St. Catherine University

Our world swirls with a tumult of discordant messages competing for our attention and exhausting our emotional capacities. As educators we desire to move our students beyond this clamor that distracts and dulls our senses toward spaces that bring us closer to clarity and generative action. As we aspire to create pathways for our students to promote human and planetary flourishing, justice, and peace, finding meaningful entry points for exploration is paramount. This chapter explores ways that the arts offer revelatory avenues for critical inquiry and at the same time augment students' yearning for healing, hope, imagination, and justice. Providing opportunities for looking, being, and doing with art inspire ways to move through the tumult. An encounter with art is not only rich in its capacity for cognitive exploration, but also invites a posture of "beholding," and, as theologian Alejandro García-Rivera asserts, "moves the human heart."[1]

1. Alejandro García-Rivera (1951–2010) viewed theology as a living aesthetic in which the continuity of the beautiful includes the ordinary, the artist and their community, the work of art and craft, and the natural world, in addition to creations made by human hands. See Alejandro García-Rivera, *Wounded Innocence: Sketches for a Theology of Art* (Collegeville, MN: Liturgical Press, 2003), ix.

In this chapter, I offer three ways that illustrate how student engagement with the arts facilitates meaningful experiences that link mind and heart with their own personal and collective learning. The examples presented here are drawn from my own teaching experience; however, my intention is to offer them as ideas that may resonate across disciplines and be adapted for different purposes of learning.

These practices have emerged over my forty years in education where my interests have been interweaving art, spirituality, and justice. Underlying the examples shared in this chapter is this interdisciplinary triad. I situate myself as someone who took a circuitous route to higher education, by first garnering degrees in studio art and art history, then gaining professional experience as an art instructor, arts advocate, and museum educator, before stepping into my current position in theology. I maintain that art and creativity are not superfluous, nor the sole privilege of the elite. They are inherent in our condition as humans and prevalent throughout our lives, as evidenced by our varied inclination to create at any age.

In my own Hispanic family, I witnessed the ways women carried out the quotidian faith practices and traditions of our Catholic-mestiza roots. They did this with reverent intentionality, creating beauty and meaning-making memories with ingenuity and modest resources. From this upbringing, an appreciation of art as an expansive and ubiquitous expression of beauty was cultivated and felt. Now, in higher education at a Catholic women's university in the Midwest, I work purposefully to incorporate the arts in my classroom. I do this through the selection and careful curation of images, cognizant of art that may resonate with my students. Thus, with an intent to affirm the cultural and creative contributions of the diverse communities my students represent, I am attentive to their issues and concerns and the distinct expressions that they respond to.

I also recognize how images used within the classroom shed light on the contextual and emotive complexity of a community's histories and worldview. Thus, it is within a humanities classroom like theology that the arts are an especially rich resource. Visual art provides a point of entry to illuminate an issue, unpack challenging concepts, or raise questions related to power or the status quo. In short, images work to stimulate deeper thinking, evoke fresh insights, ignite the imagination, and move our human hearts. All these experiences are examples of generative processes that move students toward healing, hope, imagination, and justice.

Cultivating Practices of Looking

Cultivating practices of looking within a classroom environment involves focused viewing on an image and thoughtful reception of what is seen and heard. This process can make thinking and feeling visible and garner valuable insights through shared discussion or personal reflective writing.[2] It is a practice that students are intuitively inclined toward as their lives are steeped in social media, yet they may find themselves less invested in judiciously interpreting the messages. Cultivating practices of looking through art can nudge students toward discerning the explicit and implicit meanings of images to gain new insights.

In the classroom I guide my students through a process of describing, analyzing, and interpreting works of art. As in other disciplines where written text is read and analyzed, the aim in cultivating practices of looking is to begin with a process and proficiencies needed to move students toward "close-reading" of images. This effort first involves curating a collection of spirit-inspired works of art related to particular course themes and rich in capacity for eliciting affective responses.[3] Students respond well to opportunities to pause, "look closely," and delve into the intersectional and revelatory aspects of works of art, evidenced by their engaged discussions and focused writing.

To do this effectively, it is essential to begin by providing time for students to pause and "look" in silence at an image that fills a screen in its entirety. This is an important first step toward cultivating a practice of slow looking.[4] The quiet time may be awkward at first, but the process itself proves settling

2. Ron Ritchart, Mark Church, and Karin Morrison, *Making Thinking Visible: How to Promote Engagement, Understanding, and Independence for All Learners* (San Francisco: Jossey-Bass, 2011). See "Routines for Exploring Ideas," 53–108, particularly the section on "See—Think—Wonder," 55–63.

3. I have found the following sites useful as resources for images and keep a digital collection of selected images stored for use: JSTOR/Artstor Collections (https://www.jstor.org/images); SmArthistory (especially Reframing Art History [https://smarthistory.org/reframing-art-history/]); Google Arts and Culture (https://artsandculture.google.com); and links to museum collections (e.g., The Metropolitan Museum of Art), to digital exhibitions (e.g., "Immigration Stories" at the Smithsonian National Museum of the American Latino), or examples from local galleries (e.g., The Catherine G. Murphy Gallery at St. Catherine University, "Latino/Latinx MN: Re/claiming Space in Times of Change").

4. Shari Tishman, *Slow Looking: The Art and Practice of Learning Through Observation* (London: Routledge, 2017).

and centering. I move through a sequence of three steps that begins with naming and describing what is seen, noticing and analyzing what visual "tools" the artist used, and inviting discussion about the possible meanings of the work. This last step can be extended to include summative interpretations or carried out through personal reflective writing. This approach adapts an exploratory method of looking at art that moves from what is objectively evident in a work of art to subjective interpretation.[5] There are often students who initially want to begin with extrapolating, contextualizing, or interpreting what they are seeing. However, slowing them down and guiding them through describing, analyzing, and then interpreting the art invites contributions from students who process information in different ways. It also allows space to invite students to participate in the discussion wherever they feel most comfortable. With time, students became more adept at the process, seeing more details, noting artists' more nuanced ways of communicating, and offering interpretations that are evidence-based or directing their peers to the idiosyncratic or the intersectional overlays they see and understand. Students become more willing to explore the meanings the art prompts and more candid in claiming new perceptions. They are enthused about the new information garnered and find themselves more comfortable and affirmed in sharing their own resonant experiences that they bring to the image.

Time spent with an image allows students to follow their curiosity into areas that may be uncomfortable as they become participant-observers within a supportive community of peers to discover new understandings and insights.[6] When students are invited to "step into an image"

5. This process is an adapted approach of aesthetic criticism set out by Edmund Burke Feldman, *Varieties of Visual Experience* (Englewood Cliffs, NJ: Prentice-Hall, 1987), 471–94. I also draw on Michael J. Parsons, *How We Understand Art: A Cognitive Developmental Account of Aesthetic Experience* (Cambridge: Cambridge University Press, 1987). Another source that supports methods of viewing art conversationally is Philip Yenawine, *Visual Thinking Strategies: Using Art to Deepen Learning Across Disciplines* (Cambridge, MA: Harvard Education Press, 2013). Also see Visual Thinking Strategies: Critical Thinking and Inclusive Discussion (https://vtshome.org/about/).

6. I acknowledge the Wabash Center for Teaching and Learning in Theology and Religion for the opportunity to participate in two Wabash Fellowship Workshops, which culminated in pedagogical projects in which I explored the connections between art and empathy: "Images that Transform: The Use of Art in Teaching Theology in an Online

and guided through an experience of slow looking, they are moved into perspective-taking, empathy, and collective listening (without judgment). We have an inherent facility for empathy, and these practices of looking at art contemplatively support this capacity to move the human heart.

Creating Spaces for Belonging

My second example demonstrates how art can facilitate learning while enabling a sense of belonging within a classroom. This example is centered on an introductory learning activity and class community building experience where students identified, selected, and then shared a work of art with their peers. The artwork became a means to locate the work within a historicized context, address unanswered questions that the art provoked, and reveal connections that the art elicited. This experience was situated within an interdisciplinary humanities honors course called *Decolonizing Art and Religion in the Americas: Resistance, Reparations, and Repair* that my colleague, art historian Dr. Amy Hamlin, and I co-taught in the fall of 2023.[7]

A pre-class inventory confirmed that our students had minimal exposure to Latin American or Latinx art and nominal experience with religion. We turned to a unique opportunity in our community that coincided with the launch of the new semester. A special exhibit at the Minneapolis Institute of Art was in its final three weeks and was generously providing free access for students. The exhibit, titled *ReVisión: Art in the Americas*, included over 130 pieces of Latin and Central American art and was organized thematically.[8] Ancient pieces were juxtaposed with contemporary pieces and intentionally placed in conversation with one

---

Environment" at the Early Career Workshop for Faculty Teaching Undergraduates, 2020–2021, and "Art as a Catalyst for Cultivating Empathy Related to Issues of Justice" at the Early Career Latinx Workshop for Faculty Teaching Religion, 2021–2022.

7. I am grateful to my colleague, Dr. Amy Hamlin, and the seventeen students who participated in *Decolonizing Art and Religion in the Americas: Resistance, Reparations, and Repair*, Fall 2023, at St. Catherine University.

8. *ReVisión: Art in the Americas* at the Minneapolis Institute of Art, July 1–September 17, 2023 (https://new.artsmia.org/exhibition/revision-art-in-the-americas). Other museum or gallery exhibits, in the local community or those on campus, hold potential for carrying out this pedagogical process. Online exhibits are also valuable and accessible resources.

another to provoke connections. The exhibition proved an ideal entry point to our course, where the artistic expressions of the peoples of Latin America could be appreciated while exploring themes of struggles, exploitation, and oppression, as well as diversity, creativity, and resilience.

Within the first three weeks of the semester, we visited the exhibit twice during our ninety-minute class period. The students' first encounter served as an introduction to the collection with no foregrounding about the art. The students' task was simply to walk through the exhibit and photograph a piece they were particularly drawn to. A week later we returned to the exhibit for some special time set aside with its curator, Dr. Valéria Piccoli. She explained how the exhibit was meant to "formulate tentative answers to the complex question of what makes the Americas the Americas."[9] She spoke about the shape of the exhibit's "narrative" that she and her team worked to create. Students had opportunities to ask her questions about the installation and about specific art pieces. Time was allowed for everyone to revisit their previously selected piece with this new information.

The second step took place in the classroom. Students were asked to prepare a brief presentation with no more than three slides and explain what drew them to their selected piece. They were also asked to delve into the exhibition catalogue and other resources to assemble pertinent information about the artwork, the artist, and from what context the art emerged. Most importantly, they were to share why the piece mattered to them. Amy and I each modeled a brief presentation about the artwork we were drawn to, offered some of the contextual information related to our selected piece, and explained why the art resonated with us. We each shared a particular "community of concern," which revealed an issue we carried with us into the classroom. In the process, we disclosed to our students our own questions and vulnerabilities, revealing who we were as their instructors. With each student presentation, time and space were given to share what students learned about their selected piece. In this way, we were all introduced to a wealth of information about the histories, contexts, and

9. As viewers left the exhibit, a wall text, titled "Notes from the Curator," provided Piccoli's final statement. This is an excerpt. For more on the exhibit, see Tim Gihring, "How ReVisión Challenges the Narrative of American History and Looks Great Doing It," July 13, 2023, https://new.artsmia.org/hub/collection-exhibitions/how-revision-challenges-narrative-of-american-history.

salient issues connected to the Americas. Most importantly, students were invited to unveil as much about themselves and their identities as they wished, including their own "communities of concern."

This activity underscored that every preference was grounded in a personal experience or perspective. It showed how each work of art was an avenue for revealing a significant contextual and intersectional story. As students unveiled their personal choices and their new knowledge, it was clear that every selection was valid. As we learned more about one another, we gained deeper respect and appreciation for all we carried with us into this supportive and attentive space. We walked away from this experience bonded by the personal stories we heard, the shared practice of collective listening, and a deeper appreciation of who we were as a class community.

Laura Rendón, in *Sentipensante (Sensing/Thinking) Pedagogy: Educating for Wholeness, Social Justice, and Liberation,* speaks of the importance of "first-person" learning, where emphasis is placed on the student's own mind activated by their senses to learn and connect to the world around them.[10] Sentipensante, a Spanish word meaning "to feel and think," is an example of a pedagogic approach that, according to Rendón, "fosters both academic and inner-life skills and abilities, self-knowledge, critical consciousness, presence, team building, and creativity."[11] We learn from one another when we recognize how a student's own knowledge arises.

Sentipensante is an example of a pedagogic approach suited to promote academic prowess that combines critical inquiry with self-knowledge. It affirms inner-life skills and the compassionate concerns that students need for navigating an increasingly complex world fraught with unresolved challenges. Evidence shows that when students' voices are validated and hearts are acknowledged, each student's perspective and expertise is honored.

10. Laura Rendón, *Sentipensante (Sensing/Thinking) Pedagogy: Educating for Wholeness, Social Justice, and Liberation* (New York and London: Routledge, 2023). "A key aspect of third person learning is that it privileges intellectual reasoning, rationality, and objectivity, while first-hand experiences are related to subjective ways of knowing which reengage a learner's own mind, activate the senses, and allow learners to connect with the world around them" (2).

11. Rendón, *Sentipensante*, 6–7. As Rendón explains, "[S]entipensante merges sentir (sensing) and pensar (thinking) to create an epistemological framework that magnifies the learning experience so that the learner is fully present and engaged using the full capacities of mind, body, and senses" (3).

Inspiring Ways of Doing

My final example describes how student-engaged art exhibitions may serve as a catalyst for moving through the tumult and outward into generative action. This effort begins with students' in-class learning and the experiences and interests they bring with them. An exhibition project as a cooperative activity within the course acts as a platform to extend their learning to the wider school community. This pedagogical strategy is co-curricular, cross-disciplinary, and collaborative since it acknowledges and enlists the students' interdisciplinary expertise that resides in the classroom and draws on the support and engagement of entities beyond the classroom, such as campus organizations, academic resources and centers, and student services.

An art-focused exhibit begins with the content and aims of a course and encourages the emergence of important and relevant questions. Two exhibition examples centering on spirituality, justice, and religion from two separate classes are illustrated here. No matter the discipline, it is always a worthwhile endeavor to take students' learning experience beyond the classroom into a wider venue.[12]

A cohesive visual display of art and artifacts allows students to shape their own narratives or assert their own perspectives. A collection of images attentively assembled and intentionally curated can be used to affirm, unsettle, and disrupt static ways of thinking or raise questions about our understanding of the world. Within teams, students determine the thrust of the narrative or the ideological framework they wish to communicate grounded in the learning that has taken place.

As course instructors for *Decolonizing Art and Religion in the Americas,* Amy and I had access to a collection of art and artifacts as a resource for further investigation, a work space for students to use as a study room, and a library gallery reserved for them.[13] Students selected a piece of

12. Pedagogical strategies like exhibitions center learning around teaching skills, acquiring knowledge, and assessing tasks that are authentic and relevant to life. Some of these methods include High-Impact Programs (HIPS), Community-Engaged Leading (CEL), and Performance-Based Learning (PBL).

13. These works of art were a combination of a small collection of folk art from Latin and Central America donated by Sister Barbara Cervenka, OP, and the author's own collection.

art or an artifact to research from our study collection, which included embroidered textiles such as huipils and molas, amate bark paintings, wood-carved religious sculptures and alebrijes, ceramic figurines, painted gourds, retablos, and paintings of saints on tin. Each piece of handcrafted art carried within it a particular history and spirit. We drew on the expertise of our art department's exhibition members, who explained the logistics that are needed to curate and mount an exhibit. The rationale for this venture was made explicit as follows:

> As we learned in our thinking with and about the artworks in *Re-Visión: Art in the Americas*, an art exhibition is an exercise in storytelling. The curators and artists co-create a narrative told through the juxtaposition of resonant objects in space and time, as well as in the wall labels and chat labels next to the artworks.
>
> Central to this community project will be to collaboratively determine what "story" you wish to tell, identify a collective question you wish to pursue, select a theme or idea you want to highlight, or create a particular way you wish to engage your audience.[14]

Students delved into their personal research related to their selected artworks, which deepened and further informed their engagement with the content of the class. They then collaboratively determined the story and scope of their exhibition. As the project unfolded, it drew on the conceptual and spiritual process that we uncovered individually and together as we determined the specific thrust of the exhibition and its narrative. The result was a theme-driven exhibit focused on the relational worldview of the Indigenous cultures of the Americas. With the title *Pacha: Decolonizing our Cosmos,* the framework was in place.[15] The introductory text captured its essence and purpose:

> The complex idea of worlds and cosmologies has evolved and changed throughout human history, and the concept of this world

14. From an excerpt from the instructions for this project, "Exhibition: An Integrated Community Project," authored by Amy Hamlin.

15. See the student-created site for *Pacha: Decolonizing our Cosmos*: https://honorsexhibition2023.wordpress.com/.

> and other worlds holds significant meaning for every culture and civilization. The Quechua word *pacha* exemplifies this complex idea. Pacha roughly translates to "world." In ancient Incan beliefs, there were three distinct *pacha*: the *hanaq pacha* (world above), the *kay pacha* (this world), and the *ukhu pacha* (world below). These worlds are distinct from the Christian idea of heaven and hell.
>
> In Central and South America, "world" can represent many ideas. One is the worlds of the Incan and Mayan traditions, as well as the hundreds of other tribes and civilizations that have resided in Latin America. Another is the idea of the old world of Europe sailing to the new world of Latin America to colonize and exploit the land and the people.
>
> In decolonizing the art, history, and religion of Latin America, we work not only to deconstruct and analyze the world presented by the colonizers of these lands, but also the worlds that were obscured, erased, and lost but are now being reclaimed.

Exhibitions like this address salient issues, invisible histories, and the overlooked contributions by marginalized communities and their artists to raise awareness, educate, and inform.

Another exhibition project illustrates the creative potency of art to enact awareness and envision new ways of standing with others as we move through the tumult. This project took place within a class called *Maiden, Mother, Crone: Life Stages of Women's Spirituality*. The course included the study of spirituality in connection with the life stages of women and the spiritual journeys of exemplary figures, as well as individuals who, as guest panelists representative of life stages, shared their journeys. It also included the exploration of questions that emerged from the students' reflections on their own interior lives. Recognizing that their lives as spiritual seekers were directly related to women throughout the globe, students acknowledged that not all women lived privileged lives like theirs to have the luxury of carrying out a focused and intentional study of spirituality. Some women's lives focus on maintaining a livelihood for themselves and their families. Nonetheless, even in their quotidian lives, women often gathered in collectives for communal support and the making of crafts for sale. Through various examples, the students recognized that creating art together was a way for women to assess their exterior and interior lives individually and together in community.[16] Thus, an exhibition titled *Stitching Stories of Spirituality and Resilience* was organized to honor these tangible efforts and expressions of the spiritual lives of women beyond our classroom and throughout the globe. The exhibition was meant to situate ourselves in solidarity and relationship with these women.[17]

This exhibit was organized around the artistic expressions of women's textiles from three areas of the world: fabric pictures called *cuadros* from Peru, embroidered garments from Afghanistan, and flower cloth, or *paj ntaub*, from Southeast Asia. Examples were intentionally selected from these regions because they reflected the three key cultural and faith traditions represented at our university: Christian, Muslim, and Hmong.

From the introductory text:

> The art seen here is inspired by the women's worldviews and spiritualities grounded in Christianity, Islam, and Animism. Their creativity is reflected in their efforts to collectively remember their stories and traditions and mark the beauty and the realities that surround them. To do this, they draw on their unique visual language, using cloth and thread to ingeniously craft pictures or stitch garments. The creative work seen here also represents their entrepreneurial

16. Here I draw on the work of Brazilian theologian Ivone Gebara, who notes, "Resistance is also expressed in collective ways of working at various crafts, sharing responsibility for production, and selling and also sharing the profits. This becomes more than a work initiative because these small organizations become cells for personal and communal change. Within these cells women dare to talk about themselves, about social and political organization or disorganization. They have the freedom to reflect, agree, or disagree and then their consciousness, lulled by the clatter of plates and pans, begins to awaken. It finds words and feels the urge to reorganize this world differently." Ivone Gebara, "Option for the Poor as an Option for the Poor Women," in *The Power of Naming: A Concilium Reader in Feminist Liberation Theology*, ed. Elisabeth Schüssler-Fiorenza (Maryknoll, NY: Orbis Books, 1996), 142–49.

17. This exhibit was inspired by the content of the class and was organized and prepared with the assistance and expertise of teaching assistant Sofia Gibson and research assistant Kiara Gomes. Both students were supported by the Mellon Grant, a humanities-driven initiative focused on anti-racist pedagogy. This project was intended to situate our class community in solidarity and relationship with the women artists represented in the exhibition and all women's determined efforts to actualize their dreams.

> efforts to provide a livelihood for their families. Thus, their art reflects a resilience grounded in and sustained by a spirituality directed toward a thrust toward life, beauty, and hope.[18]

Both exhibitions are examples that consciously employ an approach that focuses on the life experiences of the creators and the common humanity we share—whether it be ancestral-past or contemporary-present. Students curate and showcase the creative work of members of communities who historically have had little access to power. Emphasis is placed on the artists' creative ingenuity, spiritual acumen, and resilience. The exhibitions inform viewers, support solidarity, and inspire different ways to think about justice as a global prerogative. In both examples, encounters with art deepen engagement in a way that "moves the human heart." This is an important step toward transformational change.

This pedagogical method merges the content of the class with the students' personal and collective reflective work, outward to a public project. This strategy finds resonance in what literary theorist and decolonialist Gloria Anzaldúa calls *conocimiento*.[19] Anzaldúa asserts that *conocimiento* is a deeper way of knowing that gives simultaneous attention to theory and praxis and to inner work and public acts.[20] For Anzaldúa, the combination of spiritual practice and political action is essential in enacting a transformational shift toward spiritual activism. The arts, in their varied expressions and intersectional connections, contribute to this transformational shift, which Anzaldúa notes here:

18. *Stitching Stories of Spirituality and Resistance*, April 1–28, 2023, Coeur de Catherine Library Gallery. See the article written by student Leah Keith, "Stitching Stories of Spirituality and Resistance: A Global Interreligious and Community-Orientated Exhibit," in *The Wheel*, April 14, 2023, https://www.stkateswheel.org/home/stitching-stories-of-spirituality-and-resistance-a-global-interreligious-and-community-oriented-exhibit?rq=stitching%20stories.

19. For an excellent summary of Gloria Anzaldúa's life and work as it pertains to this discussion, see "Spiritual Activism as Conocimiento," in Christopher D. Tirres, *Liberating Spirituality, Reimaging Faith in the Américas* (New York: Fordham University Press, 2025), 67–86.

20. Gloria E. Anzaldúa, "now let us shift . . . the path of conocimiento . . . inner work, public acts," in *Light in the Dark/Luz en lo oscuro: Rewriting Identity, Spirituality, Reality*, ed. AnaLouise Keating (Durham, NC: University Press, 2015), 117–59. In this chapter, Anzaldúa outlines this seven-step reflexive consciousness process.

> A form of spiritual inquiry, conocimiento is reached via creative acts—writing, art-making, dancing, healing, teaching, meditation, and spiritual activism—both mental and somatic (the body, too, is a form as well as site of creativity). Through creative engagements, you embed your experiences in a larger frame of reference, connecting your personal struggles with those of other beings on the planet, with the struggles of the Earth itself. To understand the greater reality that lies behind your personal perceptions, you view these struggles as spiritual undertakings.[21]

"Inspired by ways of doing," the two exhibitions described above open channels for exploring the interrelatedness of our world and social change. Art fosters an appreciation of the creativity and skills of its makers, but art also gives expression to deeper ways of knowing and understanding by reminding us of the spirituality, memory, and relationship that is inherent in the making. Anzaldúa points to this process of critically knowing our connection to one another through her usage of the Spanish word "*nosotros*," meaning "us." But writing it as "*nos/otras*," "us/others," she emphasizes it is "who we are together." "[C]onocimento," Anzaldúa explains, "motivates you to work actively, to see that no harm comes to people, animals, ocean—to take up spiritual activism and the work of healing."[22] This deeper way of knowing is the critical, relational, and holistic worldview necessary to transform oneself and our world. Art-centered pedagogies contribute to this process and to the spiritual activism that it motivates.

Conclusion

Art is a vital pedagogical tool—and gift—for reflecting on the nature of the human condition, examining salient issues related to social and personal existence, and considering the questions of how we are to contribute to a world where all persons and creation flourish. Experiences with art offer our students opportunities for fostering spiritual practices

21. Anzaldúa, "now let us shift . . . ," 119.

22. AnaLouise Keating, "'I'm a Citizen of the Universe': Gloria Anzaldúa's Spiritual Activism as Catalyst for Social Change," *Feminist Studies* 34, vol. 1/2 (Spring 2008): 53–69. Note the epigraph to this essay.

that restore attention, build relationships, and center peace. As Gloria Anzaldúa reminds us, "Our spirituality does not come from outside ourselves. It emerges when we listen to the 'small still voice' within us, which can empower us to create actual change in the world."[23] By reclaiming and nurturing this inner spiritual power through art, we can say that, instead of beneath the tumult or above the tumult, the arts provide us a spirit-driven way to "move our human heart" through the tumult.

23. Gloria Anzaldúa, "El Mundo Zurdo," in *This Bridge Called My Back: Writings by Radical Women of Color*, ed. Cherríe Moraga and Gloria Anzaldúa (New York: Kitchen Table/Women of Color Press, 1983), 195.

“Prophets of a Future Not Our Own”

Toward a Life of Meaning, Purpose, and Learning from the Other through Study Abroad

Ana Fonseca Conboy
College of Saint Benedict and Saint John's University

As educators, we are called to be models for our students: models of lifelong learning, discipline, passion, and finding a vocation and meaningful purpose in life. We bring our whole selves into the classroom, with our gifts and imperfections. While what we say is important, it is our actions that truly speak. It is our way of being that most stays with, and impacts, our students long-term. In the end, we desire that our students garner the skills necessary to engage meaningfully in their own lives. Irrespective of discipline taught, we strive to develop our students' transformative learning, equip them with tools, and instill in them values and behaviors that will serve them (and those around them) in the future. As such, it is not always possible to assess the outcomes of our objectives in the immediacy of meeting and working with students. Only time will tell if our efforts bear fruit.

While all academic areas offer the possibility of cultivating transformative behaviors, the field of languages and cultures, and in particular the study abroad experience, may afford especially potent paths for our students to become intercultural citizens, gifted with global awareness and a grounded humility.

Intercultural awareness and humility both require an openness to difference and an availability to notice and acknowledge such difference.

This nonjudgmental attitude implies a profound respect for the differences encountered. We ask our students to step away from their preconceived notions and assumptions, to draw out of themselves. We encourage them to dive into new experiences, into fuller existence, to embrace the newness and potential of seeing things through the eyes of the Other. In this process, we hear echoes of Walter Brueggemann's call to a "reframing" and prophetic imagination.

One set of techniques for confronting cultural assumptions and seeing through the eyes of the Other is provided by the practice of mindfulness. Mindfulness can be described as "the awareness that emerges through paying attention, on purpose, in the present moment, and non-judgmentally to the unfolding of experience."[1]

A complement to the mindfulness strategy is the concept of intercultural citizenship.[2,3] True intercultural citizenship (ICit) involves not only attitudinal change, but also implicit social and/or political action, aroused and mobilized by the interaction with a host culture. The concept of ICit also echoes the prophetic imagination.

In this chapter, we explore how a study abroad curriculum, when applied as transformational praxis anchored in mindfulness and ICit, can act as a prophetic vision in higher education.

The Program

The College of Saint Benedict/Saint John's University (CSBSJU) is a Benedictine institution located in Minnesota. The activities described below were part of a study abroad seminar-taught program in France during the fall semesters of 2018 and 2023. The activities aim to focus students' attention in the experiential opportunities of the study abroad experience. By doing so, students' concrete encounters will be rendered

1. Jon Kabat-Zinn, "Mindfulness-Based Interventions in Context: Past, Present, and Future," *Clinical Psychology Science and Practice* 10, no. 2 (2003): 145.

2. Michael Byram, *From Foreign Language Education to Education for Intercultural Citizenship: Essays and Reflections* (Clevedon, UK: Multilingual Matters, 2008).

3. Fan Fang and Will Baker, "A More Inclusive Mind Towards the World: English Language Teaching and Study Abroad in China from Intercultural Citizenship and English as a Lingua Franca Perspective," *Language Teaching Research* 22, no. 5 (2018): 608–24.

more meaningful, through personal beholding, contemplation, and reflection. While the activities were used in the study abroad context, a similar organization may prove effective and equally engender a sense of belonging and connection to the surrounding community in an in-home college classroom. These activities foster students' metacognition, availability to new ways of seeing, and action towards a more just community and future.

Inspired by Ignatian and Benedictine spirituality, as well as writings on mindfulness by Thich Nhat Hanh[4] and Jon Kabat-Zinn[5], the theoretical background for the study abroad seminar included readings from David Brooks,[6] Deepak Chopra,[7] Albert Camus,[8] and Brené Brown,[9] as well as Karen Eifler and Thomas Landy's *Becoming Beholders.*[10] The seminar was organized around the theme of mindfulness and the five senses and was structured around three axes: *Who Are THEY? Getting to Know the Host/Other*; *Who Am I? The Self through the Other*; and, *Who Are WE? Paying It Forth—the Self to/for the Other.* Students engaged in ongoing reflection, individually through writing and collectively through discussion.

Experiential opportunities and assignments were planned to catalyze and enhance the relationship between students and the host culture. The practical aspects of the seminar included excursions to and activities at local museums, concerts, markets, parks, and vineyards, where students were able to participate in a grape harvest. In these opportunities, students experienced an aspect of the host culture and reflected on it through

4. Thich Nhat Hanh, *The Miracle of Mindfulness*, trans. Mobi Ho (Boston: Beacon Press, 1975).

5. Jon Kabat-Zinn, *Mindfulness for Beginners: Reclaiming the Present Moment—and Your Life* (Boulder, CO: Sounds True, 2011).

6. David Brooks, *The Road to Character* (New York: Random House, 2015).

7. Deepak Chopra, *Seven Spiritual Laws of Success* (San Rafael, CA: Amber-Allen, 1994).

8. Albert Camus, "The Guest," in *Exile and the Kingdom* (New York: Vintage Books, 1965).

9. Brené Brown, *The Gifts of Imperfection: Let Go of Who You Think You're Supposed to Be and Embrace Who You Are* (Center City, MN: Hazelden, 2010).

10. Karen E. Eifler and Thomas M. Landy, *Becoming Beholders: Cultivating Sacramental Imagination and Actions in College Classrooms* (Collegeville, MN: Liturgical Press, 2014).

written assignments and in-class discussions. Through them, students cultivated awe to counter the indifference and apathy common in today's world, to exercise hospitality, and be at once host and guest to the Other.

Intercultural Citizenship and the Prophetic Imagination

The notion of ICit, championed by Michael Byram, stems from the concept of intercultural communicative competence (ICC). ICC requires linguistic and cultural competencies, cultural awareness and sensibility, and emotional intelligence. These attributes allow the student to acquire the knowledge, skills, and attitudes necessary to behave appropriately and effectively in multiple complex contexts and negotiate meaning across difference.[11,12] Critical cultural awareness and self-reflection supplement experiential learning and promote intercultural learning, encouraging a deeper understanding of the host culture and of the self. Being interculturally competent is demonstrated by respect, openness, and curiosity toward others and toward diversity.

Intercultural citizenship, a goal of language education, goes beyond the concept of ICC, adding a component of required social and/or political action catalyzed by interaction with a host culture.[13] Besides personal transformation through attitudinal change, it requires societal engagement. This urgency for constructive action toward the improvement of local and global communities echoes the prophetic imagination. Working towards ICit, whether in the language classroom or in the study abroad context, embraces the prophetic vision of the contemporary world.

Mindfulness as Foundational Attitude

Mindfulness cultivates perceptual acuity, attentiveness, and appreciation of life so that learning from, and with, the host culture can occur in

11. Darla Deardorff, *The Sage Handbook of Intercultural Competence* (Thousand Oaks, CA: Sage, 2009).

12. Michael Byram, *Teaching and Assessing Intercultural Communicative Competence* (Clevedon, UK: Multilingual Matters, 1997).

13. See Byram, *Foreign Language Education*; and Fang and Baker, "More Inclusive Mind."

a more meaningful and impactful way. With proper guidance and scaffolding, the study abroad setting can be inherently conducive to practicing mindfulness. Students enrich their identity through their relationship to the Other, through embodied encounters in the host culture. When we follow this approach in study abroad, students become "sojourners," rather than "tourists." As such, they can "learn and be educated, acquiring the capacity to critique and improve their own and others' conditions."[14] In this way, the study abroad context can hone students' senses to identify societal shortcomings and, at the same time, impel students to implement meaningful action to expand justice: in short, to enable students to adopt a prophetic imagination.

CSBSJU study abroad experiences are not merely "sign up and go" programs. Students are selected through extensive interviews and preparation. The aim of the interviews, beyond simply confirming that students are a good fit for the program and vice versa, is to introduce them to the framework adopted and discern how the group can form community, as a body of individuals bringing their own strengths and gifts to the working of the whole. From the very first encounter with the students, at the interview stage, mindfulness is the foundational attitude.

Before going overseas, the students explored the concept of mindfulness theoretically, through primary and secondary readings, and practically, through guided meditations, journaling activities, and student-led exercises. The pre-departure emphasis continued in-country, where students in the programs were urged to forge relationships with the world around them, nonjudgmentally, intentionally, and moment by moment, following Pope Francis's urging of a "culture of encounter."[15] A main takeaway from the pre-departure workshops is that every encounter, whether with another person or with one's surroundings, is an opportunity to pay attention, reflect on oneself, transform, and be transformed. And to accomplish this, one needs to exercise vulnerability.

14. Byram, *Teaching and Assessing*, 2.

15. Pope Francis, "Vigil of Pentecost," May 18, 2013, https://www.vatican.va/content/francesco/en/speeches/2013/may/documents/papa-francesco_20130518_veglia-pentecoste.html.

Inspiring Vulnerability

Brené Brown, whose text *The Gifts of Imperfection* provided food for in-class discussions, indicates the value of being vulnerable and embracing vulnerability as a strength rather than a weakness. In the context of study abroad, the ability to live and lead vulnerably frees us to be more open, patient, and accepting towards differences and different mindsets, and it may even inspire a shift in perspective. By experiencing vulnerability, we can be kinder to ourselves and others and more open to embracing our own brokenness and that of the world around us.

As a step in forming community, we engaged in simple icebreaker activities to inspire vulnerability in the students. The intent was for students to create a relationship of equity, to be comfortable with each other and with sharing a space, and to engage in respectful dialogue. An effective tool to forge community is "listening for understanding." In this activity, inspired by a workshop on the UNESCO methodology of Story Circles, led by Darla Deardorff (April 4, 2023, CSBSJU), students exercise vulnerability, authenticity, and confidentiality. As they engage in intentional listening, holding off on forming judgments and predetermined reactions to what they hear, they are open to learning and fostering deeper relationships. After establishing ground rules (maintaining confidentiality within each small group, giving complete attention to the person speaking, no note-taking, and no comments or interruptions when another is speaking), the guidelines are explained. In each three-to-four-person group, everyone takes turns sharing. The first speaker is the person whose birthday is closest to the day of the activity. The timekeeper is the person whose name follows alphabetically the first speaker's. The timekeeper then becomes the second speaker and so forth. The exercise consists of three timed rounds:

- **First round** (1 minute or less per speaker): Share two words or phrases that are crucial to your identity—to who you are—and why they are important to you.
- **Second round** (2.5 minutes or less per speaker). Share a memorable experience you had with a person who is different from you. What did you learn about yourself and/or about the other person in this experience?

- **Third round** (15 seconds per speaker): Finish the sentence, "The most memorable part of your story (from the second round) for me was. . . ." Share just the facts, not the *why*.

In the final (lightning) round, participants respond to their peers' contributions. They do not need to explain or support their response—they simply state what most struck them.[16] This activity helps distinguish between "listening for understanding" and mere "listening for responding." Proper listening for understanding can reveal how there is more to each of us than what we assume. Through "listening for understanding," participants realize that in our unique stories, there is a shared humanity. The activity requires that the students be open, mindful, and intentional, fully present to listening for understanding, rather than listening for responding.

Paying Attention

The world around us is complex and chaotic. We are bombarded with environmental stimuli that seek the continual attention of our eyes, ears, nose, tongue, fingers. . . . Though unable to reduce the flow of so much outside cacophony, we often protect ourselves by turning off its reception and interpretation. It becomes important to hone the skill of paying attention with intention and focus, to discipline our senses, and to be honest with ourselves and the reality that encircles us. We need to be countercultural and move beyond taking things for granted, beyond the cultural imagination.[17]

Each of the five senses is given priority at different times during the program. While in France, students were asked to visit a local market at least six times during the semester, each time focusing on a different sense, noticing, and journaling about the experience. In addition to honing perceptual acuity and cultivating their sensibilities, the market activity also encouraged students to support what the local community has to offer, a form of what Eggemeier describes as "commutative justice."[18]

16. Darla K. Deardorff, *Manual for Developing Intercultural Competencies: Story Circles* (New York: UNESCO/Routledge, 2020).

17. Matthew Eggemeier, *A Sacramental-Prophetic Vision: Christian Spirituality in a Suffering World* (Collegeville, MN: Liturgical Press, 2014).

18. Ibid., 169.

The sense of taste, so intricately linked to all other senses, was also explored through "blind tastings." Removing the sense of sight—our go-to and first interaction with food—allows for a more attentive relationship with the other senses, and, in this case, especially with that of taste. It forces students to focus on the smells, textures, and tastes, rather than the appearance, of what is in front of them. The logistics of a full "blind dinner" can be complex, but a simpler activity can reap the same benefits. Students bring a bandanna or some form of blindfold to class and place it over their eyes. We engage in a short collective meditation to bring students' attention into focus, calm the body, and prepare the mind and senses for the exercise. I have used morsels of Turkish delight (*loukoums*) in the past, in part due to the unfamiliarity most students have with them, but also to introduce class content related to migration and how it can change the culinary landscape. In this way, it serves the development of intercultural awareness. Slowly, deliberately, students are asked to take one *loukoum* from the box and first explore it with their senses of touch, smell, and hearing before gently bringing it to their mouth and taking a small bite to savor it intentionally. Students are taken out of their comfort zones and must trust. This exercise in mindfulness, using the *loukoums* and the five senses, is followed by brief journaling, where students expound on the little things they noticed to develop perceptual acuity.

In light of the Benedictine charism of our home institution, the senses of sight and hearing were also explored through *visio* and *audio divina*. In pre-departure workshops, students learned about and were guided through contemplative techniques by a member of the Benedictine monastic community. Once abroad, and using what they had learned, students conducted *visio divina* in a museum, choosing a work of art that most spoke to them, and *audio divina* at a local classical music concert. These contemplative strategies draw on the encounter with art and music to reveal interior movements. They allow for self-revelation while providing a learning opportunity about the culture that created the art.

Giving the gift of attention to another being or thing expresses respect and esteem for them. It is an acknowledgment of their existence, and that we are connected to them. It can also open one to seeing through a different perspective.

Reframing and a Shift in Perspective

Brueggemann speaks of a need for "reframing so that we can re-experience the social realities that are right in front of us, from a different angle," and experience genuine humanness.[19] In the context of study abroad and ICit, this can be accomplished by experiential opportunities in direct contact with the host culture, which are guided and scaffolded by the faculty director. Once students are keen on paying attention in the moment, intentionally and nonjudgmentally, they can more readily see through the eyes of another and describe the world differently according to their new insights and experiences.

One of the quotes that opens the course syllabus is Marcel Proust's, "Le véritable voyage de découverte [. . .] ne consiste pas à chercher de nouveaux paysages, mais à avoir de nouveaux yeux."[20] The citation, from *In Search of Lost Time*, continues, " . . . de voir l'univers avec les yeux d'un autre, de cent autres, de voir les cent univers que chacun d'eux voit, que chacun d'eux est . . ."[21] Perhaps such "seeing" is facilitated by leaving one's home and embarking on a voyage to another country. Much of the foundational work can be completed prior to departure and for this reason, pre-departure preparation is fundamental.

The pre-departure workshops prepare the students to explore social and cultural differences they will experience while abroad. We begin with a discussion of the familiar, of the local culture and differences of which they are already aware. In one of the first meetings, we discuss the concept of culture and its parameters and distinguish individual cultures from collective cultures.

Prior to departure, discussions also focus on assumptions, preconceptions, unrealistic expectations, and stereotypes of the host culture

19. Walter Brueggemann and Krista Tippet, "The Prophetic Imagination," December 22, 2011, in *On Being with Krista Tippet*, produced by American Public Media, 51:53, https://onbeing.org/programs/walter-brueggemann-the-prophetic-imagination-dec2018/.

20. "The true voyage of discovery [. . .] is not one of seeking new landscapes, but rather of acquiring new eyes."

21. " . . . of seeing the universe through the eyes of another, of a hundred others, of seeing the hundred universes that each of them sees, that each of them is . . ." Marcel Proust, *La Prisonnière [À la recherche du temps perdu]* (Paris: Éditions de la nouvelle revue française, 1923).

and the students' culture(s). By identifying and naming anticipations, one becomes more conscious of and attentive to them and less likely to allow them to become normative behavior once in the host country. The adoption of a mindful outlook and way of being fosters the availability and openness necessary to accomplish such tasks respectfully. Through activities, discussion, and reflection, students cultivate the understanding that one's culture is highly dependent on past personal experiences and ingrained values, that we tend to see the world through our own lenses and filters, and, as a consequence, any encounter with another culture can lead to learning that is influenced by our established notions. As we perceive our world differently from the way others do, our behavior and decisions depend on our lived experience.

Moreover, the importance of repetition in learning and consolidation of knowledge is stressed in activities such as "Finding the Unfamiliar in the Familiar." Partially inspired by Alain de Botton's chapter on traveling in one's own room,[22] this exercise can be repeated at different stages of the students' experiential learning. Pre-departure, the exercise involves exploring a familiar space and finding newness, the unexpected. In country, the exercise can be done a few weeks into the stay and later on, once students have had the chance to become acquainted with their surroundings. Students read de Botton's chapter and emulate the author's journey into the familiar, then reflect and write, which supplements an in-class debrief on the experience and discoveries. Students change into their proverbial "pink-and-blue cotton pyjamas,"[23] and explore their room by getting to know it all over again and discovering new things. This encourages receptivity and humility, as de Botton suggests. Through the activity, students hone their awareness of the environment around them and come to the realization that there is always more, always difference, always newness beyond what we (think we) know. It invites students to be guests in their own environment, to welcome any difference, and to be in awe at surprising elements they may encounter. Such an exercise can also prepare students to experience a "mysticism of open eyes," as

22. Alain de Botton, "On Habit," in *The Art of Travel* (New York: Random House, 2002), 238–49.

23. Ibid., 249.

described by Johann Baptist Metz.[24] Students are invited to see anew, fully awake in the present moment, with open eyes.

While in country, students journal regularly. Students reflect on their experience of the host culture in its multiple facets, and they come to conclusions about the Other. In the process, they also reflect on themselves to exercise metacognition. In the assignment "Become an Anthropologist," inspired by Richard Carlson's chapter of the same name in *Don't Sweat the Small Stuff*,[25] students take time to observe their surroundings as witnesses and let themselves be drawn in by a particular human interaction that captivates them. They are to do so nonjudgmentally, as objectively as possible, and contemplate the interaction with a "prepared mind,"[26] one that is open and ready to dig deeper beyond appearances. The observation is followed by intentional journaling, where students reflect on the "what," the "why," and the "what now." After describing the event, students reflect on what caught their attention and why (one to two pages). Finally, they reflect on what they beheld, trying to do so from the perspective of the Other, and then redirect their thoughts to themselves. Using their imagination "in order to picture alternatives to the present order," [27] they explain what they perceive from a different viewpoint. After beholding a man on a garden bench for several minutes, one student wrote:

> I was concerned for him and pondered the source of his pain. I said a prayer for him and left. I felt strange and almost guilty for not saying goodbye to him. I had spent time with him, even though he didn't know it, and I thought about him for a little while after leaving my spot in the park across from his bench. I worried about him and said a few more prayers. I had observed him as objectively as I could because, of course, it is impossible for humans to do anything completely without judgment. I noticed that my questions and any interpretation often stemmed [from] my empathy for others. I also noticed

24. Johann Baptist Metz, *A Passion for God: The Mystical-Political Dimension of Christianity*, trans. J. Matthew Ashley (New York: Paulist Press, 1998).

25. Richard Carlson, *Don't Sweat the Small Stuff. . . . and It's All Small Stuff* (New York: Hyperion, 1997).

26. Kabat-Zinn, *Mindfulness for Beginners*, 74.

27. Eggemeier, *Sacramental-Prophetic Vision*, 5.

> that I looked for things that made him strange. Maybe I should change that? Either way, I enjoyed 'becoming an anthropologist.'

The exercise draws students outside of themselves and asks them to shift their perspective, to reframe, so that they may honor another's viewpoint. Moreover, as exemplified above, it can lead to empathy and a sense of compassion for others. This student's engagement was her prayer. Her action exemplifies a shared sense of humanity and concern for the Other.

Exercises of this nature may have implications for the students' behavior and viewpoints and equip them with the courage to rethink and imagine what is possible for them. In a reflective essay on the topic of cultural identity, one student wrote, "I think this practice [saying "Bonjour" and "Merci, au revoir" in stores] shows respect for one another and I value this norm very much [. . .] I wish Americans would pick up on [it] and practice more often."

Intentional scaffolding of cultivating vulnerability, attentiveness, and openness to other mindsets, in tandem with self-reflective exercises, nurtures students' metacognition. In turn, it can also foster students' emotional maturation and empathy towards others.

Opening at the Close: "What brings me joy? What am I good at? What does my community need me to do?"

To fuel continued reflection, students watch Fr. Michael Himes's short video on "The 3 Key Questions."[28] This video is a good tool for engendering productive discussion in any group seeking to explore questions of personal gifts, passions, and vocations. Himes walks the audience through three key questions for discernment and creating a life of meaning and purpose: What brings me joy? What am I good at? What does my community need me to do?

Supplemented by readings from Deepak Chopra's *Seven Spiritual Laws of Success* and David Brooks's *The Road to Character*, students discussed the three Himes questions in the context of their approaching transition back to life "at home," and their potential actions for a more distant future.

After a semester of honing their metacognitive skills and practicing their attention and perceptual acuity, students were better conditioned to listen

28. Michael Himes, "The 3 Key Questions," Center for Student Formation, April 20, 2016, video, 30:35, https://www.youtube.com/watch?v=P-4lKCENdnw.

to their inner voice. "What brings me joy?," as Himes explains, is quite different from "What brings me happiness?," and the answer to the former is a first step in giving meaning to life. It requires an acute awareness of self, of inner movements and reactions. It also necessitates self-honesty.

After self-reflection, the second question shifts the focus outward: "What am I good at?" Often the answer is not self-evident and will require paying attention to others' praise or constructive criticism. Paying attention can be nurtured by the Benedictine practice of "listening with the ear of the heart" (RB Prologue). Accepting the answer requires humility and an availability to hear what we might not want to hear. What are our gifts? Our skills? With that knowledge, how can we best put them into practice to serve others?

The third question, "What does my community need me to do?," shifts to an even broader perspective and brings with it a sense of urgency, to nourish a personal vocation and transform behavior so that it will be beneficial for the common good, for those around us, whether at the local or global level.

After a semester of mindfulness practice, of encountering the Other nonjudgmentally, and of self-learning, the first two questions may find answers. The third may remain unanswered. The purpose is not to construct concrete answers but to let the questions simmer in students' minds, with the fierce hope that, in time, they will reach their own conclusions, be true to themselves and interdependent with others, and—using their gifts—serve those they encounter on the way, welcoming them as guests.

One of the last activities of the semester is to read together, and aloud, selections from the prayer "Prophets of a Future Not Our Own."[29] The prayer ends with, "We are workers, not master builders, ministers, not messiahs. / We are prophets of a future not our own." What does this mean to the students? We then invite a dialogue between the prayer and the ideas of Rebecca Solnit, for whom

> hope locates itself in the premises that we don't know what will happen and that in the spaciousness of uncertainty is room to act. When

29. Ken Untener, "Prophets of a Future Not Our Own," in Homily of the Mass for Deceased Priests, October 25, 1979, https://www.usccb.org/prayer-and-worship/prayers-and-devotions/prayers/prophets-of-a-future-not-our-own.

> you recognize uncertainty, you recognize that you may be able to influence the outcomes—you alone or you in concert with a few dozen or several million others. Hope is an embrace of the unknown and the unknowable.[30]

Equally, one could invite dialogue with Parker Palmer's definition of hope as an action, "holding a creative tension between what is and what could and should be, each day doing something to narrow the distance between the two."[31] At the heart of each of these statements lies the notion of action: We are "workers," as Untener's prayer states, who "may be able to influence the outcomes" by acting to narrow the distance between reality and an imagined reality of what "should be." We have the ability to act and effect change—slowly, surely, with a hopeful outlook.

In a society that is rooted in consumer culture and that puts so much pressure on our young adults to compare themselves with others (often in unrealistic ways), to succeed, to choose a career that will be financially stable, to have a life filled with material possessions and wealth, ending on this note can provide a sense of relief for the students. They come to understand that "[w]e cannot do everything, and there is a sense of liberation in realizing that. / This enables us to do something, and to do it very well."[32] This realization is especially poignant after having spent several months together focusing on things that often go unnoticed and cultivating an ethics of attention. Bringing meaning and purpose to life involves contemplating and reflecting on experiences, and then acting to serve the common good.

With Himes and Untener, we open at the close. The study abroad experience comes to an end and new life begins. We allow for the gentle knocking to continue, to move the students to persistent self-reflection, with an eye to the Other's well-being. We go forward together, and always with hope.

30. Rebecca Solnit, *Hope in the Dark: The Untold History of People Power*, 3rd ed. (Chicago: Haymarket Books, 2016), xiv.

31. Parker Palmer, interview by Einhorn Team, "Through the Prism with Parker J. Palmer," Einhorn Collaborative, June 22, 2021.

32. Untener, "Prophets."

At the end of the semester, one final conversation sought to integrate all individual and collective experiences, reflections, and learnings. Modeled after the Ignatian pedagogical paradigm inciting to experience, reflect and act, and as a culminating moment, I invited the students to follow the AWE strategy: to be fully Attentive and Aware of surroundings, noticing details and Acknowledging them; to allow oneself to be in Wonderment of them, grateful for them, be they good or bad; and, finally, to Engage with those surroundings, using one's gifts in such a way that will perpetuate the host-guest-host dynamic and bring improvement to all involved. In other words, we concluded the semester with the invitation to go forth and act for the betterment of students and their communities. We ended with a fierce hope to be prophets of a future not our own.

One discerns how the activities described call for a sacramental view of the world. It is from the tension, described by Brueggemann and Eggemeier, between the sacramental and the prophetic imaginations, that generative work can happen. By inspiring a sacramental vision via mindfulness, embodied encounters, and a contemplative focus, students reach the openness, attentiveness, and self-reliance necessary to adopt a prophetic vision of the present world and exercise respect for human dignity. Working toward ICit implies working toward active engagement in today's complex world and seeing the beauty of creation in a suffering world. While that engagement may not be immediately evident, we, as educators, can live with the fierce hope that the seeds planted will grow in the years ahead, and that we, as prophets of a future not our own, have done our job.

Teaching in Our Frightening Time

bell hooks and Spiritual Practices for Classrooms

William McDonough
St. Catherine University

> I talk about spirituality more now than ever before, because I see my students suffering more than ever before. . . . Feminism does not ground me. It is the discipline that comes from spiritual practice that is the foundation of my life.
>
> bell hooks (2017)[1]

Introduction: A story for our time, and the claims of this essay

A story that Patricia Hampl tells in her 2018 memoir *The Art of the Wasted Day* helps me understand why I have been so drawn to the later writings of bell hooks (1952–2021) in the past decade of my teaching.

More on hooks presently, but first to Hampl's story. She and I are at home in the Twin Cities of St. Paul and Minneapolis. Here she describes events during a January blizzard early in her own teaching career at the University of Minnesota. Hampl had scheduled writing conferences that day. Her husband tried to talk her out of making the trek across town to school, but duty called, and she relates:

1. George Yancy, "bell hooks," *On Race: 34 Conversations in a Time of Crisis* (New York: Oxford University Press, 2017), 23.

> I went foolishly through a killer Minnesota snowstorm to get to the university. The university had closed by the time I arrived. I sat in my office in the empty building cursing my ruinous work ethic. Then a knock on my office door. I opened it and there, like an extra out of Dr. Zhivago, stood my eleven o'clock, a quiet sophomore, Tommy.
>
> He looked anxious. He was really glad I was there because he had a big problem with the assignment. I had asked the students to write short autobiographies. "I just can't write about my life," he said, head down, boots puddling on the floor. . . . "See," he said, miserably, "I come from Fridley," one of those nowhere suburbs beyond the freeway north of Minneapolis. Nothing had ever happened to him and I was asking him to write about it.
>
> "I have good news for you, Tommy," I said. "The field's wide open—nobody has told me what it's like to grow up in Fridley. It's all yours." . . .
>
> The little world you alone can bring into being, bit by broken bit, angles into the great world. It's voice, your style. Or, call it what it is—your integrity.[2]

Hampl doesn't say how it turned out for Tommy. She does suggest that, especially now, we all face Tommy's challenge:

> In times of peace the age itself is the story—busy, busy, busy with its social self, making massive formal shapes. In times of terror like ours, we seek instead the sane singular voice, maybe to assure ourselves that sanity does exist somewhere, and the self, the littleness of personhood is somewhere alive. We know the awful part.[3]

I do know the awful part. Part of it is that very few of my students see the value of a theology course in the great world. More chillingly, many of them do not believe anything at our university can help them. As a 2022 study has it, Generation Z's distrust of higher education is at "red flag level."[4] But the most awful part of all is knowing that, for many years,

2. Patricia Hampl, *The Art of the Wasted Day* (New York: Penguin, 2018), 184–86.

3. Ibid., 97.

4. Katherine Knott, "Gen Z's Distrust in Higher Ed a 'Red Flag,'" *Inside Higher Education*, August 11, 2022, https://www.insidehighered.com/news/2022/08/12/survey-highlights-gen-zs-distrust-higher-ed.

the way I taught contributed to what we will see bell hooks call university students' pervasive sense of disconnection.

How to move beyond our own and our students' disconnection is the topic of this essay. It is here that bell hooks is my guide. Her later writings come from what a faculty colleague calls—in some impatience with both hooks and me—the "Buddhist period" of hooks's life. This essay asserts and unpacks ways that those writings are relevant for our teaching across the curriculum.

My argument has three parts: (1) hooks's own growing commitment to spiritual practices in her teaching, (2) adapting Catholic theologian John Shea's call for health care professionals to learn and model "foreground spiritual practices" to our role in higher education, and (3) describing specific spiritual practices I have used in the classroom over the last several years, practices that are exportable far beyond theology classrooms. Finally, this essay's conclusion underscores its connection to the book's larger theme of developing prophetic imaginations by circling back to the "Tommy" in me, who is slow to trust that the path to the great world runs through my own life. Suspecting that other academics are also sometimes slow in this regard, I claim that our willingness to take this path is the measure of our prophetic imaginations, that only our own spiritual practices can ground an imagination deep enough to sustain us for our tasks in this frightening, even terrifying, world.

ONE: bell hooks's movement from a self-propelled, abstract, activist understanding of practice to something deeper, quieter, and more personally costly

bell hooks's self-understanding as a teacher shifted in her later writings. While a long theoretical argument is out of place here, a brief examination of writings from three different times in hooks's life shows the evolution in her understanding of practice.

First, early on and before hooks wrote about her interest in Buddhist practices, spiritual practice for her was a rather solitary enterprise aimed at remaking the world according to her understanding. In a chapter in her 1994 book *Teaching to Transgress*, she writes:

> Living in childhood without a sense of home, I found a place of sanctuary in "theorizing," in making sense out of what was happen-

> ing. I found a place where I could imagine possible futures, a place where life could be lived differently. This 'lived' experience of critical thinking, of reflection and analysis, became a place where I worked at explaining the hurt and making it go away. Fundamentally, I learned from the experience that theory could be a healing place.[5]

We notice how intrapersonally (as opposed to relationally) grounded and monological hooks's approach is here. We also notice its activism: with good theory, "we will have no difficulty building a mass-based feminist resistance struggle."[6]

By the early 2000s, hooks was experimenting with spiritual practices in her own life, and theorizing communally and dialogically with her students. She begins a 2003 essay with the story of a university failing a young African American woman, asserting that many students experience disconnection in higher education:

> June Jordan longed to have college be the place that would connect all the fragmented pieces [of her life]. . . . She hoped that college would either give her the connection between the apparently unrelated world of white and Black, or that it would enable her to make that connection for herself. Her hopes were dashed. She found that none of the courses of study, nothing about the teaching facilitated her discovery of a connection. . . . For many smart students from backgrounds that are marginalized . . . college continues to be a place of disconnection.[7]

hooks writes that the antidote to disconnection is to "ground education within [students'] experience. Examining closely our perceptions, emotions, and beliefs—our experience—awareness and insight naturally arise. We are already endowed with the qualities of seeing, recognizing, feeling, and knowing. Spiritual identity arises in and of itself from identification with experience."[8] We should notice two things. First, practice here is

5. bell hooks, *Teaching to Transgress: Education as the Practice of Freedom* (New York: Routledge, 1994), 61. The book's fifth chapter is entitled "Theory as Liberatory Practice."

6. Ibid., 75.

7. hooks, "Spiritual Matters in the Classroom," in *Teaching Community: A Pedagogy of Hope* (New York: Routledge, 2003), 177.

8. Ibid., 182.

much less a solo enterprise than in her earlier writing; together we find connection in education. Second, the process here remains quite activist. Reflecting on experiences naturally lets students act from their depths.

In what seems to me a third period of her writing, hooks was not at all sure that reflection on experience naturally brings connection to ourselves or anyone else. In her 2009 book *Belonging: A Culture of Place*, she writes of her life after leaving home for college:

> My college years began the process of feeling split in my mind and heart which characterized my life in all the places I moved to. . . . Much of my life away from Kentucky was lived in a trance state, as though I was always there and not there at the same time. . . . Away from Kentucky my heart was spinning and it was only when the spinning stopped that I could see clearly and heal.[9]

In that book's preface, hooks writes that she experiences such disconnection everywhere in our culture: "I am stunned by how many citizens in our nation feel lost, feel bereft of a sense of direction, where they are going."[10]

Soon enough, though, she was recalling people who loved her—particularly, her maternal great-grandmother (Bell Blair Hooks—whose name, though in lowercase, Gloria Watkins adopted as her own). She writes:

> Even though life in my dysfunctional primary family was an endless series of hurts and heartbreaks, all the knowledge and wisdom that was shared with me by the old ones . . . from church and community, was empowering . . . I began to realize as I wandered from place to place, trying to find myself, that I had been given these precious gifts from the elders. . . . This wisdom remains life sustaining even though many of the elder teachers are long gone.[11]

In 2004, hooks moved home to teach at Berea College, 200 miles across Kentucky from her birthplace. Her return was largely contemporaneous

9. bell hooks, *Belonging: A Culture of Place* (New York: Routledge, 2009), 15, 18.

10. Ibid., 1–2.

11. Ibid., 204.

with her taking up regular Buddhist practice—as she writes in *Belonging*: "Seeking a place of spiritual grounding from Buddhist and Christian practice in my life today, I experience stillness as a path to divine mind. I want to live in that experience of knowing unity with the divine in stillness."[12]

Belonging is an astounding book, with all but six of its twenty-one chapters written after hooks moved home. The book's closing words recommend developing gratitude practices as an antidote to our disconnection: "Gratitude allows us to receive blessings; it prepares the ground of our being for love. And it is good to see that in the end, when all is said and done—love prevails."[13]

Gratitude is a spiritual practice for hooks. So, already in 2009, and especially by 2017, when she claims that spiritual practice grounds her, she means practice in a very different way than she had in 1994. Practice is not theorizing, but stepping away from theory into a more receptive place.

Her increasing focus on practice did not mean that she thought things had improved since the early 1990s. When she told Yancy in 2017 that her students were suffering "more than ever before," she added that white supremacy and patriarchy are our society's pervasive "mental illness. . . . We are a culture in crisis . . . a spiritual crisis as much as a political crisis."[14]

There is no blueprint here, but hooks gives teachers an opening to think about our spiritual lives.

TWO: What has this to do with us? Health care professionals (and teachers) as generalist spiritual practitioners

Just about when hooks began describing spiritual practices in her life, American health care began exploring such practices in its work. I now look briefly at what happened in health care, convinced that we and our students need something similar.

In his 2000 book *Spirituality and Health Care*, Catholic theologian John Shea noticed that American hospitals' regulating agency had, just the year before, claimed that "an individual's spiritual, cultural, and social value

12. Ibid., 65.

13. Ibid., 230.

14. Yancy, *On Race*, 19.

system is the key ingredient to understanding the individual's perception of treatment outcomes and continued stability."[15]

Shea also noticed that palliative care physician Christine Puchalski was asking health care to adopt a "dimensional view of human beings as biopsychosocial-spiritual beings."[16] In fact, by 2009, Puchalski had convinced the body overseeing palliative care to require that all of its "clinicians be able to distinguish when the patient presents with spiritual issues. . . . The model is based on a generalist/specialist model of care in which board-certified chaplains are the trained spiritual care specialists."[17]

Shea provides an extended argument that all health care would be improved (and its professionals happier) by adopting such a biopsychosocial-spiritual understanding of persons. A summary of Shea's call for health care professionals to understand themselves as "generalist" spiritual practitioners offers an analogy, that we ought to think about ourselves the same way.

Shea's most fundamental claim is that being human simply does have a spiritual dimension and we misunderstand ourselves if we ignore it: "The spiritual is a 'given' in human existence. . . . The only options are to include it or ignore it. But whether it is included or ignored, it is still 'there.' The spiritual has to be taken into account if health care is to treat individuals in their concrete particularities."[18]

Second, Shea acknowledges that the spiritual dimension was pushed out of health care in the twentieth century because of its advocates' bad behavior, but, appropriately chastened, it is time for the spiritual to be let back into health care: "The suspicion is that people in health care need to open themselves to the spiritual. . . . to stay spiritually healthy in an environment that paradoxically has ongoing invitations into spiritual depth and also ongoing invitations into soul blindness."[19]

15. John Shea, *Spirituality and Health Care: Toward a Holistic Future* (Chicago: Park Ridge Center, 2000), 43.

16. Ibid., 73.

17. Christine Puchalski et al., "Improving the Quality of Spiritual Care as a Dimension of Palliative Care: The Report of the Consensus Conference," *Journal of Palliative Medicine* 12, no. 10 (2009): 890–91.

18. Shea, *Spirituality*, 72–73, 77.

19. Ibid., 132, 135.

Shea's third point is that, in attending to the spiritual dimension of human beings, health care should notice its distinctiveness:

> In the unfolding agenda of self-care, it is appropriate to think and plan about how to care for our bodies, minds, and . . . relationships. However when it comes to the spiritual dimension, a different approach is needed. The spiritual is the deepest center of the person. It is the place from which we care; it is not an "object" we care for. . . . Therefore, it is more appropriate to say that the spiritual cares for us than to say we care for the spiritual. . . . We work with the mind and the structures of consciousness in order to open into soul and Spirit. Once this happens, a reverse flow occurs. Spirit gives itself into the soul, mind, body and world. . . . This is the distinctiveness of the spiritual.[20]

This sense of a "reverse flow" means that all grounded action has a prior passive moment. Think of Tommy needing to listen into his own life.

Fourth and most practically, Shea distinguishes foreground practices from background ones. People learn background practices within specific spiritual traditions, but those practices are less relevant to the public lives of professionals. Unlike background ones, foreground spiritual practices do two things: they "awaken spiritual consciousness in the midst of social interactions" and they help us "bring the resources of the soul space into the outer world of the everyday."[21] Shea proposes that health care professionals remain in touch with the spiritual by developing three broad types of foreground spiritual practices. A summary of these provides examples of how I have used similar practices in my teaching.

First, he proposes practices of self-remembering, "the ability to not lose touch with soul as you become more in touch with the world." Such contact does not happen naturally for anyone; we often lose it and must find our way back to ourselves and those around us. One way of self-remembering proposed by Shea is for us to go back to people we have harmed and "redo" our actions.[22]

20. Ibid., 108, 110–11.
21. Ibid., 128.
22. Ibid., 138–39.

Second are what Shea calls practices of knowledge, which do not add to what we know. Instead, they help us "become aware of what is in the mind and loosen our attachment to it. Often, it is our attachment to what we know that makes us 'blind and deaf' to what we most deeply desire as it knocks upon our door."[23] Shea again suggests specific ways of loosening our attachments, including learning to watch the flow of thoughts in our minds as we interact with others.

Third, Shea describes practices of compassion to help health care professionals experience their connection to the people they serve: "Conventional perception stresses our separateness and difference from others. Spiritual consciousness recognizes a fundamental communion within which separateness exists. When we are aware of this communion, it overflows into the experience of compassion."[24] He again suggests specific compassion practices, including quieting ourselves to experience how much like others we are.

Shea sums up: "People in touch with the spiritual are more excellent in every way. They embody the values that are essential to medicine and healing in a way appropriate to the gracefulness of the spiritual."[25] Is this not also true of us as teachers?

Before I make connections to our teaching, it is useful to reflect on bell hooks's developing understanding of practices in light of Shea's claims—perhaps particularly his claim that practices connect us to a "reverse flow," which grounds us for the hard tasks we face. It is only in hooks's "Buddhist period" that she notices gratitude for elders flowing into her. Before such practices, hooks acknowledges that she worked for years in a trance. She would understand this claim of Shea's: "Often we are simply missing. We are not there as we act."[26]

THREE: Foreground spiritual practices for us and our students

Teachers know about soul blindness—both our own and our students'. We need spiritual practices of our own. I must acknowledge that such

23. Ibid., 144–45.
24. Ibid., 150–51.
25. Ibid., 131.
26. Ibid., 135.

practices are not panaceas. I claim rather that we need centers of practice. And just as Shea asked hospitals to become centers of foreground spiritual practices, I ask Catholic colleges and universities to become such centers.

I reflect here on the two courses I have taught most—each at least fifty times over the years: a first-year theology course (Theological Questions) and an introductory ethics course (Theological Ethics). I acknowledge that for many years my teaching was nonrelational, monological, and abstracted from my students' lives. I organized Theological Questions around (my own) big questions; Theological Ethics was just as nonrelationally and abstractly organized around case studies from which students could choose and give their view. Somewhere along the way, predetermined theological questions and ethical cases gave way to a more relational approach, with practices designed to help us open to a reverse flow of energy. My students and I have come to cherish these practices.

I now describe three specific examples, each linked to at least one of Shea's three foreground spiritual practices. First, both courses now begin with the same short online survey, which I use as a practice of both self-remembering and compassion. Before the first day of class, I ask students to read bell hooks's essay *Spiritual Matters in the Classroom* and to respond to two questions. I assure them that their anonymity will be protected as they take the survey and in our classroom use of it. While I share a collated list of responses, no one is ever asked to divulge her own responses. Here are the questions:

> *Please briefly describe an experience from any time in your life that relates to the story about June Jordan that bell hooks tells near the beginning of her essay. In a paragraph, please describe a time when you were hoping for connection but experienced disconnection.*
>
> *Now, in the opposite direction, please describe a time when you were hoping for connection and found it. In a paragraph: What happened? What was it like?*

Our opening class session is devoted entirely to considering the collated student responses. As we read the responses aloud, I ask each student to listen for and mark two texts. First, they identify one response (not their own) to the question about disconnection. They tell many stories of dashed hopes for connection—both before and during their time at our school. Second, they are to listen for one response (not their own) to the question about connection that surprises them and evokes some happiness in them. As they read each other's stories and as I tell a story or two of my own, I hope the conversation helps students touch our shared humanity. I also hope they have a self-remembering experience, being brought back to something about themselves they may have forgotten.

Then I tell them that I hope the whole course will be more connecting than disconnecting and that we will write anonymously at least two more times about their experiences of connection and disconnection—this time in the course itself. Having named Shea's practices explicitly and linked our first day's experience to them, I aspire to some self-remembering of my own when we repeat the survey. I tell students that when they name times I have caused disconnection, I will ask to redo what happened. I often do not see these coming.

As a second example, both courses have a text explicitly linked to practices of self-remembering, inviting students back into their own depths. In Theological Questions, most recently we have used Brian Doyle's posthumous essay collection, *One Long River of Song: Notes on Wonder*, dedicating each of this three-times-a-week course's fourteen Fridays to two of Doyle's essays. The essays are focused on wonder; as Doyle puts it: "We are only here for a minute, for a little window. And to use that time to catch and share shards of light and laughter and grace seems to me the great story."[27] I want students to see a connection between their own stories and the great story. On "Wonder/Mystery/Theological Questions Fridays," we come back week after week to Doyle's short essays and to experiences of mystery they evoke for students. Each student writes their own "note on wonder" late in the semester—graded only on whether the student does what is asked of her.

In Theological Ethics, we have used hooks's *Belonging* for the last several years, and I make connections between it and Shea's foreground practices. But for the last few years, our main "practice book" in that course has been Buddhist-influenced psychologist Kristin Neff's book *Self-Compassion*. It is filled with exercises (spiritual practices!) that help us be grounded in self-compassion. The central practice of the book is a five-minute "self-compassion break," in which we call to mind a difficult

27. Brian Doyle, *One Long River of Song: Notes on Wonder* (New York: Little, Brown, 2019), xx.

situation in our own lives and silently speak three phrases to ourselves: *This is a moment of suffering; suffering is a part of human life; may I be kind to myself in this suffering.*[28]

There is a "reverse flow" here, as both self-remembering and compassion reduce the sense of distance between us. There is an assignment here as well. Students select two exercises from the book they will practice outside of class. Twice during the semester, students report on any one exercise they have found helpful.

Finally, both courses end with a project involving the foreground spiritual practice of knowledge. Each student chooses a question important in their own life. In Theological Questions, the question is to be about mystery; in Theological Ethics, it is directed at a practical moral challenge important to the student. Students receive all the points if they articulate their question in a nonrhetorical way (as a genuine form of self-inquiry), explain why the question is important to them, name at least one course source that influenced their thinking on it, engage in a conversation with someone from outside the course who they think can help them go deeper with their question, give their own best response to the question at this point in their life, and present all this to the rest of us.

I conclude with two examples of what students have done with this assignment, one from each course in the spring semester of 2024. First, in Theological Questions, a Muslim student used one of our optional course visits to a Zen Buddhist meditation center to pose a question to the guiding teacher. After we sat in silence and heard a dharma talk, the teacher invited conversation. My student's hand shot up. She asked: *What does it feel like to be fully present as one sits in meditation or prayer? This is very important to me.* The teacher smiled, thanked the student, spoke about experiences of knowing what it is like not to be present while meditating, and invited further conversation with the student. The question became the student's final project. When she reported her experience in class, other students applauded spontaneously.

Second, in Theological Ethics, one student articulated her final course question thus: *How can I be useful in efforts to reduce gun violence in this country?* The question arose because she had stood next to her best friend

28. Kristin Neff, *Self-Compassion: The Proven Power of Being Kind to Yourself* (New York: Harper Collins, 2011), 234–35.

in a bar a couple of years before and watched in horror as her friend was shot and killed, caught in the crossfire between two men shooting at each other. With respect to learning from another, the student had spoken with our state's attorney general about legislation mandating metal scanners in all bars and accepted his invitation to serve on a task force to that end. And because her friend loved basketball, the student also established a fund to support young local girls interested in playing basketball but unable to afford the costs involved. When she reported this in class, many asked to donate to the fund.

While these examples are extraordinary, it is always a spiritual practice to ask ourselves what is most important to us and wait for insight. Listening to these and so many other stories has become a spiritual practice for me. I am convinced that foreground spiritual practices of self-remembering, knowledge, and compassion are transportable across the disciplines.

Conclusion: Foreground spiritual practices as source and measure of our prophetic imagination

Spiritual practices like these are students' and our way to connect our little worlds to the one great world. For too long, I tried to use education to leap out of my small life into a greater world. But, twenty-six years ago, I was privileged to come to St. Catherine University. Soon, I was reading bell hooks. A little more slowly, I began trusting myself and my students enough to engage in foreground spiritual practices with them. Then such practices became the foundation of my teaching.

What does this have to do with the prophetic imagination? There is no thinking our way into such an imagination. It grows only as we help each other listen for and open our hearts to whatever truths emerge from our own small lives. I ask students what they are learning in such practices and tell them what I am learning. Most of all, we tell each other about our growing sense that love really is at work in our small lives and that it is bringing us further into the great world, even in times as terrifying as ours.

Energized for Freedom

Hospitality and Antiracist Pedagogy

Mary M. Doyle Roche
College of the Holy Cross

Cultures of belonging in college are fostered by attending to classroom ecology. Changes in course content (including the topic of racism on syllabi, decolonizing the canon of disciplinary literature, and espousing an intersectional approach to social analysis) are crucial for inclusive pedagogy but are insufficient if habits of classroom engagement and assessment remain unchallenged. Antiracist teaching practice disrupts the power dynamics of the learning relationship, which involves a radical rethinking of assignment development and evaluation. Resistance to classroom cultures and grading schemes that flow from and perpetuate systems of white male supremacy in the guise of intellectual "rigor" is vital. A culture of belonging in higher education in an antiracist key also prompts a radical rethinking of hospitality as we acknowledge that many of our institutions reside on stolen land and reap ongoing benefits from the sale of stolen people.

I am an avid consumer of mysteries and police procedurals. When I hear the word "rigor," my first thought is that we are determining how long something or someone has been dead. It is a word used at the scene of a crime. Classroom as crime scene is a chastening image. What if *vigor*, rather than *rigor*, is the goal of a course? What if the task is not mere survival of a strict regimen that results in physical and emotional exhaustion, but rather an invitation to flourishing marked by *energy* and *freedom* for everyone (student and teacher alike)? What if teaching and learning could be genuinely *vigorous*, that is to say, healthy and energizing?

This chapter will draw on the work of education scholars in the vanguard of antiracist and anti-misogynist pedagogy and critiques of corporatized higher education to offer a reflection on strategies that invite educators in any discipline to leverage university mission and religious charism to advance antiracist practice toward what education scholar Bettina Love calls "freedom dreaming." Though I share my experience within the humanities (specifically, theological ethics), the strategies themselves are practical and portable across disciplines.

Antiracist and Abolitionist Pedagogy

In recent years, I have become further acquainted with the work of a number of antiracism activists and critical race and feminist theorists, including Layla F. Saad, Brittney Cooper, Ibram X. Kendi, Tarana Burke, Ayo Tometi, Alicia Garza, Ijeoma Oluo, Michelle Alexander, Isabel Wilkerson, Nikole Hannah-Jones, Rachel Swarns, Marc Lamont Hill, Clint Smith, Lorgia Garcia-Peña, Tricia Hersey, and Bettina Love, and icons such as bell hooks, Angela Davis, and Kimberly Crenshaw. Love examines school policy and practice through an intersectional critical race feminist queer lens. Advocating for the abolition of what she terms the "Educational Survival Complex" (ESC) in K–12 schools, Love calls on allies to become co-conspirators in the construction of education as the practice of "freedom dreaming."[1] Her vision shares resonances with bell hooks's transgressive education as the practice of freedom, M. Shawn Copeland's enfleshing freedom, Bryan Massingale's calls to the welcome table, Willie Jennings's pedagogical ecology of belonging, and many other Black theologians in the United States, including theologians on the Black Catholics Syllabus compiled through the labor of Tia Noelle Pratt (including Collins, Eugene, Harris, Hayes, Mosely, Phelps, Segura, White, and Williams).[2] As Massingale notes in his essay, "Toward a Spirituality

1. Bettina Love, *We Want to Do More than Survive: Abolitionist Teaching and the Pursuit of Educational Freedom* (Boston: Beacon Press, 2019).

2. M. Shawn Copeland, *Enfleshing Freedom: Body, Race, and Being* (Minneapolis: Fortress Press, 2009); bell hooks, *Teaching to Transgress: Education as the Practice of*

of Racial Justice," "the goods, lands, and material wealth of nonwhite peoples exist for the benefit of white people and can be seized by any means they deem fit."[3] Here I must acknowledge that my "use" of the work of Massingale, Jennings, Love, Lorde, and others is an example of such seizure. As a white, straight, cis-woman, I am guilty of misappropriating the insights of BIPOC and LGBTQIA+ scholars to further my arguments. That indictment sticks to me always, even as I strive to be an abolitionist co-conspirator in writing this essay.

Love calls for the abolition of an ESC that is racist and white supremacist, sexist and patriarchal, LGBTQIA+-phobic, ableist, and neoliberal capitalist. Higher education's complicity in the perpetuation of the ESC operates on institutional and systemic levels and influences college culture and policy. It also lives in student-teacher interactions, necessitating abolitionist practices of resistance in the classroom. The Underground Railroad provides a helpful if limited analogy. Abolitionists strove to end the institution of slavery but also engaged in civil disobedience by securing immediate, if precarious, safety for people day by day, night by night, house by house. Faculty can strive for antiracist pedagogy course by course, class by class, and connect with others who attempt to do the same. Colson Whitehead invites us to imagine the Underground Railroad as a "magnificent operation," a "marvel to be proud of," where both those who escaped and those who abetted "found salvation in the coordination of its stations and timetables." Radical hospitality indeed.

Abolitionist pedagogy resists the false opposition between choosing an education that prepares students for a "real world" of high expectations and an inclusive abolitionist pedagogy. The goal of energizing for college freedom dreaming is *freedom for the whole community.* It is sustained by a firm commitment to education as a common good that requires equitable access and full participation of all learners (including students, faculty,

---

Freedom (New York: Routledge, 1994); Bryan Massingale, *Racial Justice and the Catholic Church* (Maryknoll, NY: Orbis Books, 2010); Willie James Jennings, *After Whiteness: An Education in Belonging* (Grand Rapids, MI: Eerdmans, 2020); and the Black Catholics Syllabus, available at https://tiapratt.com/blackcatholicssyllabus-2/.

3. Bryan Massingale, "Toward a Spirituality for Racial Justice: The Transformation of Consciousness and the 'Souls of White Folks,'" in Laurie Cassidy and M. Shawn Copeland, eds., *Desire, Darkness, and Hope: Theology in a Time of Impasse* (Collegeville, MN: Liturgical Press, 2021), 335.

staff, and administrators). Writing about theological and ministerial education in particular, Willie Jennings says,

> A teaching life can be a powerful intervention into the structures of racial antagonism that shape the West, but only if we can find a way to overturn our colonial legacies and draw the dominant trajectories of Western educational institutions toward more life-giving ends. A life that teaches in this racially agonistic moment must be angled in a new direction beyond simply building intellectual capacities, toward presenting an embodied desire to learn from and join others. To be teachers who live by faith at this moment is to be those who speak a word of belonging not simply by their words but by their lives.[4]

Antiracism also upends many assumptions in the practice of hospitality. Jennings lays down a spiritual challenge to theological educators who "still imagine our students as guests in a world that we host, rather than as the host of a world we have entered as guests."[5] For Jennings, "the invitational character of our work" is inescapable and is animated by "an embodied desire for life together." He continues,

> We who teach are guests who again and again enter the worlds of our students and we must create and perform a pedagogy that shows that entrance in honor and love. We share this world with our students; this is the truth that must find its way more tangibly in the pedagogy of the academy and into our lives.[6]

Jennings's insights nuance Massingale's image of the welcome table in his calls for racial justice in the Catholic Church, "Justice is that state wherein the despised and outcast are respected and treated as worthy to dine as honored guests at the table."[7] Together, Massingale and Jennings challenge visions of educational hospitality that take for granted the centrality of the professor and neglect to acknowledge that the resources that colleges share were never really theirs to begin with.

4. Willie Jennings, "Race and the Educated Imagination: Outlining a Pedagogy of Belonging," *Religious Education* 112, no. 1 (2017): 58.

5. Ibid., 63.

6. Ibid., 64.

7. Massingale, *Racial Justice*, 139.

The ESC and Higher Ed Grind Culture

In *We Want to Do More than Survive: Abolitionist Teaching and the Pursuit of Educational Freedom*, Love writes,

> America's educational history is overrun with dark suffering. Native American boarding schools, school segregation, English-only instruction, *Brown v. Board of Education*, No Child Left Behind, school choice, charter schools, character education, Race to the Top . . . all have been components of an educational system built on the suffering of students of color. I call this the educational survival complex, in which students are left learning to merely survive, learning how schools mimic the world they live in, thus making schools a training site for a life of exhaustion.[8]

Love highlights key characteristics of the ESC: the "disposability of Black and Brown children," "no excuses" character education that values grit as a premier virtue, and the bullying of minoritized students by other students, faculty, and administrators.[9] Disposability and bullying are grave issues, but it is the particularly seductive lure of "no excuses" character education in higher ed that I wish to challenge here. Love argues that the drivers behind character education are "wealthy philanthropists, corporate foundations, and Wall Street hedge fund managers who believe dark children need discipline, character education, rudimentary academic skills, and full submission to White economic demands."[10] At the college level, I have begun to question whether interest in a "rigorous education" is simply "no excuses" in disguise, especially when "rigorous" is essentially a synonym for white, cis-male, and Eurocentric. It is unforgiving in its assessment of everything that deviates from that ideal. In *After Whiteness*, Jennings provides powerful examples from his experience as a dean interacting with faculty and students devastated by the casual cruelty of their professors and teaching assistants.[11] Love calls this "spirit murdering." She writes, "What I am describing is a life of exhaustion, a life of doubt, a life of state-sanctioned violence, and a life consumed with the objective of

8. Love, *More than Survive*, 27.
9. Ibid., 30.
10. Ibid.
11. Jennings, *After Whiteness*, 54–57.

surviving. It is trying to survive in, and at the same time understand and make sense of, a world and its schools that are reliant on dark disposability and the narratives necessary to bring about that disposability."[12]

Exhaustion. Self-doubt. Depression and anxiety. Does any of this sound familiar? Even white, straight, cis-gendered, affluent students are crumbling under the weight of zero-sum competition and grind culture in nearly every sphere of life.[13] Refusing to face the ways in which grind culture is shaped by and advances white supremacy, patriarchy, and rape culture on our campuses fails to meet the challenges of antiracism.[14] The relentless challenge of simply existing in a white, male, heterosexist, cis-centric world with its overt violence and microaggression is exhausting on a different scale. Framing an exhausting survival mode as the "virtue of grit" serves the status quo, simultaneously romanticizing the struggles of white students and dismissing the suffering of BIPOC and LGBTQIA+ students.[15]

At many of our institutions, faculty have a degree of relative autonomy with respect to their courses and classrooms. Any ethical analysis of the ESC must include attention to the role that faculty choices play in its entrenchment. Here are a few examples from my experience: courses designed to weed out students from majors or that have the practical consequence of sorting students prematurely,[16] faculty in the humanities insisting that students take these courses as "seriously" as they do courses in STEM and signaling this in the workload and complexity of course material, overcorrecting African American vernacular English and other ways of speaking and writing that do not conform to the habits of white language,[17] tolerating and enacting microaggressions within classrooms,

12. Love, *More than Survive*, 39.

13. See Angela Duckworth, *Grit: The Power of Passion and Perseverance* (New York: Scribner, 2018), and Heather McGhee, *The Sum of Us: What Racism Costs Everyone and How We Can Prosper Together* (New York: One World, 2022).

14. See Ijeoma Oluo, *Mediocre: The Dangerous Legacy of White Male America* (New York: Seal Press, 2021), and Megan McCabe, "A Feminist Catholic Response to the Social Sin of Rape Culture," *Journal of Religious Ethics* 46, no. 4 (2018): 635–57.

15. Tricia Hersey, *Rest as Resistance: A Manifesto* (New York: Little, Brown Spark, 2022).

16. Alo C. Basu, "Are We Ready? The Future of Inclusive Excellence in STEM," *The Thinking Republic*, March 2021, https://www.thethinkingrepublic.com/fulcrum/are-we-ready.

17. Asao Inoue, *Labor-Based Grading Contracts: Building Equity and Inclusion in the Compassionate Writing Classroom* (CSU Open Press, 2019), and *Antiracist Writing Assess-*

adopting costly course materials, maintaining a Eurocentric curriculum and/or recolonizing the work of minoritized scholars, making ableist and classist assumptions in course design and implementation, allowing "rigor" to go unchallenged as an absolute value that creates false choices between excellence and inclusion and mistakes "high standards" for the shared production of knowledge, and refusing to explore the impact of unconscious bias on assignments and practices of assessment. The outcomes of these habits that Jennings refers to as "refined brutality"[18] are clear and are being studied most closely in the STEM fields where BIPOC and women students withdraw from or are forced out of these courses of study and out of fields that enjoy high remuneration and status in society.[19]

Abolitionist Ethics and the Common Good of the Classroom

There are numerous resonances between critical antiracist praxis and themes in Catholic social thought, though antiracism does not derive its legitimacy from these resonances. Each asserts the absolute intrinsic dignity of persons who are profoundly relational and interdependent with other persons, communities, and social structures. Each takes embodied experiences seriously as sources of ethical reflection without which any vision of justice will be found wanting. Each demands a bias in favor of those who are most vulnerable and who have been brutalized by patterns of systemic violence throughout history. Each demands solidarity and practical action at every level of social organization. Each recognizes that all human relationships and organizations are marred by injustice (though institutions are reluctant to acknowledge their complicity in the evils of racism, white supremacy, sexism, and gender-based injustice).

An *antiracist and feminist common good tradition* can transform our classrooms. The common good, understood as "the sum total of social conditions" in which persons and communities can pursue flourishing most easily, is undermined by racism, white supremacy, misogyny, homophobia,

---

ment Ecologies: Teaching and Assessing Writing for a Socially Just Future (Parlor Press, 2015).

18. Jennings, "Race and the Educated Imagination," 64.

19. Basu, "Are We Ready?"; and C. Singh et al. "Changing Social Contexts to Foster Equity in College Science Courses: An Ecological-Belonging Intervention," *Psychological Science* 31, no. 9 (2020): 1059–70.

poverty, and violence.[20] If a course is a common good marked by antiracism and feminism, then it honors everyone's participation in making that good a reality: professors, students, administrators, and those who produced the books, articles, films, artwork, and the rest of the course's materials. As a common good, the course must be easily accessible and facilitate the participation of every unique member. Courses are successful only if everyone contributes and learns. The insights of teaching theologians like Jennings and Massingale harken to a celebration at which everyone can find the table, pitch in, take a seat of honor, and dine. The professor could be the host who sets the table for a meal that is nutritious and delicious. The risk is that the menu may be limited and harm rather than satisfy. Instead, the course could be more of a potluck affair. The professor is not the host but rather a guest, whose experience at lots of celebrations prepares them to find a spot on the table for every dish, a seat for every celebrant, and a holding space for the guests' coats, hats, and bags. This image of the common good classroom is attractive because it reminds us that classrooms can be pleasurable, joyful places where everyone engages in an exhilarating and generous gift exchange and is enriched by it.

What this image fails to capture adequately is the place of power in classroom dynamics. The expectation of dominance on the part of some (the professor) and the expectation of struggle on the part of others (especially BIPOC, first-generation, and LGBTQIA+ students) contribute to the abuse of power.[21] It is the task of professors who hold the responsibility for evaluation to "transform power so that it is no longer producing misery."[22] As Jennings so powerfully claims,

> A shared space of learning does not mean that we have nothing to teach our students. It means that the work of teaching must always be embedded in the work of learning, learning not only our students' abilities and interests, but the worlds—social, cultural, geographic—out of which they come. It means learning the deep histories of place

20. *Gaudium et Spes*, par. 26, https://www.vatican.va/archive/hist_councils/ii_vatican_council/documents/vat-ii_const_19651207_gaudium-et-spes_en.html.

21. Massingale, *Racial Justice*, 79.

22. Alicia Garza, *The Purpose of Power: How We Come Together When We Fall Apart* (New York: One World, 2020), 269.

> where we teach and live, and it means being open to the expansion of our identities toward the life-worlds of our students.[23]

How then might professors adopt a pedagogy in which power is leveraged on behalf of students, with a bias in favor of minoritized students?

Adventures in Antiracist, Abolitionist Pedagogy

According to Love, "Abolitionist teaching is the practice of working in solidarity with communities of color while drawing on the imagination, creativity, refusal, (re)membering, visionary thinking, healing, rebellious spirit, boldness, determination, and subversiveness of abolitionists to eradicate injustice in and outside of schools."[24] It is also "choosing to engage in the struggle for educational justice knowing that you have the ability and human right to refuse oppression and refuse to oppress others, mainly your students."[25] There are numerous opportunities to make concrete changes that move in the direction of abolition of the ESC. Many of them wed the approaches of universal design for education and inclusive excellence.[26] They shift from a deficit mindset, in which the focus is primarily on what students lack and how the teacher fills the void, toward an asset-based perspective.[27]

Abolitionist pedagogy takes seriously insights such as those of Mary Jo Iozzio, who awakens us to the kaleidoscopic diversity and fecundity of all creation, and Bryan Massingale, who professes that "the diversity of the human family is a divine blessing and mirrors the inner life of God."[28] Without minimizing the obstacles people might face, universal design and inclusive excellence assume that all participants in a learning community have resources to share. They welcome as strengths the

23. Jennings, "Race and the Educated Imagination," 63.

24. Love, *More than Survive*, 2.

25. Ibid., 11.

26. Universal Design for Learning, accessed December 1, 2024, https://www.cast.org/impact/universal-design-for-learning-udl.

27. Carol S. Dweck, *Mindset: The New Psychology of Success* (New York: Ballantine, 2016).

28. Mary Jo Iozzio, "Thinking about Disabilities with Justice, Liberation, and Mercy," *Horizons* 36, no. 1 (2009): 32–49; and Massingale, *Racial Justice*, 127.

experiences and qualities that higher education has repeatedly devalued. Jennings has challenged us to rethink relationships with students that further paternalistic and colonial mindsets that focus on overcoming students' deficiencies in knowledge, experience, and skill. What follows are examples of changes I have made to specific course elements: introductions, grading, and syllabi.

Introductions

A modest attempt in my classroom begins by highlighting all of the strengths that each participant in the course brings in order to reframe what is valuable for learning. During classroom introductions, I invite students to provide their major (or academic interests) not as a mere descriptor, but as a chance to name the skills and perspectives they can contribute from that discipline. We do the same with other interests and experiences. I share some of the experiences and preparation that draw me to this particular subject. Classroom introductions that include knowledge of other languages and cultures, family and work experiences, hobbies, and sports are not merely about sharing fun facts but about positioning students to make unique contributions. I hope that this practice, repeated throughout the course, will challenge, in Jennings's words, "the racial image of intelligence born of colonialism" and "the necessity of imagining exception inside of the process of being educated; that is, the educated nonwhite person must imagine herself as an exception or be imagined as an exception both as one who has not lost her cultural identity through assimilation and as one who has indeed been truly educated and is therefore not a counterfeit."[29]

Grading

Grading, onerous for all involved, will likely remain a fact of college life at most institutions for the foreseeable future, but it can be undertaken in ways that no longer systematically disadvantage BIPOC and first-generation students in particular.[30] As bell hooks notes,

29. Jennings, "Race and the Educated Imagination," 62.

30. Resources include Susan Blum, *Ungrading: Why Rating Students Undermines Learning (and What to Do Instead)* (West Virginia University Press, 2020); Inoue, *Labor-Based Grading Contracts*, and *Antiracist Writing Assessment Ecologies*; and Linda Nilson, *Spec-*

> In traditional terms that [power to grade, judge] *is* the source of power, and judging is something we all do as students and as teachers. That's not really the source of power in the successful classroom. The power of the liberatory classroom is in fact the power of the learning process, the work we do to establish a community.[31]

There are numerous examples of antiracist grading practices that include multiple means of assessing knowledge that take advantage of the media with which students are familiar and engaged, opportunities for continued revision or retaking of exams, not penalizing students for work early in the course when they have demonstrated improvement throughout, restraint in correcting language patterns such as African American Vernacular English or the common "mistakes" made by international students and heritage speakers of languages other than English, restraint in rewarding the habits of white language over substantive intellectual work, and transparency that decreases the uncertainty around grades that depletes the intellectual and emotional energy that could be used for learning.[32] I have adapted labor-based grading for my courses. Successful completion of various written and oral communication exercises along with course engagement form the basis of evaluation, and the final grade is determined by how many elements the students decided to undertake. Individual assignments receive feedback from me but are not graded. My goals are to reduce stress around grades, keep the focus on learning, empower students' agency, and allow them to enjoy learning and taking intellectual risks. I hope that it makes the grading process transparent and positions all participants as members of a cooperative rather than competitive enterprise. It is jarring for students at first, and I don't think that they believe me. As we build trust, the students report experiencing some relief from grading stress and we are all able to celebrate our contributions to learning.

---

ifications Grading: Restoring Rigor, Motivating Students, and Saving Faculty Time (Stylus Publishing, reprint, 2014).

31. hooks, *Teaching to Transgress*, 153. Italics in text.

32. Inoue, *Labor-Based Grading Contracts*.

Syllabi

It is critical that the material we share with our students represents diverse voices and perspectives on elements of what I continue to hold is our shared humanity. Here again, this takes great care and attention. Tacking on the work of BIPOC scholars is insufficient and can be used to recolonize and exploit their labor while reinforcing their perspectives as "other" or outside the dominant Eurocentric tradition. Our syllabi should also reflect that BIPOC, LGBTQIA+, and women scholars work in every area of [insert your discipline here], not just on race and gender. This calls for "flipping the script" in which these scholars are limited to a "unit" that comes later or last on the syllabus and functions as a reaction to other scholarship which remains normative.[33]

The intrinsic dignity of the human person is foundational for all of my courses in ethics. Rather than leading students through scholastic developments and papal documents, we begin with Nigerian author Chimamanda Adichie's TED talk, "The Danger of a Single Story," and reflections on human dignity from Cole Arthur Riley's *This Here Flesh: Spirituality, Liberation, and the Stories that Make Us.*[34] These women of color set the stage for the course, their authority is established at the outset, and their insights assist our critical assessment of other sources. In my experience, these materials have a lasting impact on the students who frequently return to them throughout the course of the semester.

These few abolitionist practices respond to Jennings's insistence that "[w]hat we need is a vision of education that aims at cultivating deep structures of belonging."[35] They recognize and take seriously Massingale's point: "Racism is not merely or primarily a sin of ignorance, but one of advantage and privilege" that requires more than "education, dialogue, and moral persuasion."[36] They acknowledge that we must not only teach about racism, sexism, and gender discrimination but that we must allow

33. Thanks to my colleagues in the Catholic Theological Society of America who shared generously of their classroom practices during a 2021 online video gathering.

34. Chimamanda Adichie, "The Danger of a Single Story," accessed December 1, 2024, https://www.youtube.com/watch?v=D9Ihs241zeg. Cole Arthur Riley, *This Here Flesh: Spirituality, Liberation and the Stories That Make Us* (New York: Convergent, 2023).

35. Jennings, "Race and the Educated Imagination," 63.

36. Massingale, *Racial Justice*, 75.

intersectional critical theories to shape our courses from the ground up and guide every element of the lived experience of the class. They provide a foundation for other engagements at the institutional, structural level. These include advocating for colleagues who adopt these strategies when we participate in decisions about hiring, reappointment, tenure, and promotion; discontinuing the use of racialized standardized testing in the admissions process;[37] exploring cluster hiring; and institutionalizing sabbath practices that resist grind culture for all members of the community, but especially for BIPOC and LGBTQIA+ members. Love is clear, "Pedagogy, regardless of its name, is useless without teachers dedicated to challenging systemic oppression with intersectional social justice."[38]

Conclusion

There are many details of antiracist pedagogy about which faculty will disagree, and we will need evidence-based approaches to minimize the probability that the best intentions of faculty and administrators (especially "well-meaning" white, straight, cis- folks) will go awry. However, many of the facile responses to proposals like these are familiar and always unsatisfying. "We have always done it this way." "This is a slippery slope." "This is unrealistic." "People will take advantage of you." "But we have to prepare them for the real world, and the real world doesn't work this way. Employers/customers/patients/clients are demanding and unforgiving." All of that may be true, but I have realized how presumptuous it is of me to proceed on the assumption that somehow students, especially our BIPOC, first-generation, and LGBTQIA+ students need to be schooled in real life.

Our task in the academy, especially on religiously inspired campuses, is not to mimic reality with all of its injustices, but to imagine new ways of living, learning, and connecting with one another. It is to cultivate the virtues and habits we and our students need to transform the world. Transformation for justice and mercy is the goal. What students and colleagues are asking for, as I have heard it, is to know that there are people

37. See Lani Guinier, *The Tyranny of the Meritocracy: Democratizing Higher Education in America* (Boston: Beacon Press, 2015).

38. Love, *More than Survive*, 19.

who will resist all patriarchy, white supremacy, and neoliberal capitalism at every opportunity.

Yes, my proposals might mean that faculty will be taken advantage of. It is true that some students will be able to manipulate a more merciful system of grading, but privileged students are doing that already. Privileged students know that their financial and social capital, racial, and gender privileges will generate opportunities for them irrespective of whether they do well in this or that course. Solidarity is a risky business. Faculty with privilege, especially the privilege that comes with whiteness, maleness, cis/straightness, rank, and tenure, need to absorb more of the risk. To the extent that faculty participate in shared governance in our institutions; participate in hiring, tenure, and promotion; formulate academic programs and syllabi; and assess student work, we have some real power, and we ought to use it on behalf of students and colleagues who are struggling. At Catholic institutions, we ought to be able to model the Teacher whose yoke is easy and whose burden is light, who came as a guest to feasts, and who transformed "fragments" into abundance to nourish everyone.[39]

Love's freedom dreaming is not wishful thinking, nor is Jennings's "fantasy work of imagining the educated."[40] It "honors the emotional, physical, spiritual, and financial struggle" of living under white supremacy and "finding one's humanity within the struggle against it."[41] Energized freedom-dreaming faculty take their lead from "the indomitable spirit of the abolitionist who engages in taking small and sometimes big risks in the fight for equal rights."[42]

Time will tell if these interventions will have an impact on academic culture and benefit those groups of students who have been systematically disadvantaged and devalued. The lasting transformation to which I can attest is in my instructor mindset. When I enter my students' lives as a guest and accompany them on a journey in which they are honored as whole people and their worth is not measured in grades, every aspect

39. Jennings, "Race and the Educated Imagination," in particular, 63–65, and *After Whiteness*, 23–46.

40. Ibid., 62.

41. Love, *More than Survive*, 64–65.

42. Ibid., 89.

of my life as a teacher is energized. The burden is lighter and so we are able to journey farther together.[43] I take inspiration from the prophet bell hooks, resting now in peace and power, who wrote:

> The classroom, with all its limitations, remains a location of possibility. In that field of possibility, we have the opportunity to labor for freedom, to demand of ourselves and our comrades an openness of mind and heart that allows us to face reality even as we collectively imagine ways to move beyond boundaries, to transgress. This is education as the practice of freedom.[44]

43. I am indebted to my colleagues at Holy Cross working toward inclusive excellence, especially Alo Basu, Madeline Vargas, Michelle Mondoux, Jumi Hayaki, and Lauren Capotosto.

44. hooks, *Teaching to Transgress*, 207.

Out of the Miry Clay

How Catholic Social Teaching Lifts Us from Essentialism, Moral Injury, and Suspicion

Esteban del Río
University of San Diego

I waited patiently for the LORD;
  he inclined to me and heard my cry.
He drew me up from the desolate pit,
  out of the miry bog,
and set my feet upon a rock,
  making my steps secure.
He put a new song in my mouth,
  a song of praise to our God.
Many will see and fear
  and put their trust in the Lord.
    Psalm 40:1-3

The "dangerous pit" and the "deadly quicksand," or, in other translations, the miry clay, is perhaps the best metaphor for our current national conversation about differences such as race, ethnicity, gender, sexuality, class, religion, or ability in higher education and beyond. The mire also characterizes my own experience as an academic, confident in my scholarly and pedagogical approach to understanding the politics of human difference, but also someone who wrestles with the frustrations and opportunities germane to institutional diversity, equity, inclusion, and justice

(DEIJ) efforts. As a communication scholar, I teach and write about how information and entertainment culture constructs categories such as race and ethnicity. My students approach these categories not as necessarily coherent variables, but as sites of analysis: Under what conditions and for what purposes are differences constructed and contested in the culture? But I also served for seven years as associate provost responsible for DEIJ work on my campus, where my academic approach to difference encountered routines of institutional storytelling and strategy that were not critical, but administrative, in nature. I found myself stretched between competing logics, grasping for something solid to steady myself.

In what follows, I draw on my experience serving as both the institutional diversity officer and a member of the faculty at a Catholic university during our time of accelerated change to reflect on the miry clay we often find ourselves in when it comes to confronting hierarchical relationships that operate through human difference. I offer two interventions in my work, reflecting on my own successes and failures. The first has to do with how I heard prophetic voices who held me accountable to DEIJ commitments; the second is how I navigated moral injury by self-deporting from institutional DEIJ work, focusing on the students and colleagues I could accompany not in theory or strategy, but in material ways—and with whom I could create new possibilities for undertaking the work of truth, justice, and understanding. While my discipline and administrative experience lend themselves to a critical analysis of difference, Catholic thought and culture is usable by anyone in Catholic higher education who wishes to leverage institutional missions to ground the prophetic imagination and advance radical hospitality in their work. I propose that we recommit to Catholic social teaching (CST) as a foundation for a different kind of DEIJ approach and operationalize educated hope to fuel our collective work in Catholic higher education.

Our Challenging Times

> Bad times, hard times—this is what people keep saying; but let us live well, and times shall be good. We are the times. Such as we are, such are the times. (St. Augustine)[1]

1. Cited in *Nicene and Post-Nicene Fathers, First Series, Volume 6*, ed. Philip Schaff (Buffalo, NY: Christian Literature, 1888), 352.

In the United States, the word "persistence" best characterizes the long struggle to ensure that the nation's founding principles are manifest for all people. The opportunity that colleges and universities afford the nation, both in knowledge creation and in the lives of students who move through our curricula, makes a campus a key site in this struggle. In higher education, so much has changed so quickly when it comes to institutional DEIJ efforts. New initiatives, pithy slogans, detailed strategic plans, and grand announcements of new hires' ebb and flow have taken on new guises and provoked emotion as well as complacency in the thirty years since I was an undergraduate student who became interested in these issues in the context of the culture wars of the early 1990s. More recently, racial justice in particular has taken a sharper focus: in 2014, the murder of Michael Brown in Ferguson, Missouri, led to the emergence of Black Lives Matter; a year later, events at the University of Missouri sparked national student activism and ushered in a new era of institutional sensitivity and responsiveness to demands made by constituents. Policies and posturing pursued under the first Trump Administration, the tumult of 2020 and its accompanying racial reckoning after the murder of George Floyd in Minneapolis, and the rancor and resignation that accompanied the reelection of Donald Trump in 2024 all create a context for the tenor and content of the prophetic imagination and the mechanics of institutional procedures on our campuses.

Now, well into the twenty-first century, as prophetic voices have become more emboldened and university administrations have become more "responsive," we have painted ourselves into corners in such a way that barely distinguishes Catholic colleges from secular institutions. Prophetic voices make demands and institutional leaders react with defensiveness; activists assume essentialist notions of identity and assert political binaries while managers respond with tokenism and virtue-signaling; faculty confidence in political and moral righteousness supersedes the attention to nuance necessary for inquiry; students expect their universities to issue statements that reaffirm their missions in tumultuous times while institutional neutrality appears to be the better option for administrators. All the while, we have become acculturated to blind spots and groupthink by way of routines: taking up habits and assumptions on our campuses which are increasingly characterized by illiberalism and corporate antiracism.

Our times are indeed challenging. The DEIJ consternation on campuses is often stoked by opportune reactionaries or conservative provocateurs who are met by reliable opposition from energized students, as well as the tepid management of cautious administrators. Journalists cannot be blamed for telling the stories that encapsulate national distrust in elite institutions so well: the elites vs. regular folk, the privileged vs. the oppressed, racism vs. antiracism. University administrators have come to rely on an increasingly professionalized class of diversity managers, specialized strategic assessment tools, and communication tropes to quell controversy. Diversity statements in hiring, strategic diversity plans, campus speech codes, and implicit-bias training are often bracketed by mission-derived language in programs at Catholic colleges. But such language often functions to shroud the same kind of rote tactics that are agnostic when it comes to Catholic thought or culture, easily employed at other institutions, whether secular, religious, or for-profit. There are benefits to following "best practices" across the higher education sector, but some of these programs have begun to be called into question as ineffective, creating hostility and backlash or cultivating suspicion on campus as people carefully navigate surface-level cautions about language, biases, political opinions, or nuance. Some critics who champion inclusion argue that current DEIJ efforts are an anathema to critical thinking, and there is growing support for alternative ideas such as Danielle Allen's notion of confident pluralism.[2] Allen argues that we must become confident in our values but understand that others are also operating from values as we attempt to find common ground, rather than falling into the toxic disagreement that characterizes our times. Regardless of the features of these debates, it is clear that we find ourselves at a difficult decision point about how to proceed.

But we are the times. I often see mission-centered language used to explain why we do already-formed DEIJ work. Why not allow Catholic thought and culture to function as the taproot for this work, determining both its rootedness and the direction of its branches? It is time to transplant the sapling into the earth. We could cultivate a more profound

2. Danielle Allen, "We've Lost Our Way on Campus. Here's How We Can Find Our Way Back," *Washington Post*, December 10, 2023, https://www.washingtonpost.com/opinions/2023/12/10/antisemitism-campus-culture-harvard-penn-mit-hearing-path-forward/.

commitment to each other in Catholic higher education, to accompany those experiencing marginalization, to encode a politics of mercy[3] in our habits and routines, and to center Catholic social teaching as the logic for the why and how we do what we do.

Centering Catholic Thought and Culture

When I began as associate provost in 2012, I had minimal direction, a lot of freedom, and very little direct administrative experience, having just been granted tenure and focused on planning my sabbatical research. Prior to my appointment, DEIJ commitments were separated, in concept, from our Catholic character, particularly by faculty advocates. This was especially the case with matters of gender and sexuality, which were not perceived to have the clarity of alignment with our Catholic identity in the same way that the sin of racism or the accompaniment of immigrants seemed to hold. I decided to bring these mission-critical values into dialogue by integrating Catholic concepts such as mutuality, solidarity, accompaniment, and radical hospitality into the secular assumptions central to DEIJ work. I insisted that the university take matters of gender and sexuality seriously *because* of our Catholic identity, not despite it. This meant that DEIJ would be more difficult to treat as an "add-on" to our work at the university when convenient or when one becomes interested, but instead it would become integral to what we do across the institution in ways that might provoke commitment—and the change that commitment entails. I leaned heavily on Catholic social teaching as a foundation for our work. I continue to believe that, in particular, the four principles as articulated in Mark Shea's *The Church's Best-Kept Secret: A Primer on Catholic Social Teaching*[4] can provide the determining logic for both why and how we take up DEIJ efforts on our campuses and classrooms. In my two-person office, here are brief examples of how we proceeded:

The dignity of the person. We understand that all people hold inherent dignity, have been created by God as they are, and are loved by God.

3. Matthew Eggemeier and Peter Joseph Fritz, *The Politics of Mercy: Catholic Life in an Era of Inequality, Violence, and Racism* (New York: Herder and Herder, 2020).

4. Mark P. Shea, *The Church's Best-Kept Secret: A Primer on Catholic Social Teaching* (New York: New City Press, 2020).

We are called to advance the dignity of all people, and as Pope Francis remarks in *Fratelli Tutti*, we are obliged to "ensure that every person lives with dignity and has sufficient opportunities for his or her integral development."[5] This provides a foundation for why we advance diversity and radical inclusion on our campuses in student and employee recruitment, in order to manifest more justly the beauty and variety of creation. It compels us to invite and include all, especially those whose perspectives and experiences are underrepresented or are cast to the periphery of our communities. When my university was weighing how to provide LGBT students more official, strategic support (as opposed to the more informal, contingent support they reported), we centered advocacy on the dignity of LGBT people as created and loved by God, eventually resulting in the establishment of an LGBT student center.

The common good. The common good refers to "the sum total of social conditions which allow people, either as groups or as individuals, to reach their fulfillment more fully and more easily."[6] Equity is a flexible and useful tool to work toward justice, and I situated equity as a function of the principle of the common good. The common good is not a zero-sum game with winners and losers but an opportunity to create conditions where all can reach their God-given potential, which benefits everybody. Our first-generation and low-income student programs, which provided summer college-preparation experiences and targeted academic support, were expanded and sustained because of our commitment to the common good.

Subsidiarity. This principle tells us that larger institutions should not dominate or dictate the lived experiences at the more local, vernacular level. When we developed my university's first strategic diversity plan, we relied heavily on the principle of subsidiarity. Sometimes, it is easy to fall into thinking that DEIJ across campus should resemble departments of sociology or ethnic studies or take on the tone and tactics of the multicultural student center. But there are ways to advance DEIJ from

5. Pope Francis, *Fratelli Tutti*: Encyclical Letter on Fraternity and Social Friendship, October 3, 2020, par. 118, https://www.vatican.va/content/francesco/en/encyclicals/documents/papa-francesco_20201003_enciclica-fratelli-tutti.html.

6. Pope Paul VI, *Gaudium et Spes*: Pastoral Constitution on the Church in the Modern World, December 7, 1965, par. 26, https://www.vatican.va/archive/hist_councils/ii_vatican_council/documents/vat-ii_const_19651207_gaudium-et-spes_en.html.

political science to physics to the physical plant that are germane to those departments' logic and operations. We asked departments and programs to set their own goals and develop strategies to meet those goals (with my office's help) that came from their own professional logic. Subsidiarity allows for more than empowerment: it also facilitates action that matters most to those operating at the lived-level of experience and expertise.

Solidarity. Solidarity asserts interconnection and our shared responsibility for advancing human dignity and the common good. Solidarity also promotes acting to find common ground across differences to achieve others' fullest flourishing. The preferential option for the poor and vulnerable presents a challenge for colleges and universities, who valorize achievement through external validation and whose ivied walls and ivory towers come at a high cost in terms of tuition. One way we pursued solidarity is through community-engaged learning. We determined that DEIJ and community engagement were interdependent, rather than distinct spheres of activity. Community engagement, a mature and self-reflexive field in higher education, has much to offer DEIJ offices and programs. Community partners often exemplify solidarity as a practice; in their diverse contexts, organizing means not all people or groups achieve the totality of outcomes they seek, but they organize with others to find common ground.

In my administrative role, I became rather proud of this framing. CST provided a rationale for the DEIJ achievements that quietly unfolded. I had rejected grand pronouncements and "town halls," which had dominated this work for the previous twenty years. I decided it was time to act; situating the work solidly within CST began to pay dividends, in my estimation. The campus saw a marked increase in the share of students and tenure-track faculty from underrepresented racial and ethnic groups; we established an Office of Tribal Liaison, grew our strategic student support for underserved populations, enhanced our core curriculum to include DEIJ commitments, and altered some rank and tenure guidelines to factor in inclusive teaching and mentoring in faculty evaluation. But my strategy was not hoisting up many flags signaling its success. Rather, positive outcomes unfolded more gradually, coming from changes to the routines of institutional work rather than from grand pronouncements. Centering Catholic thought and culture meant that change resulted from people's reflection and discernment related to the responsibilities they already held, rather than relying solely on adding new personnel, programs, or novel branding exercises to things that were already happening.

At one important point, however, my pride got the best of me. In the fall of 2015, events at the University of Missouri sparked a national student movement contesting anti-Black racism and demanding that institutions of higher education do more to realize stated DEIJ commitments for all students. I was asked by administrative managers to mount a response to these events, even though I often advised leadership to avoid putting themselves in a "responsive" position.

Regardless, I organized a faculty panel to explore the interdependence of free speech and equity. Student protesters interrupted our panel to read their demands for the university, which was a tactic repeated on campuses across the country. We gave them the floor. As prophetic voices spoke their truth, internally, I allowed myself to become defensive and not reflective; I felt as though I had to "respond" rather than accompany. Part of this had to do with student activists' suspicion and statements that painted in broad strokes, insisting that the university had done *nothing* to support their cause. Part of it had to do with my centering of self and administrative priorities such as reputation or strategy that I had unconsciously adopted. I became alarmed when I saw my default mindset mirrored in deliberations among administrative managers shortly after the interruption: harboring suspicions of faculty puppet-mastering, blaming students for the incomplete picture they held, and treating their protests as a public relations problem. What I heard from others might as well have been a recording of my own internal thoughts and feelings. But hearing it from others made me listen more critically, recognizing my own pride and defensiveness as a barrier to listening to the students.

I pivoted and invited student protesters to my office without any agenda. After some time, a few first-year students who were involved in the protest started eating their lunch in the common area in our office, and I began simply spending time with them. Before long, we were talking freely, and I invited them to join a few of us who were attending a racial justice conference in the days that followed the 2016 election. From there our relationship continued, even though the specific urgencies of 2015 had faded from headlines and protest agendas. I learned that there is more to centering Catholic thought and culture than explaining CST principles, although that is important. If one seeks to operate in DEIJ spaces leveraging an institution's Catholic mission, one ought to move beyond reciting principles and instead embody broad pastoral values associated with CST such as accompaniment, empathy, patience, and a willingness to listen.

Coming Home to the Classroom

Reflecting on my time as associate provost, I found myself in a position that may be familiar to readers: a newly tenured person of color entrusted with DEIJ responsibility for the whole campus but given little to no authority to make the changes necessary to fulfill my area's goals. Ultimately, when it became clear that the kind of transformational, vernacular, cultural work that I thought was necessary would not be taken up in any meaningful way by leadership, I decided to step out of the role, as moral injury overwhelmed my experience. Moral injury occurs when a values-driven organization does not provide constituents the resources or opportunities to fully manifest those values in their contributions to that organization. The term gained currency during the 2020 public health emergency, as employees reassessed their work/life situations and companies increasingly relied on "mission" language to motivate their employees. Moral injury is useful in identifying the kind of suspicion, exhaustion, and disengagement that is not uncommon among faculty and staff at Catholic colleges and universities, particularly in relation to DEIJ commitments. My own experience with moral injury was surprisingly deep and lasting. I found myself profoundly and personally disappointed in decisions made at the institutional level, and my moral injury began to pollute my own sense of belongingness at my university to the point of not really wanting to be on campus.

Exiting my administrative role was not an easy decision professionally, as I cared about the work, and my resignation interrupted my trajectory of leadership positions with "increasing responsibility." Reclaiming the coherence and goodness of my place at my university, however, made the decision obvious. And if there is one thing about my professional life that I truly and joyfully relish, it is teaching undergraduates. It is easy to get caught up in institutional manifestations of what a college or university does in the world, but we can always ground our work in what we can do: our own commitments and our own agency. Ultimately, and particularly in DEIJ work, there is great value in building community and capacity to define what it is to be at a Catholic institution from below, rather than to become entangled from what it means as defined from above. Meaningful teaching and mentoring relationships with students create opportunities for material accompaniment around ideas: to listen attentively, to journey with students, to ask probing questions—all these go beyond theory or strategy. Teaching regrounded my commitments, and I found myself taking the same tack with faculty and staff colleagues, with more listening, more questions, and fewer speeches and statements.

I regularly teach a course titled Media and Conflict. It critically examines how reality-based media such as journalism or documentary video represent and construct social conflict, influence human action, and shape public opinion and policy. Course content investigates the relationships among media practices and difference, democracy, ethics, and social justice, employing the lens of historically situated examples of political violence and social control. The first day I taught the course at my university was September 11, 2001. From that day on, class conversations and ways of understanding power dynamics have been an intellectual salve for students and myself as we navigate war, disasters, tragedies, elections, and protests. The course is filled with prophetic energy, fulfilling the DEIJ requirement in our core curriculum.

As I returned my focus to teaching, I decided that my Media and Conflict students and I deserved a more productive way out of the morass of encountering power dynamics, subjugation, and suffering over and over again with mostly explanatory tools. I began to operationalize an educated hope that is stripped of the fiction of idealism and rooted in reality. We would take criticism seriously but try a new flavor of critique: one of hope and possibility. I turned to cultural studies scholar Henry Giroux, who argues that we must help students "view cynicism as unconvincing and hope as practical" and see hope as "the precondition for imagining a future that does not replicate the nightmares of the present, for not making the present the future."[7] I brought hope into my teaching not with a special exercise, community engagement experiences, or some innovative pedagogical technique. Rather, I placed the study of hope

7. Henry Giroux, "Cultural Politics and Public Intellectuals in the Age of Emerging Fascism," *Communication and Critical/Cultural Studies* 21, no. 1 (2024): 16.

within the normal flow of the reading schedule, included essay questions about hope on exams, and added an upshot in assignments that helped students think about hope. This normalized hope as part of what we do in the class—what we start with rather than something we might adopt at the end of our study as compensation for the suffering we encounter. Taking educated hope seriously with students leads to peer habits of mutuality, listening, accompaniment, and compassion in our discussion in and outside of the classroom, including debates! For a course that covers matters of intense political disagreement, and with students who represent a variety of viewpoints and experiences, our conversations are characterized by mutual respect as much as they are filled with passionate arguments. Hope can transform conversations and help students see common ground across differences in the direction of goodness and justice.

I invite readers to reflect on how hope might be conceptualized to serve their teaching, research, creative activity, or collegiality. Hope provides a generative arena to leaven prophetic practices that advance DEIJ. For now, I will offer four sources of inspiration. First, Giroux's notion of hope as a *precondition* for agency situates hope at the beginning of any endeavor, rather at the end. Second, educator and organizer Mariame Kaba teaches that hope is a discipline and a practice, rather than an emotion.[8] Hope in this way becomes accessible to the students in academic disciplines that fill their curricula and syllabi with attention to methodology, procedure, and process. Third, theologian Orlando Espín argues that "Christianity stands or falls on hope, a reasonable and realistic hope and not wishful credulity, that Jesus of Nazareth was right" that God is compassionate. Espín continues, "Christianity exists because of the effectively subversive hope that God really does care for the most vulnerable and disposable members of humankind, that God is really compassionate, and that the ultimate moment of history will be compassionate and not the now all too frequent abuse of the poor and vulnerable."[9]

Espín, my undergraduate Catholic theology instructor, does not deal in low stakes here. Instead, hope is reasonable but also subversive and

8. Kelly Hayes and Mariame Kaba, *Let This Radicalize You: Organizing and the Revolution of Reciprocal Care* (Chicago: Haymarket Books, 2023).

9. Orlando O. Espín, *Idol and Grace: Traditioning and Subversive Hope* (Maryknoll, NY: Orbis Books, 2014), 6–7.

countercultural; the very message of Jesus was hope for God's compassionate intervention in the world. Finally, hope is different from optimism, as described by Pope Francis:

> Hoping, in fact, is not a mere act of optimism, like when we sometimes hope to pass an exam at university ("Let's hope we make it") or when we hope for good weather for the trip out of town on a Sunday in the spring ("Let's hope for good weather"). No, hoping is waiting for something that has already been given to us: salvation in God's eternal and infinite love.[10]

In these ways, we begin with hope, learn to put hope into practice, recognize that hope subverts power in the Christian worldview, and take hope seriously: yearning to better manifest God's love in the world rather than merely developing a plan we think might work. Hope—in the classroom, on campus, and in the community—is the precondition for action that creates a more just and compassionate world for one another, and hope will carry us through the trials and troubles that characterize the journey to realize justice and mutuality in this world. For me, there is no more direct way to cultivate the values of DEIJ than what I can do as a teacher and a mentor. The cultivation of an educated hope in young people, and the conversations that transpire from there, make me feel as though I have escaped the miry clay of our times and am now standing secure on firm ground to build a compassionate future with others.

10. Pope Francis, "Hope Is a Gift and a Duty of Every Christian," *Vatican News*, November 6, 2024, https://www.vaticannews.va/en/pope/news/2024-11/pope-francis-hope-is-a-gift-and-duty-for-every-christian.html.

PART II

THE EPICENTER

Welcoming who and what have been excluded as we cultivate hospitality

The *Management Exercises*

Bringing Our True Selves to Our Real Work

Kimberly Rae Connor and Richard W. Stackman
University of San Francisco

In order to "bring our true selves to the table and to the work," we need first to identify what our true self is and what constitutes, in the words of Wendell Berry, "our real work."[1] We also need to engage our identities in ways that are enduring and renewable. Today we face seemingly insurmountable economic, social, and environmental challenges that need educated people willing and able to fashion a more humane and just world. Communities demand more from organizations and the leaders of these organizations. Organizations and their leaders ask more from those hired to work in these organizations. And students and graduates of our universities seek more from their education in order to better fathom the world's inherent complexity and contribute to its peace and prosperity. This "more" we all seek risks becoming trivialized unless we define it in terms of *magis*, a "holy boldness," as described in the proceedings of the 34th General Congregation of the Society of Jesus.[2] Building sustainable and inclusive communities is at the very heart of a Jesuit university education.

1. Wendell Berry, "The Real Work," in *Standing by Words* (Berkeley, CA: Counterpoint Press, 1983), https://writersalmanac.publicradio.org/index.php%3Fdate=2012%252F08%252F04.html.

2. Portal to Jesuit Studies, "General Congregation 34," https://jesuitportal.bc.edu/research/general-congregations/general-congregation-34/.

Our Ignatian values not only infuse what we do daily as educators but also call upon us to harness the resources already at our disposal.[3]

Although applying any wisdom tradition out of context can be a risky proposition, the *Spiritual Exercises* of St. Ignatius of Loyola—a compilation of meditations, prayers, and contemplative practices to help people deepen their relationship with God—are uniquely positioned by form, function, and intent to be adapted for secular settings. For centuries the *Spiritual Exercises* were most commonly given to priests as a "long retreat" of about thirty days of solitude and silence. In recent years, however, there has been a renewed emphasis on the *Spiritual Exercises* as a program for lay people and non-Catholics who can substitute "good" for "God" in their quest to deepen their awareness of what matters in their lives and what actions matter. St. Ignatius wanted as many people as possible to benefit from the *Spiritual Exercises*, so he included annotations in his text that offered a flexible approach towards guiding seekers that invites all to participate, regardless of their faith commitment or status.

Offering the *Spiritual Exercises* as a "retreat in everyday life" is now a common practice among Jesuits. At the University of San Francisco (USF), our mission statement strongly endorses a welcome to all persons of any faith or no faith; we also hope that students who attend USF will benefit from the spiritual and intellectual resources derived from Ignatian spirituality and the wisdom traditions that accompany it. With this encouragement from St. Ignatius himself to adapt the *Spiritual Exercises*, the School of Management recognized that our Jesuit tradition provided the content and method to shape a value-enriched experience for our students. Through the *Management Exercises*, we introduce the global and humanistic traditions on which our university was founded and provide an opportunity for students to engage this tradition in ways that are also relevant to their ongoing academic and professional development.

3. Given the possibility that the content may evoke a strong response or trigger an unresolved issue or conflict, we recommend that the instructor have completed the *Spiritual Exercises* themselves or at least be conversant in Ignatian spirituality techniques. Ideally, the instructor would be trained in spiritual direction, comfortable guiding seekers through spiritual retreats, and willing to invite students who may be triggered or inspired by the content and who wished to engage in a deeper conversation about their experience to reach out to the instructor for a private conversation or be referred to someone in university ministry who can offer the same kind of support and accompaniment.

In a recent *New York Times* essay, "Can Everyone Take a Sabbatical?," Silicon Valley entrepreneur Olatunde Sobomehin recognized the value of sabbaticals: "They offer a path 'to rest and restore our connection to our God and our calling on earth, and to birth new iterations of our purpose and find new layers of our calling.'"[4] Resourcing and incorporating sabbaticals into our busy work lives and packed academic curricula, however, isn't easy. In order to offer students a version of a sabbatical as an Ignatian "retreat in everyday life," we wanted to provide the benefits of a sabbatical but allow students to maintain their responsibilities. We also wanted to establish a model for how they could continue to explore their interior lives as distinct from the professional identities they are cultivating.

Recognizing that our students were likely headed to jobs in the corporate sector that may not offer the opportunities for renewal and refreshment that come with a sabbatical, the *Management Exercises*[5] help students acquire perspectives, tools, and techniques to sustain their ongoing need for restoration.[6] The program encourages them to reconnect with their identities and personal missions in order to proceed forward as engaged global citizens. Students can be unaware that their studies have been influenced by the "dominator paradigm"[7] that has prevailed for millennia. Therefore, our management students study how to be compassionate instead of callous, how to respond instead of react, how to serve the common good instead of serving only shareholders' interests. While most management gurus refer to these traits as "soft skills," we redefine

4. Tish Harrison Warren, "Can Everyone Take a Sabbatical? We All Need a Rest," *New York Times*, June 25, 2023, https://www.nytimes.com/2023/06/25/opinion/sabbatical-work-life-balance.html.

5. The *Management Exercises* can be offered as a co-curricular program or a stand-alone course that engages either undergraduate or graduate students at a key point in their academic career.

6. While we have found it effective to build the content into an online platform that students can access at their convenience, and indeed the entire program can proceed in an online/virtual setting, we also recommend that each module be introduced and students guided through the content. If possible, given the group dynamics and setting, we also recommend that the final reflections be shared in person, perhaps with a corresponding activity, as a way to build community and to break down barriers that prevent students from revealing their innermost selves.

7. Riane Eisler, *The Chalice and the Blade: Our History, Our Future* (San Francisco: Perennial Library, 1988).

them as "core skills."[8] Our goal is to orient students toward what Flannery O'Connor calls a "habit of being"[9]—a life of questioning, learning, and engagement. Participating in the *Management Exercises*, students learn to exercise discernment, build character, and enact citizenship.

The *Management Exercises* combine three perspectives in its overall design: Ignatian spirituality, Catholic social teaching, and terms commonly applied in management settings. These three categories are then gathered under broader categories that introduce four modules building from self, to others, organizations, and society, and establishing the perspective from which students are invited to engage relevant and diverse content in multiple modalities—taking on a contemplative practice, watching videos, listening to podcasts, reading essays, and reflecting in a project-based activity.

When he established the Society of Jesus in 1540, St. Ignatius provided his followers the *Spiritual Exercises* as a kind of handbook that offered a set of directions for how to make decisions and act based on core character dimensions, what he called "movements of the soul." As a companion to management education, the *Management Exercises* are intended to support a similar function: to be a whole-soul workout that enhances the educational experience of students by asking them to consider their professional development from multiple points of view. In adapting the *Spiritual Exercises* for a management education, we are answering the question: "How do we help our students learn to manage themselves so that their lives are aimed not only at the pursuit of a career but also focused on a journey towards human fulfillment?" The structure of the *Management Exercises* offered below offers a glimpse into how we proceed to respond to this question. The terms that appear in regular font are derived from Chris Lowney's Ignatian-inspired management treatise, *Heroic Leadership*.[10] Terms that are *italicized* are derived from the tradition of Catholic

8. Jennifer Parlamis and Matthew J. Monnot, "Getting to the CORE: Putting an End to the Term 'Soft Skills,'" *Journal of Management Inquiry* 28 (2018): 225–27, https .doi.10.1177/1056492618818023.

9. Flannery O'Connor, *The Habit of Being: Letters of Flannery O'Connor*, ed. Sally Fitzgerald (New York: Farrar, Straus and Giroux, 1988).

10. Chris Lowney, *Heroic Leadership: Lessons from a 450-Year-Old Company That Changed the World* (Chicago: Loyola Press, 2005).

social thought. Terms that are **bold** are from the Ignatian tradition, and those that are in ***bold italics*** come from a language other than English.

Module 1: Self (How shall I lead myself?)

Self-Awareness—I understand my strengths, weaknesses, values, and worldview.

Synchronicity—Is my decision true to my deepest values and uncompromising principles?

Discernment—A process for making choices often not between good and evil, but among several possible actions that are potentially good. The process of discernment that relies on multiple human faculties helps us identify the greater good.

Module 2: Others (How shall I accompany my stakeholders?)

Love—I engage others with a positive, compassionate attitude.

Solidarity—Is my decision respectful of others and inclusive?

Cura Personalis—From the Latin for "care for the person," this attitude encourages us to establish personal relationships with respect for the dignity of each individual.

Module 3: Organizations (How shall I contribute to our cultures?)

Ingenuity—I confidently innovate and adapt to embrace a changing world.

Subsidiarity—Is my decision empowering others and promoting leadership development in my organization?

Cura Apostolica—From Latin, the counterpart to ***cura personalis***, which refers to the personal care of individuals, this one is concerned with the care of our organizations or collective missions.

Module 4: Society (How shall I summon a higher purpose?)

Heroism—I energize myself and others by embracing courageous and spirited ambitions.

Sustainability—Is my decision making a positive change for communities and future generations?

Magis—From the Latin for "greater," ***magis*** was traditionally used by Ignatius of Loyola. Jesuits continue to use the term to suggest the spirit of generous excellence in which our work should be performed.

How the *Management Exercises* Begin

The *Management Exercises* begin by inviting students to practice mindfulness techniques derived from many wisdom traditions, including our Jesuit tradition, framing the meditations as an **Examen**, a form of prayer created by St. Ignatius. Each module includes an **Examen** particular to the core concepts of the week and positions students to begin working the module in a balanced and receptive state.[11] Because each module begins with an **Examen**, we offer students some context and explanation for why we engage in this practice and describe its origins in the Jesuit tradition.

There are many types and variations of techniques to develop self-awareness, originating in multiple cultures and traditions. More recently, meditation has been shown to improve happiness, health, and performance. Meditation helps us become more connected and this improves our ability to collaborate in our families, at work, and anywhere. Indeed, the chief executive officer (CEO) of Aetna, Mark Bertolini, has extolled how mindfulness and related practices not only helped him heal his body after a traumatic injury but also helped shape his approach to doing business as a health care insurer and management leader.[12] Marc Benioff, the founder of Salesforce, has installed meditation rooms throughout Salesforce Tower in San Francisco. He approaches management with a "beginner's mind," which allows him to "listen deeply," "step back," and "be here in the moment."[13] These are not the only CEOs embracing mindfulness; the practice extends throughout the workforce in a variety of settings. Among the mindfulness or meditative practices that emerged from the *Spiritual Exercises* that can be adapted to many settings is the **Daily Examen**, a technique of prayerful reflection on the events of the day in order to detect the presence and discern the will of God's/the Good's direction for us.

11. Because students will be experiencing a "retreat" more than a class, we encourage a Pass/Fail assessment of assignments so students do not feel judged when it comes to expressing their interior thoughts and feelings or be driven by a competitive performance.

12. "Yoga, Mindfulness, and Leadership with Aetna CEO, Mark Bertolini at Wisdom 2.0 Business," October 17, 2013, video, https://www.youtube.com/watch?v=4A87XJ7iPMI.

13. "'Maintain Your Beginner's Mind,' Salesforce Chair and CEO Marc Benioff Advises on the Hello Monday Podcast," October 12, 2020, https://www.salesforce.com/news/stories/maintain-your-beginners-mind-salesforce-chair-and-ceo-marc-benioff-advises-on-the-hello-monday-podcast/.

The basic steps of an **Examen** practice that we have adapted for the *Management Exercises* are:

1. Recall your blessings. Give thanks.
2. Reflect on your challenges; consider your feelings.
3. Review your thoughts; ponder your actions.
4. Regret your mistakes; ask for help.
5. Renew your character. Hope for the future.

An **Examen** invites us to slow down and pay attention to our day and leads to a more engaged process of discernment as a way to adjust our perspective and solve a problem more slowly.[14]

Developing self-awareness is the first task in the *Management Exercises.* The importance of continually improving self-awareness is reinforced by the **Practice** exercises included in each module. We then connect this spiritual positioning to our social positioning, relying on two sources: the *Ignatian Presupposition* and *Eloquentia Perfecta.* Applying principles from these sources leads students toward relationships and engagements that are more humane and productive. During the first week of the *Spiritual Exercises*, St. Ignatius establishes the "Presupposition" that promotes the moral purpose of communication:

> For a good relationship to develop between the retreatant and the director and for the greater progress of the retreat, a mutual respect is very necessary. This may be especially true in areas of scriptural and theological presentation. Every good Christian adopts a more positive acceptance of someone's statement rather than a rejection of it out of hand. And so a favorable interpretation by the director or by the retreatant should always be given to the other's statement, and confusions should be cleared up with Christian understanding. So, too, if an actual error seems to be held, an attempt at a better interpretation should be made so that a more correct understanding may develop.[15]

14. To help students use the **Examen** meditations that initiate each module, we introduce a video by the Dalai Lama who gently guides viewers through a simple breathing meditation at https://youtu.be/QUieZeyDLrM.

15. All quotes from the *Spiritual Exercises* are taken from David J. Fleming, SJ, *Draw Me into Your Friendship: A Literal Translation and Contemporary Reading of the Spiritual Exercises* (Boston: Institute for Advanced Jesuit Studies, 1996), 23.

The practice of an **Examen** as a tool for achieving moral poise and clarity is tied to the *Presupposition* and to the Ignatian tradition of *Eloquentia Perfecta,* the joining of knowledge and expression with virtue and morality. Applying these principles establishes the terms for a dialogue rather than an exchange; it is relational, not transactional. As students engage others during their *Management Exercises* explorations, we hope to promote a spirituality of citizenship and to adopt the advice St. Ignatius gave "to put a good interpretation on another's statement rather than to condemn it." *Eloquentia Perfecta* emerged from St. Ignatius's advice to Jesuits who were participating in the Council of Trent.[16] Simply put, we encourage students to apply these principles as they proceed through the course and throughout their lives:

- Learn the surpassing worth of conversation;
- Be slow to speech;
- Be considerate and kind;
- Pay attention to the whole person;
- Understand the meaning, learnings, and wishes of those who speak;
- Be free of prejudice;
- Argue from authority cautiously;
- Quote from important persons only if arranged beforehand;
- Consider the reasons on both sides without showing attachment to your own opinion;
- Be modest when you are certain;
- Choose to speak at the other's convenience even when certain;
- Give conversation the time it needs. Forget about your own leisure or lack of time—that is your own convenience; accommodate yourself to the convenience of your conversation partners.

16. Ignatius on Trent (1546), Instruction for the Stay at Trent, "For Helping Souls," https://jesuitportal.bc.edu/research/documents/1546_ignatiusontrent/.

How the *Management Exercises* Proceeds

Module 1: Self (self-awareness/*synchronicity*/**discernment**)

We begin every module with a poem and the first one is "The Summer Day" by Mary Oliver that poses a question that positions where students begin their discernment, asking what they plan to do with their one life.[17] In Module 1, students start simply with a **Practice** represented by a **discernment** meditation derived from Zen and Jesuit spirituality. In each module, students will be led to three additional sections—**Watch**, **Listen**, and **Read**—that comprise the core content.

In Module 1, students **Watch, Listen,** and **Read** as people in different vocations consider what they are doing with their lives and how they advise others in personal and professional settings. The final **Reflection**, like all *Management Exercises* reflections, is derived from a contemplative exercise recommended by St. Ignatius in the *Spiritual Exercises.* In advising a "way of making a correct and good choice of a way of life," St. Ignatius recommends the following:

> 186. THIRD RULE. If I were at the moment of death and so I would have the freedom and clarity of that time, what would be the decision I would want to have made now? I will guide myself by this insight and make my present decision in conformity with it.

Because he suggests answering complex moral questions by imagining ourselves on our deathbeds, we ask students to compose an ethical will. An ethical will is an informal document often included with other estate planning papers. It is a "letter to the future," in which people can share the relationships, accomplishments, and values that made their lives satisfying. Preparing an ethical will takes no special training and does not have to follow any particular format; it is simply an opportunity to tell our beneficiaries what matters to us.

Students' discernment in Module 1 will lead them to shape their self-awareness and direct them on to a path towards leadership in synchronicity with their values. This module gives students the opportunity to

17. Mary Oliver, "The Summer Day," *Library of Congress*, Poem 133, Poetry and Literature, https://www.loc.gov/programs/poetry-and-literature/poet-laureate/poet-laureate-projects/poetry-180/all-poems/item/poetry-180-133/the-summer-day/.

deepen their understanding of the moral choices they make and to articulate the principles and arguments on which they base their choices in conscious and intentional ways, culminating in a gathering during which students share their ethical wills.

Module 2: Others (love/*solidarity*/***cura personalis***)

Module 2 of the *Management Exercises* asks students to deepen their process of self-inquiry by focusing not on themselves but on others. Rather than discerning their own character, students will turn towards the many stakeholders in their lives and explore how they develop loving relationships in solidarity with them, engaging the core dimensions of their characters and recognizing their connectedness. The poem that begins this module reminds students of the most important test of their career. Drawing on the writings of St. John of the Cross for the title, the poet repeats the saint's famous dictum, "In the evening we shall be examined on love."[18]

The module's **Practice** asks students to focus their attentive mindfulness on gratitude, how they define their experience through gifts they receive from others. **Watch**, **Listen**, and **Read** all offer examples of how others, in a variety of settings, domestic and professional, encountered and negotiated their relationships and moved from attention, to reverence, to devotion—the Jesuit path we take from noticing to loving—and how we do so collectively for and with one another.

The **Reflection** asks students to compose a mission statement. We ask them to create a mission statement for themselves that could apply to their role as part of many organizational groups. Ignatius describes this process of identifying our calling as an **election**, a concept that emphasizes the freedom necessary for this kind of declaration. To arrive at an election, we first need to discern where we feel consolation and desolation:

> 335.7 As we continue to make progress in the spiritual life, the movement of the good spirit is very delicate, gentle, and often delightful. The good spirit touches us in the way that a drop of water penetrates

18. Thomas Centolella, "In the Evening We Shall Be Examined on Love," *Poetry Foundation*, https://www.poetryfoundation.org/poems/142197/in-the-evening-we-shall-be-examined-on-love-.

> a sponge. When the evil spirit tries to interrupt our progress, the movement is violent, disturbing, and confusing. The way that the evil spirit touches into our lives is more like water hitting hard upon a stone.

By leaning toward consolation as Ignatius describes, students come to envision a goal that comes from their true desires and is embodied in how they envision their "real work." We ask them to declare their professional goals and aspirations as a six-word statement, following the inspired logic of *SMITH Magazine*'s Six-Word Memoirs.[19] By applying an economy of form, students distill their complex personalities to a memorable statement of purpose that could appear on their LinkedIn profiles. We also encourage them to use their mission statement like a mantra, to repeat it when they need to be grounded. St. Ignatius gives frequent instructions for those with active contemplative lives to practice repetition as a way to unfold their interior motions and to move towards relishing—a word he uses for love on several occasions—all for which we are grateful. Love is not an attachment that can become disordered; it is a process of living in the world with purpose.

As students refine their professional ambitions in the context of their program and a deeper academic immersion in their chosen career path, they will also be identifying how all they hope to accomplish is part of a wider sense of purpose, a mission that includes and transcends their personal goals, that transforms their jobs into a calling, positioning them, in the words of Pedro Arrupe, SJ, to become "a person for others."

In developing their mission statements, students will link their identity to others and recognize that, as they mature in their professional identities, love can continue to guide them in solidarity with the multiple stakeholders who make up our world. Students demonstrate their heightened awareness by how they begin to observe the Jesuit value of care of the whole person: ***cura personalis***.

Module 3: Organizations (ingenuity/*subsidiarity*/***cura apostolica***)

Module 3 of the *Management Exercises* extends students' vision beyond caring for themselves and others to caring for institutions—what Jesuits call ***cura apostolica***. The content is designed to move students toward this

19. Six-Word Memoirs, https://www.sixwordmemoirs.com/.

more expansive vision of who they are in the cultures all around them. As students reflect and position themselves in a new organizational setting, their experience will reflect what they have learned about themselves thus far in the *Management Exercises.*

Whatever shape their career takes, students can apply the learning they encounter in Module 3, which aligns them with a larger organizational or institutional identity, no matter how ambiguous or ambitious that relationship may be. Knowing what they know about themselves and how to engage others, they can, as the poet Elizabeth Alexander advises, "walk forward into that light."[20] Students appreciate that stating a mission is not enough; they need to embody that personal mission by dedicating themselves to a public role as citizens of the world and as members of an organization they chose to join. That organization is part of a larger culture made up of diverse approaches and individuals aimed at accomplishing an organization's mission. When our leadership is aimed at subsidiarity, when we recognize how to lead through accompaniment and apply ingenuity towards providing expansive opportunity and democratic choice, we practice ***cura apostolica***.

The **Practice** asks students to meditate on how they can demonstrate dedication to a role in an organization. After encountering examples in **Watch**, **Listen**, and **Read** of remarkable individuals who model this kind of relational, rather than transactional, engagement, Module 3 asks students to move from people to places and to reflect on how we arrange the places and spaces in which we move as organizational collectives. The One Block reflection guides students in answering this question as they compose a narrative describing their professional setting from their point of view but also with a focus on someone whose experience in the same setting offers a different perspective.

In the *Spiritual Exercises*, St. Ignatius recommends a particular contemplation called "composition of place," wherein he would imagine himself in the biblical scenes he read. This was his attempt to understand more deeply the context in which Scripture emerged so that he might have a better appreciation for its meaning and how it applied to his life.

20. Elizabeth Alexander, "Praise Song for the Day," *Poetry Foundation*, https://www.poetryfoundation.org/poems/52141/praise-song-for-the-day.

> 47. FIRST PRELUDE. The first prelude is a composition, seeing the place. The composition will be to see with the sight of the imagination the corporeal place where the thing is found which I want to contemplate. The composition will be to see with the sight of the imagination and consider that my soul is imprisoned in this corruptible body.

He later elaborates that in this kind of contemplation, one should apply one's senses and "take in sights, smells, sounds, tastes, and feelings as an automatic datum for my attention. The total felt-environment . . ."[21]

We ask students to apply this contemplative technique as they reflect on their One Block experiences—to put themselves in other people's stories. We want to demonstrate how we can make connections between our environment and the privileged human act known as management—to notice patterns of interwoven human institutions and social phenomena, to recognize how managerial privilege sits atop layers of historical interconnections between human acts and the societies they inhabit, and to ask themselves if they are practicing cultural humility, which, unlike cultural competence, initiates a lifelong commitment to self-evaluation and to redressing social imbalances through new partnerships. Proceeding this way, we hope each student will have practiced perceiving as a discerning and caring human who strives to look at a situation from many points of view before deciding how to act or what to do.

Module 4: Society (heroism/*sustainability*/***magis***)

Module 4 of the *Management Exercises* concludes the program and takes students to higher ground—a vision of their lives beyond the quotidian—from which to launch from their studies. The opening and final poem by Emily Dickinson invites students to "dwell in possibility."[22] Module 4 is designed to help students find a sustainable way to practice all that they have learned in ways they have yet to discover. Students celebrate the conclusion of the course by imagining more—reaching back to the past and forward to the future and confirming their bonds in a shared meal.

21. Fleming, *Draw Me*, 101.

22. Emily Dickinson, "I Dwell in Possibility," *Poetry Foundation*, https://www.poetryfoundation.org/poems/52197/i-dwell-in-possibility-466.

The **Practice** for Module 4 asks students to embrace the Jesuit concept of ***magis***, or more, the value of striving for better, confirming their commitment to the search for excellence. The final **Watch**, **Listen**, and **Read** offers examples from poets to activists on how they reached as far away as space and prison and as close as nature and home. Students will see embodied in each a form of heroism that possesses sustainability because of a compelling higher purpose that inspires their action and promotes a society of engaged citizenship.

The concept of ***magis*** that directs this final module brings together the many aspects of students' academic experience, including who they were before enrolling in the academic program and who they hope to become after leaving the program. Thus, an **At the Table Reflection** asks each individual student to use their imagination to create a dinner party across time among themselves and four invited guests, to use the image of a dinner gathering as an occasion for contemplation.

In the *Spiritual Exercises*, St. Ignatius is explicit in emphasizing how hospitality is an essential practice for people building a civil and just society. He concludes the Third Week with "RULES WITH REGARD TO EATING," recognizing lessons one can learn from the necessary act of eating that also develop awareness: of sufficiency and waste, cleanliness and modesty, silence and conversation, freedom and attachment. In these rules and others, St. Ignatius is offering habits for living that lead to a sustainable way of life that supports our individual and collective missions. He also recommends dining as a contemplative time:

> 215. SIXTH RULE. Another time, while he is eating, he can take another consideration, either on the life of the saints or on some pious contemplation or on some spiritual affair which he has to do because being intent on such a thing, he will take less delight and feeling in the corporeal food.

Rather than contemplating the life of a saint, we ask students to imagine that they are eating with people they consider saints. Thus, this last assignment asks students to be creative in their appreciation of time and to use their imaginations to create a dinner party with guests who may be from any time or place, personal or public, famous or common. The only requirement is that students explain why they invited those guests.

Finally, we ask them to add a late, surprise guest, someone who accompanied them through the *Management Exercises* experience—a peer, a family member, even someone whom they don't know but whose words and actions have sustained them.

We invite them to extend their imaginations further, beyond the characters, and to decide other details: What is the "setting" of the dinner party? How will the "plot" unfold as students demonstrate hospitality? Does the event have a "theme" or a vision or a thought they want their guests to carry away with them? How does the event generate consciousness in the ways Ignatius describes? By imagining themselves "at the table," students can relax after a long journey and share the fruits of their labor with their fellow souls, and eventually pick up and continue their journey inspired by St. Ignatius.[23]

Final Thoughts

To illustrate the initial impact of the *Management Exercises*, consider the outcome of the ethical will reflection that we have observed. In asking students to complete this assignment, we require them to share their results with their cohort.[24] We also invite them to consider the epistolary form itself and whether there is another form that is a more accurate expression of their feelings and sensibilities. Students' responses to this invitation have been astonishing in their variety, impact, and beauty. While many write letters to family members—one even wrote her own obituary—other students created video montages and short films and mix tapes; composed original poems and songs; developed a game show to

23. A detailed version of the *Management Exercises* that includes suggested content, illustrations, and more complete descriptions of the reflection assignments can be found in the appendix of the open-source textbook *A Way of Proceeding: Ethical Decision Making for Management Students at Jesuit Colleges and Universities* by Kimberly Rae Connor at https://www.ignited.global/shared-resources/way-proceeding-ethical-decision-making-management-students-jesuit-colleges-and.

24. While discussion boards and in-person sharing of reflections are helpful to encourage conversation and build community, the kinds of disclosures the course evokes can leave students feeling vulnerable and afraid to disclose their reflections. We recommend as much transparency as possible to challenge the stigma of self-expression but tempered with a sensitivity appropriate to the context and student population.

find winning answers to life's surprising questions; prepared value-infused cocktails and meals; and came up with rules that guide virtuosity in yoga, golf, baseball, hockey, basketball, hiking, dancing, and photography—all metaphors for a life well lived. We've viewed collages and artworks such as an origami bouquet, a Diwali candle, and a Día de los Muertos altar that depict the religious and cultural inflections of our international student body. Often we listened to poignant narratives situated in the circumstances of both global and personal crises that put a face on a moral abstraction. We cried, laughed, groaned, clapped, and more than once witnessed a presentation that began, "I've never shared this kind of thing with anyone before."

In the process, we generated a deeper community of empathetic awareness. The effects of this reflection go beyond the classroom and their immediate cohort. Most students share their ethical wills with family members and often add them to their estate plans. After presenting her ethical will, one student remarked: "I didn't know how much I needed this." In each instance, students followed their own visions and found their own "way of proceeding" by accompanying one another in the steps of St. Ignatius. As they conclude their experience of the *Management Exercises*, we encourage them to consider how they can sustain the experience and continue to apply these methods for discernment and renewal—to practice the meditations, to chant their mission statements, to explore their communities, and to move beyond the roar and tumult as they bring their true selves to their real work and their one wild and precious life.

Opening the Door

Making It Possible for Students to Remain Catholic While Staying True to Themselves

Anna Lännström and Jessika Crockett-Murphy
Stonehill College

Despite being both queer and deeply suspicious of religion, Jessika Crockett-Murphy ended up at Stonehill College, a small Catholic college in the Holy Cross tradition located outside of Boston. In the fall of her sophomore year, she decided to take Anna Lännström's course, attracted by the provocative title: "God Is Dead."

Jessika was delighted. What better way to get that oppressive Catholic intellectual tradition general education requirement out of the way? She was expecting a class that would uphold her antireligious beliefs, discuss the irrelevance of faith in the modern day, and give her ammunition to use in conversations with the religious people at the college. She thought she knew what the church was all about and what it stood for. After all, she had read so many news stories on social media about the actions of Christian groups: picketing at funerals, yelling at women outside Planned Parenthood, and objecting to Pride parades.

In many ways, Jessika's attitudes were typical of Stonehill's students. Like hers, their impressions of the Church are often both negative and muddled: "The Church is hypocritical, sexist, and anti-gay." "It reads the Bible literally and it rejects evolution." "It thinks that it's bad to examine your religious beliefs." "Having faith means having no doubts, and it requires that you don't question your religion at all." When Anna started teaching at Stonehill in 2003, almost all of the students in her required first-year intro classes (four sections a year) were practicing Catholics. But now, few are. And those who were raised as Catholics are often suspicious of classroom discussions of Catholicism because they see them as thinly veiled attempts to bring them back into the fold. An increasing number are like Jessika, baptized but raised without a religious community and lacking even basic knowledge about the differences between Catholicism and, say, the Westboro Baptist Church.

For her part, Anna had successfully avoided teaching Catholic intellectual tradition courses for fifteen years. She's a philosopher, not a theologian. She's not Catholic. And dealing with all that hostility and all those misunderstandings sounded difficult and exhausting. How do we provide a safe space for students to discuss their anger at the church while also correcting their misunderstandings? How do we talk about the ways in which they are right, the ways in which the church has failed to treat all of us as fully made in God's image? And what do we do about the church's failings? Good questions, but not for her to answer. She was content to let the Catholics sort out that mess themselves.

She got pushed into teaching the classes, though. By the time Jessika enrolled, Anna had made not being Catholic the centerpiece of her pedagogical strategy for the course, realizing that being an outsider made it easier for her to create that much-needed space for an honest dialogue about religion, the church, and students' experiences with the two, and to at least get a start on some of those other questions.

Jessika walked into that class and that space. She was disappointed at first. It turned out that she had misread the course title. It wasn't a proud atheist proclamation at all, but just a question: "Is God dead?" And the course wasn't the repository of the antireligious arguments that she had been hoping for. Anna spoke positively of religion, and while she sometimes challenged and critiqued it, she never did so in a dismantling or hostile manner. Jessika realized that the class would not uphold her assumptions and beliefs, but that it would instead challenge them.

She might have left. But she was intrigued, and it helped that she learned in the very first class meeting that Anna wasn't Catholic and that she has no interest in making anybody more or less Catholic—or even more religious. It also helped that Anna said that she disagreed with the church's positions on LGBTQ issues and that she expressed feminist objections to the Church— and to a lot of organized religion. And it helped that she stressed that the students didn't have to believe a single word of any Catholic teachings. She also said that they had to know what some of the teachings were, think them through carefully, be as fair and open-minded as possible, and then articulate their criticisms and responses clearly. That sounded reasonable. It seemed that Jessika would be allowed to question Catholic beliefs and assumptions. Plus, the class fit her schedule. Jessika decided to stay.

Anna very intentionally began the course with those comments because she had students like Jessika in mind. Too many students assume that Catholic intellectual tradition courses are about indoctrination and preaching, and they enter with all their defenses up. Pointing to her outsider status and signaling that there would be no Catholic evangelizing agenda enabled the students who had concerns about Catholicism to feel safe enough to listen and speak less defensively. They may still end up rejecting the church, but whatever decision they make will have been better informed.

Less important to Jessika was something else that Anna said that first day. After expressing her reservations about Catholicism, she talked about what she admires about Catholicism. Bringing that up in the very beginning was also a strategic decision, made to reassure students who *are* practicing Catholics that she doesn't have an anti-Catholic agenda either. She talked about the logic and intellectual rigor exhibited in the Catholic intellectual tradition, about the two thousand years of applying reason to religion, and about brilliant theologians and philosophers wrestling with difficult questions, arguing, and disagreeing with one another and with non-Catholics. And she reiterated that her goal wasn't to make anybody more or less religious but to help them think through the positions involved—including their own.

Next, it was the students' turn to speak. What had been their experiences with religion and Catholicism—what did they like, and what troubled them? To frame that discussion, adding background and context, Anna assigned Jean Twenge's "Irreligious: Losing My Religion (and Spirituality)."[1] Twenge's extensive survey data supports Anna's classroom

1. The information in this paragraph is from "Irreligious" in Jean Twenge's *iGen: Why Today's Super-Connected Kids Are Growing Up Less Rebellious, More Tolerant, Less Happy—and Completely Unprepared for Adulthood—and What That Means for the Rest of Us* (New York: Simon & Schuster, 2017), 119–42.

observations: Gen Z is significantly less religious than previous generations were at their age. They are much less likely to be religiously affiliated, to have been raised by religious parents, to believe in God, to pray, and to identify as spiritual. It has become much more acceptable to be an atheist, and more people than ever are completely secular (one-third of American college students). In addition to reviewing extensive survey data, Twenge also interviewed Gen Z members about their reasons for avoiding organized religion. They told her that it conflicts with their individualism and with science, and they objected to its old-fashioned attitudes and especially its stance on LGBTQ issues.

Anna asked the students in the class if the reading resonated with them and asked them to share some of their own experiences with religion and Catholicism.

Then she stepped back and listened carefully. The students had a lot to say, some of it positive but most of it not. Anna has heard too many painful and troubling stories over the years. Most of them center on LGBTQ issues. One of her students was an altar boy and was handed a brochure about conversion therapy by a priest who told him to try it. Another student was kicked out of his religious education class for asking too many critical questions. The family of a third student had been asked to leave their church because the student had two moms.

In these situations, Anna listens, empathizes, and learns. She explains that Catholics do not have to interpret the Bible literally, that the church accepts evolution, and that the church is not opposed to questioning, even though probing and persistent questions may indeed make some church leaders uncomfortable. (The class discusses all this in more detail later in the semester.) In response to troubling stories about what students have been told by religious authorities, she explains that parish priests and people who teach religious education classes to young teens sometimes don't know as much theology as she would wish and that, as a result, they can misrepresent the diversity of views and complexity of theology available in the church. She gets especially blunt when students have been told that a loved one is going to hell.

Jessika's class tackled LGBTQ issues directly because they were at the core of students' painful experience and objections to the church (Anna finds that they usually are). Some students are queer themselves; others have queer friends and family. They or people they love have been insulted, rejected, and excluded by people who claimed to be speaking for their church and their God. After listening carefully to the stories, Anna began correcting some of the misunderstandings, explaining what the church is and is not teaching. Many of her students have trouble telling different Christian denominations apart, unaware of the differences between the fire-and-brimstone preachers of the Westboro Baptist Church and the progressive female pastors one can find in the Lutheran Church. And so, the Catholic Church is frequently blamed for what other denominations practice and preach. Some students, Jessika included, initially don't even realize that there *are* significant differences between different denominations. They also have no idea that there are different ways of practicing Catholicism, that it can be different on college campuses than in parishes, and that different priests have very different attitudes and interpretations of doctrine. Some Catholic priests attend Pride parades, whereas others condemn homosexuality. The class doesn't go deeply into such differences, but it highlights their existence and the wide variety and diversity of Christian views, making it as clear as possible that neither Christianity nor Catholicism speaks with a single voice. It also introduces the idea that one might choose to be part of something even though one does not love all its parts, especially if one believes the organization has other deeply valuable parts.

In Jessika's class, as in most of Anna's classes, some students come in believing that the church hates gay people. To arrive at a more nuanced understanding, the class read the catechism's discussion on homosexuality. Anna pointed out that there is plenty of disagreement within the church about this and other issues. They read James Martin, SJ, noting that he is a priest in good standing.[2] They read Bryan Massingale's discussion of his experiences as a gay and Black Catholic priest.[3] The Massingale reading became Jessika's favorite text from the class, because it showed how Massingale chooses to remain in the church while also being sharply critical of its treatment of its members of color. She loves

2. James Martin, SJ, *Building a Bridge: How the Catholic Church and the LGBT Community Can Enter into a Relationship of Respect, Compassion, and Sensitivity* (New York: HarperOne, 2017).

3. Bryan N. Massingale, "The Challenge of Idolatry for LGBTI Ministry," July 4, 2019, https://www.dignityusa.org/articles/the-challenge-of-idolatry-for-lgbti-ministry.

how Massingale shares his own anger at God and the church and how he talks openly about his identities and the struggles they brought with them. She resonated with how he expressed rage, discomfort, confusion, and fear—all things she had grown up feeling. And she was intrigued by how he does not let his rage control him and how he does not let it drive him away from the church. He holds his identities, accepts them, and speaks openly about them, but he also embraces God and the church.

The main goals of these discussions and readings are to correct misunderstandings and to open the door to religion in general and Catholicism in particular for the students in the class. Anna explained that she knows many thoughtful LGBTQ Catholics, some of them priests, who remain in the church despite their strong objections to its teachings on homosexuality. She noted that she is not quite sure how they do it, but that they somehow make it work. And she made the point explicit: "There is space for you in the church too, if you want to be there. If one place or person isn't welcoming, try another. But don't leave because you think there is no place for you because that is not true. (And if you can't get past the official teachings,[4] remember that many non-Catholic churches are more welcoming to LGBTQ people.)"

These opening discussions took up the first couple of weeks and they set the tone for the entire class. Anna repeated over and over again that she's OK with the students being atheists, theists, or agnostics, but that she wants their position to be based upon good reasons and on a deep understanding of the intellectual possibilities. She told them that they likely have been exposed only to narrow and simplistic "kiddie" versions of religion up to this point, and that she doesn't want them to reject religion before they have encountered "adult" religion. And so, the class explored the gap between God and our images of God, and the difficulties inherent in grasping something so transcendent and so far beyond us. It explored the differences between literal and figurative readings of the Bible. Anna explained over and over again that Catholics do not have to take everything in the Bible literally (and that most Protestants don't either). And she explains that Catholics are encouraged to use reason, and that part of what that means is that they are allowed and encouraged to consider thorny issues of translation from ancient languages and a very

4. *Catechism of the Catholic Church* (Vatican City: Libreria Editrice Vaticana, 1993).

different historical context before deciding how to understand particular biblical passages.

As the class progressed, Jessika's misunderstandings kept being challenged. She was glad to hear that Catholics didn't have to believe those horrible lines condemning homosexuality, even though they were in the Bible. She came to realize that the Christians saying horrible things about gay people did not speak for all Christians—and that many of them were not even Catholics. She noticed that the Catholics in class didn't want to burn her at the stake for being queer. On the contrary, they were OK with her identity. Many of them even became strong allies. And while she shared Anna's feminist concerns about organized religion, she noticed that the actual priests on campus seemed very supportive of women in leadership roles. She started to realize how many different faith practices and different denominations there were and that their beliefs were strikingly different from one another. She learned that lots of Christians read big chunks of the Bible contextually and started to see how complicated the problem of how to read the Bible was. And she noticed that God seemed so much . . . *bigger* . . . than the people speaking for God and the images of God they defended. It looked like religions were not so cut and dried—they existed in many ways, they could be interpreted differently by everyone, and they often did not actually believe the things she had assumed they did.

Something else was tugging at her attention too, a line from Fr. Martin's book: The Church had been rejecting the LGBTQ community, but hadn't the LGBTQ community then rejected the Church? She thought about her own hostility towards Fr. Tim, the priest assigned as her first-year advisor. Perhaps both rejections were too hasty? It just led to more pain on all sides. Was there a way for the church and the LGBTQ community to understand each other better?

Another thing that Anna said also caught her attention: Religion can be a force for good in individual lives and the world but, too often, we allow unkind and narrow-minded voices to speak for religion in general and Catholicism in particular. So, for example, we pay a lot of attention to the tiny but loud Westboro Baptist Church, and we don't notice all the other Christians who treat gay people with kindness, respect, and dignity. Anna had also told the class that each of them has a choice. They can leave religion behind and allow people they don't agree with to speak for it and to continue shaping it. Or they can stay and fight to shape it into something better. Jessika started worrying that we increasingly are allowing people on the far right to be the main voices speaking for religion in the public discourse.

As Jessika was engaging with the course materials and talking to the other people in the class, and especially as she started paying attention to the work of campus ministry and people like Fr. Tim, she was able to see all the good religion could do and all of the ways people could benefit from it. And she could see that she might benefit from being part of it herself. She trusted Anna enough to think that it was *possible* to be a practicing Catholic and an out queer woman. But to explore that possibility, she had to reach out to actual Catholics. Like, actually *talk to* Fr. Tim about faith. Here, luck (or grace?) was required. Anna always holds her breath when she promises young queer students that there is a place for them and their identities in religion in general and in Catholicism in particular because the people they reach out to may not agree— especially outside the campus community. Instead of Fr. Tim, Jessika could have encountered somebody less supportive. In a worst-case scenario, she could have reached out to somebody like the conversion therapy priest, or the priest who excluded Anna's other student and his two moms from the community.

But she didn't. Stonehill has a great campus ministry team, and when Jessika did speak with Fr. Tim, he welcomed her and answered her questions, opening the door to the church for her a little further. And over time, she decided to walk through it. During her junior year, she found a safe and welcoming community with Stonehill's campus ministry, and by the time she graduated, Jessika had found a home and a calling in the Catholic Church. Now, three years after finishing the class, Jessika is at Villanova University, preparing for a career in collegiate ministry by pursuing a master's in Ministry and Theology and a certificate in Higher Education Leadership.

Jessika credits Anna's class with helping to open the door to the wide world of religion for her and the other students, and especially to Catholicism, which is so often misunderstood. She likes the way that the course made religion less scary and presented it as something that they could explore openly, criticize freely, and learn about in a welcoming manner. Jessika proposes that Anna add an opportunity in the class to interact with Catholic priests in the controlled classroom environment. It took many months for her to begin talking about faith with Fr. Tim, even though she knew that he was a kind and approachable person, because she couldn't see past his Roman collar. If Anna had brought some of the priests into the classroom, that may have humanized them and made the interaction less daunting.

Jessika is struck by the selflessness of the campus priests who offered their help to her around the clock with any issues she faced on her faith journey. She reflects on pictures of priests in the midst of active war zones offering comfort and support to soldiers and civilians, and stories of priests generously hearing confession for strangers in airports or taxis. All of this leaves her with an overwhelming sense of awe for the compassion and community the priesthood held. Its core belief in genuine human love and equality holds deep and good possibilities and it made Jessika fall in love with the church.

Jessika still believes that the church's teachings about women's empowerment and queer acceptance leave much to be desired. But just as we shouldn't throw out all government because we sometimes have bad politicians, we shouldn't abandon God and the church because we sometimes encounter bad leaders and priests. And the vast amount of good the Catholic Church has done in creating hospitals, schools, and orphanages, coupled with the Church's immense global range and financial resources, demonstrates that it is in a position to do even more good—even for the LGBTQ community.

She argues that the reform work needed in the church is much more likely to happen if people like her are on the inside to ignite the change, instead of making demands from the outside. And so, Jessika's work in queer ministry is rooted in her hope for a better future, one in which the resources of the Church help young LGBTQ folks who have been rejected from their families find a community where they are loved and appreciated, or help queer couples find children to adopt and complete their families. She also hopes that women's power in the church will expand—for instance, through expanding the diaconate—and she argues that such an expansion aligns with its traditions and foundational beliefs (to Anna's shock and dismay, however, Jessika is not sure if she favors female priests).

But she recognizes (better than Anna does!) that change will have to be slow. She dislikes performative activism and hasty progressive agendas.

She argues that the Catholic Church does develop, but that change will take time and patience. The Church has to evolve while also staying true to its core beliefs and commitments. But one of those commitments is to the deep humanity and infinite worth of every one of us, and Jessika trusts that the church will eventually come to enact that in its treatment of the LGBTQ community.

The beginning of Jessika's story is typical, but the ending is unusual. Most of Anna's students don't become Catholic and even fewer pursue ministry. Most of them stay whatever they were when they entered the class—atheist, Catholic, agnostic, former Catholic. But we both hope that courses like this one can help inoculate students against those who consider them "less than," showing them ways in which they can, if they desire, stay in or join the church, flourish there, and perhaps help create a better environment for others. We hope that they will learn that somebody like them can find a home in the church. And then we hope that they will make informed decisions about what religious path to travel, understanding what they are accepting and rejecting—and at what cost.

We say "at what cost" because we worry that young people are rejecting religion because they have encountered only simplistic and hostile versions of it and because they haven't understood it or the good it can do in their lives and in the world. And we think people benefit from religion as a counterweight to the pressures of the modern world and to the materialism and individualism that dominate it. We are in the midst of a loneliness epidemic, especially among young people. Religious communities can play key roles in combatting loneliness and in helping people live better lives. But they can only do that for all of us if their members and institutions treat all people as full human beings. And religious communities need to get better at that. We all do.

For those of us who teach at Catholic institutions, regardless of whether or not we are Catholic, what do we need to keep in mind when we talk to students about Catholicism?

- Start where our students are and then help them go further. To do that, we first need to create safe spaces, allowing our students to speak honestly about their good and bad experiences with the church.

- Listen to and honor their stories, but also clear up misunderstandings, correcting and deepening their understanding of religion in general and Catholicism in particular. Help them see the wide variety of beliefs, attitudes, and approaches within Catholicism, and introduce them to the disagreements and debates—or at least to their existence.
- Acknowledge that some of their criticisms of the church and religion are fair and reasonable. Speak openly about the ways in which the church has failed to treat people with dignity and respect. Highlight the goodness of what the church could become—and what it sometimes is already.
- Accept that decisions about their future relationship with the church are in their hands and not ours. But make sure they know that there can be space for them in the church, even though some people may still reject them.
- See the promise in each and every one of them, recognizing that they might be able to help transform the church into something that comes closer to living up to its own ideals.

Acknowledgment

Anna's "How Do We Teach Catholic Intellectual Tradition to Gen Z Students?" (published by the Wabash Center for Teaching and Learning in Theology and Religion) served as an early draft for this paper. See https://www.wabashcenter.wabash.edu/2022/02/how-do-we-teach-catholic-intellectual-tradition-to-gen-z-students/.

"Don't Just Do Something, Sit There"

New Faculty Orientation as Radical Hospitality

Susanna L. Cantu Gregory
Clarke University

Raise your hand if you have experienced something like the following assignment:

> *Develop a program that will introduce new faculty to the mission of their school, the tradition of Catholic higher education, and the Catholic intellectual tradition. Make sure participants learn all the policies, procedures, teaching skills, and technical know-how to do their jobs. Deliver this program in a multimodal, religiously inclusive, non-onerous way for busy people with a wide range of familiarity and comfort with Catholicism who have no free hours in common with one another during the workweek. As you plan, make the program double as ongoing faculty/staff formation in mission. Finally, since you have no budget and no paid employees, the program will run on volunteer service. Have fun!*

I am raising my hand. And shaking my head. And yet, this same assignment, in addition to inducing undeniable pressure, has sparked a labor of love and a site of radical hospitality on my campus in recent years. Since we transitioned from an administrator-led to a faculty-led new faculty orientation program a decade ago, we have attempted to fashion a radically hospitable program that bolsters our faculty's capacity for loving attentiveness, one conversation at a time. In so doing, we are nurturing prophetic imagination, seeding this ability cohort by cohort into the whole faculty.

In what follows, I share a snapshot of our program, including approaches I am proud of as well as our ongoing struggles. Along the way, I point out activities another school might find worth trying. However, the commitments and values behind our structure and pacing may be the best offering to faculty formation programs at other Catholic universities. Program design must flow from skillful, caring, on-purpose, and even radical holding of space.

We do not have the perfect program, but I see timely potential in the protected space we have cultivated. At the core of our program is an invitation to several layers of contemplative listening—listening to oneself as a person intersecting with Clarke University culture in a unique and valuable way, listening to the ways our founders' story and Catholic traditions have shaped and continue to shape our campus, listening to movements within our respective disciplines, listening to our students inside and outside the classroom, and listening to the needs expressed by the broader community in words or in silence. Each new faculty cohort builds up literacy in the local and global mission of Catholic higher education right alongside repetitive experiences of being accepted as they are and invited to more. And here is the timely potential part: It is only when we make space for new faculty to bring their full identity to intersect in fresh and surprising ways with the Catholic intellectual tradition that we can stretch one another toward "the prophetic more." When it works, our colleagues' imaginations take shape around what is possible within our common work, empowering them and giving energy to our campus.

But holding space does not always work. Sometimes the hospitality we offer does not fit every new colleague. Sometimes everyone is stretched too thin, activities fall flat, and no one wants to reflect about anything. Sometimes the gaps between our mission and vision and the messy daily work on the ground are too wide for our message to be found trustworthy. More and more new faculty stand on the perimeter of a landscape with which they are unfamiliar, and they may need to hear the basics of Catholic traditions and educational approaches. Too, most have been wired by their educational experiences for quick information download and upload. It helps to name these conditions and to articulate how different our program will be. I acknowledge that the slowness of such a formation approach can be frustrating and that listening as social action might seem strange or too passive at first. Sometimes it helps to remind a cohort that we inherited this way of contemplation in action from our founding Sisters of Charity of the Blessed Virgin Mary (BVM sisters) whose lives attest to its success.

The truth is, we develop formation programs like these because something important has receded and a need has been laid bare. With fewer and fewer faculty identifying as Catholic, we, like many schools, are calling out for common commitment and vision. In the time- and resource-bound territory of new faculty formation, a site emerges apt for building up common commitment and vision that embraces both the diverse people we have hired and the tradition we have inherited. To notice and nurture this potential, we must stretch our sense of what matters most in new faculty formation.

We Were All New Once

I see hope in new faculty formation spaces because my own professional start happened in soul-nurturing environments. I attended a small, Catholic, liberal arts university, where integration of knowledge and wisdom-seeking were shared commitments, marked by conversation and joy. There, my professional goal became clear. I wanted to teach theology in a school like the one I attended where the conversation might continue. Later, in 2007, my PhD program sent me to Collegium, where I caught a sense of possibility and empowerment along with a set of starter tools for becoming an educator in Catholic higher education. At first, my Collegium stamp manifested itself by offering presentations on Catholic intellectual tradition and mission integration in several contexts and stubbornly insisting on reciting poetry to my students.

Since 2015, I have taught in the Religious Studies program at Clarke University. I vividly recall sitting in an orientation session as a new faculty member and hearing my inner voice assert, “I want to do this. I want to lead sessions like this.” I was responding to the gentle hospitality and beauty of the space opened and guided by our leader, a seasoned faculty member and a Collegium alum. There was no rush, no pressure, no required “right” responses. I could feel his sincerity in setting an exploratory and reverential tone. He valued the mission of the school and, just as much, I could feel how much he valued the unique intersection we were having with it. I was moved by his leadership and by watching the new people—Friday afternoon–tired in the way only teachers can be, but engaged—inhabit this reflective space, brimming over with stories to tell and connections to make. Later, when our leader asked me to serve as a mentor and a guest speaker, I said yes. Then, as our leader was stepping down, I approached him with my willingness to serve as his successor. That was five years ago. At the end of this academic year, I will conclude my service in this role.

The courses I teach address topics such as Jesus, the Bible, the church, spirituality, and Catholic social teaching. Because of our religiously diverse student population and the inclusive approach of my program, I am accustomed to setting conditions for dialogue and teaching learners to honor their own responses. I habitually operate in the creative tension between holding tightly to my ecclesial commitments and just as tightly to my pedagogical commitment to hospitality in my classrooms. Theology professors need Jedi skills these days. I lean on this professional experience when I show up as a leader of our new faculty program. In both places, I am called upon to hold simultaneous stances of conviction and openness, pride and humility, my own deep joy in the work I do and holding space for whatever feelings my learners are having. Just as in my classroom, in new faculty settings, I am sensitive to the words we use and the way our stories about who we are and the work we do are always on the move. I see myself as a tender of listeners. Others of my colleagues gave me a good, long, and loving listen when I first began my job—in the doorway of my office, in the halls, on walks with my mentor, in orientation sessions with my cohort. I witnessed the strengthening and nurturing power of this gift for my own path, and I wanted to offer the same gift to others.

Since stepping into the leadership role as an unpaid volunteer teaching four classes per term I have not been funded for workshops, trainings, or credentials in new faculty development. Nonexistent budget, remember? As a result, I have learned to serve as new faculty orientation leader by leading, and somehow that from-scratch approach has mostly worked. Having had previous theological training and practice leading group reflection did not hurt. I submit that anyone serving in a new faculty leadership role should have at least some content knowledge of mission in Catholic higher education and a collegial formation experience in Catholic intellectual tradition. A leader should be equipped to guide new colleagues in what might be their first encounter with Catholic thought and culture. I have answered questions as varied as "What is a sister?" to "What is the Eucharist?" and "What is the deal with Catholics and Mary?" Other new colleagues may carry stories of ecclesial hurt and reasons for caution about agreeing to work for a Catholic institution. Sometimes, as in my classroom, it takes theological skill and humility to extend genuine hospitality. In addition to my training in theology, I have educated myself about issues that matter by talking with mission leaders and reading widely. What was most needed from me as a formation leader was to keep showing up with hope for the program, to bring a willingness to put in significant hours of detailed administrative and facilitation work, and to remain open to the perspectives of others. The role has called forth my best instructional design and delivery skills as a teacher. In fact, leading our program has much in common with teaching an extra course, but to fellow faculty members and in a fishbowl!

At one point, I was asked to tally my labor hours, arriving at a number that exceeded one hundred per calendar year, at least half of which happened over the summer, when faculty are off contract. I do not recommend replicating this aspect of our program, which has proven to be unsustainable. I had to recruit and train mentor leaders to take over that portion of the program to enable me to give adequate time for running the orientation sessions and mediating between the program and campus leaders. This year I added five volunteer session facilitators to help me design and deliver the mission-focused sessions. Let all of this be a word of warning to those at other schools: It can be difficult to find and keep stable formation leaders if such work is not spelled out in their job descriptions.

I do this work because I want new faculty to have an accurate, supportive, and hospitable first encounter with our mission. I care about the Catholic tradition and the wider educational mission to which our school subscribes. I care about new faculty members receiving a "charitable read" from their colleagues who have a longer association with Clarke. I care deeply about the process of welcoming new faculty—not just the content of the welcome. Most simply, and perhaps more profoundly, I care about my new colleagues and I am committed to walking with them.

Passing the Flame: A Faculty-Led Program

Clarke University, in Dubuque, Iowa, was founded by the Sisters of Charity of the Blessed Virgin Mary. For much of its history, sisters served as faculty members; eventually, lay faculty were hired, and they now eclipse the number of teaching sisters. I had the treat of working alongside four sisters as colleagues when I first started at Clarke, and today's new faculty tell me that they typically encounter only one or two sisters on campus. Or none. As with other universities founded by vowed religious, the need for formal new faculty formation grew in parallel with the increased numbers of lay individuals in teaching positions. At Clarke, that need has become urgent. For several decades prior to my arrival, the vice president for academic affairs (VPAA), a sister, would hold weekly new faculty orientation conversations over coffee in the early morning before classes started. From what I can tell, these conversations were enough to meet formation needs for some time, clearly a perk of serving at a school founded by sisters. Then, in the early 2010s, Clarke hired a new (lay) vice president for academic affairs just as the need increased for a more intentional handing on of the school's educational traditions.

Under this person's leadership, new faculty formation became a learning program with a topical session calendar of biweekly meetings during the fall semester. Ten years ago, I experienced this structure when I joined the Clarke faculty, the only change being the addition of a faculty co-facilitator who collaborated with the VPAA. During his term of service, this individual added a mentor program in which every new full-time colleague is paired with a volunteer faculty mentor in July. The pair are expected to meet for informal monthly conversations until May. By the time I took on leadership of the program in spring 2020, the VPAA had handed all the facilitation and administration duties to the appointed faculty leader. Our elected faculty development committee served in an advisory capacity.

Our topics are sequenced into eight seventy-five-minute orientation sessions, typically scheduled for Friday afternoons from August to April. Coffee, tea, and snacks (funded by the office of the VPAA) are served at the event, and attendance is required and supported by department chairs. I assign readings in a common book (purchased for attendees by the office of the VPAA) chosen for the purpose of giving language to common developmental stages in the new faculty experience. Sometimes I assign other short articles and lectures on Catholic higher education, the common good, and the mission and history of Clarke. A little Monika Hellwig on the Catholic intellectual tradition never hurts. Our topics and learning objectives for each session seem to be works in progress. We debate how much time to allocate to each topic and bear in mind their relevance to a newcomer trying to stay afloat in the sometimes-overwhelming currents of creating and teaching new courses. Despite our continual tinkering, the sequence has included: Mission in Catholic Higher Education, Students, the Liberal Arts Tradition and Clarke's General Education Program, Effective College Teaching, The Faculty Evaluation Process, Service and Shared Governance, The Catholic Intellectual Tradition, and The Common Good. The final session in April is usually a field trip to the motherhouse of the BVM sisters to share stories with retired Clarke teaching sisters and staff. While originally presented as a unity, I separated the overtly mission-related topics from the more policy- and procedural-related topics when I noticed the mission-related topics receiving increasingly less attention at each session. After a major program revision, we are experimenting this year with a policy/procedure session and two mission sessions per month. Recognizing the need for ongoing faculty and staff formation in mission, we have opened all our sessions to everyone employed at Clarke. While this kind of open access seems consistent with the Clarke ethic, I sometimes worry that mission content and a focus on contemplative listening may be lost by folding the care of new colleagues' experience into care for everyone else's ongoing development.

By design, the recurring reflective structure of each session has been invitational, inclusive, and unrushed. As I prepare for sessions, I center new faculty members' experience with gently paced, retreat-like time spent learning to reflect on the vocation of an educator in the context of a Catholic university. While prompts and examples vary from session to session, newbies soon learn what to expect at the opening of a session, in the transitions between topics, and in the listening and speaking I ask of them. They come to expect that I will check in on stories from their classroom, for updates on their ruminations on the good they are doing, and for their best wisdom on the good next step in their meaning-making about their jobs. Such seeding of the participants' thinking between meetings seems to do much of the formation work.

I like to start each session with short reflective teaching exercises, most of which I have adapted from exercises in my own theology courses or spirituality workshops, or, from educator friends who place a premium on reflection. Sometimes I create an exercise spontaneously, basing it on how my colleagues arrive on a given day. I explain why we are doing these exercises—to prime individual pondering—and give options for degrees of participation. I usually participate in the exercises along with my new colleagues and encourage the mentor leader, guest speaker, and any other seasoned faculty present at the session to do the same. Even with all this fine set-up, the first time I introduce a reflective prompt at the New Faculty Welcome Day, I inevitably look out upon a sea of quizzical faces. I am unfazed. They mirror my students' faces on Day One, and I know from experience that continuing to offer the prompts helps them begin to trust the sincere open-endedness of the invitation. I make it clear that there are no "right answers" in a reflective exercise and that we do the exercise to build their long-term habits of reflection. We are practicing a way of being in our work, together. I want new colleagues to hear the subtext: We are the kind of place where we honor your unique intersection with our common work. Prompts that have worked in the past follow.

- Place your hand on your heart and feel your heartbeat.
- Remember the morning. Remember the start of the teaching week. Remember the first day of the first class. How did you arrive?
- Recall a moment in a recent class that is still with you.
- Recall a humbling moment in class.
- Consider a regret you carry about a student interaction.
- Recall an unresolved situation with a student. Give your internal responses a listen.
- Recall a teacher who cared about you. How did you feel in their presence?
- Recall a recent time you learned from a student.
- How can you tell students are learning?
- Recall a healing moment in class.

- Recall the last time you were immersed in your research or creative work.
- Recall something you wish you knew before beginning to teach at this school.
- What does it feel like to have you as a teacher?
- Where do you as a learner and you as a teacher overlap?
- What do you avoid as a teacher?

After an opening exercise, the session moves to more collaborative layers of contemplating, first to a guest presentation on the session topic for about ten to fifteen minutes. The final component of each session is a guided conversation intended to give new faculty a chance to begin weaving together their experiences in the past month, the guest speaker's and their colleagues' perspectives, and insights from the assigned article or book chapter. Outside these monthly sessions, new faculty members engage in individual reflection on their work (this year guided by a first-year multimodal response assignment due in April), in reading the assigned readings, and in monthly meetings with their mentors on conversation prompts aligned with session topics.

You might be thinking that the program I have described sounds interesting but nothing special; the faculty at any school could gather regularly and talk about their jobs or even do reflective teaching exercises. But, as I hope to show here, what we do with new faculty at Clarke is not as impactful as the caring, on-purpose holding of space with which we do it.

How Hospitality Turns Out to Be Radical

Sharing our program's topics and exercises provides a start for other faculty formation leaders, but the most valuable part of Clarke's approach cannot be seen in these lists alone. Rather, it can be found in the way our program values the site of new faculty formation as radical and prophetic and takes active steps to honor it as such. New faculty are new for only a limited amount of time, and to both beginner and seasoned faculty developers I would pass along encouragement to see this time as a seedbed for all the gifts and yearnings that make up the "why" of our work.

There, at the site of the "recently arrived" having their initial talks with colleagues and gaining practical know-how for their jobs, live uncertainty, hope, care for students, passion for a discipline, questions, memories, and fresh responses to vocation. This mix of responses is treasure to me and, I hope, to others. Leaders of new faculty programs would do well to be conscious of three key attributes of newcomers' position at their university: sacredness, vulnerability, and power.

First, we can honor their arrival as new employees as a site of grace. We need to be mindful that, by their acceptance of the job offer, newcomers stand at the pinnacle of a long chain of gifts, yeses, and commitments. They have invested themselves in their education and have applied that education in a variety of contexts and experiences. They have sought another chapter in their professional growth and imagined it happening here. They have gathered up the story of who they are in their work to apply, interview for, and accept their new roles. The university has recognized and applauded their skill, potential, and "fit" with its mission. They have been offered a chance, an opportunity to *become*.

What makes the new position sacred is that it is an intersection of what is known, what has been so far, and what might be possible next. A leap of hope has happened on both sides. Before rushing into the particulars of new responsibilities and context, before flooding the newcomers with policies and procedures, it is worth honoring the goodness of their position at this intersection and encouraging them to do so as well. At Clarke, we welcome new faculty (and staff) with a resounding, "We're glad you're here!" which, at best, can be a way of giving thanks for their presence—the past that we only dimly see and that has brought them among us, and the hope they carry, full of possibilities. So, too, can their newness of sight be a sacred thing for our community. With not-yet-fixed expectations, they encounter our students, our leadership, the way we conduct ordinary days and celebrations, and the way all the components of our university work (or fail to work) together. The questions they ask, the comments they make, and the potential they see all come from a position of first encounter. This cohort of trained and passionate educators is about to encounter not only what we say about our commitments, but also the extent to which we are living out those promises. Because of them, we can see our school with new eyes and be affirmed—or challenged—by what they see. I have witnessed new faculty members respond with serious concern to aspects of the institutional church, the way our students' financial or academic situations shape what is possible, the high turnover in faculty and staff, and the ways our ideals of justice and compassion have not yet saturated our policies.

That status of newness carries vulnerability as well. Today's small liberal arts university is a vulnerable entity in several ways, and discussions of pressing enrollment issues are never far from our daily work. Those serving in visiting positions, short-term contracts, or their first years on the job may feel especially vulnerable to sudden job loss or program/university closures. Sometimes new faculty vulnerability comes through as simple unawareness of terms or recent hot-button issues, a circumstance that impedes conversation or full participation in a meeting. Sometimes it comes through as consternation when put on the spot to take a side in long-standing debates or to solve pressing problems. The vulnerability of not yet knowing extends beyond not knowing the working environment. New faculty operate for a while—sometimes even a couple of years—in a not-yet-knowing of themselves as they meet our university. So much of this intersection has to do with the ecology of a new colleague's program, department, chair, minor/major students, and courses. Unresolved questions, not immediately answerable, must be carried with openness that can generate vulnerabilities: *Is my program effective? Can I teach these students well, given the resources and time available to me? What value might I offer my students and my colleagues? Where do I detect my own limits?* I have witnessed new faculty carrying around their own questions of fit with their job for a few years, wondering if they should or could stay with their new position, being on the alert for signals to go.

In addition to recognizing and honoring the sacredness and vulnerability of the new faculty member's presence, it can be helpful to acknowledge the power that lies within that presence. Pressured to prepare courses and deliver them to students they are only beginning to know, and eager to "get things right" and thereby lay the groundwork for renewed contracts, most new faculty would deny that power is foremost among their feelings! Yet, what new colleagues do with their fresh observations and questions is especially pertinent. They can choose what to hold and keep watching, what to draw others' attention to, and what to respectfully decline. They can choose what to echo or amplify in the university's educational culture and what to critique, or when to embark on being a changemaker. Too, there is potential power in the community new faculty might build among their cohort—a community offering support and inspiration, as well as a venue for challenging expectations and assumptions about the strange new land they now inhabit. There is power in openness, in not yet knowing all the answers about their own contributions and about how effective teaching should happen. There is power in being capable of being moved by poignant classroom moments or by the pressing issues that affect higher education today.

Finally, there is tremendous power in listening. When I think of all the guest speakers, all the texts, all the conversation starters and reflection prompts Clarke's new faculty encounter over nine months, I marvel at the window through which they can peer into the university's life, its modes of being and doing, before they decide to open the door and enter. They are the ones who are asked to put together a fresh, new perception of parts and whole, and that integrative labor is powerful for them. And for us.

Sensitivity to the sacredness, vulnerability, and power of newcomers can shape the way we prepare formation sessions and arrange the space we make for "metabolizing" time in addition to content-sharing time. It is also helpful to offer new faculty members periodic descriptions of what they might be experiencing. After all, it is confusing to be both vulnerable and powerful. Program leaders can reassure new faculty by naming developmental milestones commonly experienced: the first years are hardest, with course design and delivery easing up with practice; most of us must learn to teach the student and not the subject; saying "yes" to all the invitations to serve must yield at some point to discretion and prudence. Leaders can emphasize out loud that new faculty's long, slow work of integration is honored, protected, and of benefit to the whole community.

New faculty formation as a learning program can model radical hospitality for today's fraught higher education environment. At Clarke, we take sabbath time together, just a little while during the school day and at regular intervals on our calendars. We pause our zealous planning, problem solving, and evaluating to sit with each other in this sheltered moment. We sit with each other to hold and honor in our collective awareness the work that we share. We let some things distill and other things surface. Like all skills, "just" sitting there takes practice. It is radical to give such receptivity the time and trust it needs.

Our group often meets in a room off the atrium at the center of campus. All around us is the buzz of activity. We were buzzing, too, earlier in the day, and we will resume buzzing in the hours after we depart this special space. To form new faculty, we must create little islands of not doing. This prophetic resistance is not a mere pushing back of pressures. It requires inviting one another to practice conscientious noticing, remembering, savoring goodness, and honoring responses of disquiet, not-fitting, and indignation. It requires helping each other sharpen our sense of what is and our sense of what could be but is not yet. We are seeding a common way of being as diverse educators. This is a new chapter for Catholic higher education and a hopeful one. Yet, in new faculty formation, I advocate hope with feet—equipping one another with reflective tools for guided practice. We must fill this prophetic space of new faculty formation with our best stances from the Catholic intellectual tradition: attentiveness, humility, openness, inclusiveness, patience, integration of knowledge, and commitment to our mission. Ideally, such a fine beginning finds magnification elsewhere on campus as faculty members progress from new to "seasoned."

By developing nine months of sanctuary space with multiple layers of purposeful listening, our program is forming educators as listeners for the Catholic university community. The details of the program I have experienced and describe here will surely be replaced by new variations in the years to come. As I near the conclusion of my time as leader, my hope is that future formation leaders will resist the temptation to speak more than they listen, and do all they can to safeguard the immense value in holding space. Doing so can spark truly inclusive planning and delivery. May future leaders protect radically hospitable spaces for training in loving attentiveness, spaces that serve to witness new colleagues' prophetic imaginations into being.

Trauma-Informed Pedagogy as Sacred Hospitality

Jonathan M. Bowman
University of San Diego

In recent years, the concept of trauma-informed pedagogy has gained traction in higher education circles across a variety of institution types, typically conceptualized as a useful way to more holistically engage young people who matriculate at college campuses while simultaneously acknowledging their positive *and* negative life experiences. An emphasis on trauma-informed pedagogy in the classroom allows the learning community associated with a particular course to better understand and acknowledge the diversity of perspectives, identities, and experiences that one might bring to the classroom, not only in the production of coursework but also in the engagement with both difficult and seemingly inane topics that impact the student experience. While an instructor's use of trauma-informed pedagogy might seem a practically useful strategy to simply better engage the variety of students who are likely to respond to course material and life circumstances in different ways, the transformational application of trauma-informed pedagogy can actually serve as a sacramental instance of radical hospitality in both Catholic-affiliated and secular classrooms.

Understanding Trauma-Informed Pedagogies

What, then, do we mean by a trauma-informed pedagogy, and from where does such a concept emerge? Admittedly, it must be noted that there are currently two separate discourses around the term "trauma-informed pedagogy." A common use of the term (that is admittedly less relevant for this discussion on sacred hospitality) stems from a well-developed literature around course discussions of traumatic events (e.g., topics for training counselors or clinical psychologists) which highlights the potential for retraumatization that might occur while covering these topics in the classroom setting.[1] More relevant to *this* chapter, there is a relatively distinct discussion of trauma-informed pedagogy that focuses on a collective classroom approach that recognizes both specific and general trauma that students have experienced on an individual and systematic level *while simultaneously acknowledging* that classroom content, discussions, and experiences can cause problems or even retraumatize classroom participants if not handled with grace. It is to this latter discussion of trauma-informed pedagogy as an embodied form of sacred hospitality that we turn.

In my own classrooms, I have discovered over recent years that many of the traditional teaching practices that I was taught at previous institutions are primarily meant to focus on deliverables, such as maintaining a satisfactory grade distribution and delivering content efficiently. Late assignments are marked down, assignment due dates and examination deadlines are inflexible, and students are expected to participate fully in person at every moment of every course meeting time (regardless of reason) upon penalty of grade. At the same time, these policies don't necessarily *ensure* student learning and in some cases can actually be problematic for students experiencing temporary or systematic struggles. University students are particularly susceptible to the adverse impacts of trauma-related experiences on learning, with almost half of our students reporting having experienced two or more traumatic events in their lifetime up to and during college. Yes, you read that correctly: up to 45 percent of students report *two or more* traumatic events.[2] In addition,

1. Janice Carello and Lisa D. Butler, "Potentially Perilous Pedagogies: Teaching Trauma Is Not the Same as Trauma-Informed Teaching," *Journal of Trauma & Dissociation* 15, no. 2 (2014): 155.

2. Jennifer P. Read et al., "Rates of DSM–IV–TR Trauma Exposure and Posttraumatic Stress Disorder among Newly Matriculated College Students," *Psychological Trauma: Theory, Research, Practice, and Policy* 3, no. 2 (2011): 152.

students are dealing with a world in which they are struggling not only with practical individual issues (e.g., oppression and violence based on identities like race, gender, or sexuality), or practical widespread issues (e.g., mass shootings, political instability, wage/salary gaps that foment unrest), but also conceptual widespread issues that represent an existential threat to their future (e.g., international conflict or climate change).[3]

To be fair, students aren't the only ones who have experienced traumatic events. For example, many faculty instructors collectively experienced a sudden shift in classroom experience and policy with the advent of the COVID-19 pandemic, often involving dramatic changes in delivery, content management, and course policy. Admittedly, these moments included many special institutional dispensations invoked only in case of emergency, but they also allowed for unprecedented pedagogical experimentation and shifts in classroom management. In more recent years, many institutions have walked back these dispensations with the "return to normal," leaving faculty to wonder how best to support students experiencing trauma during times that are no less tumultuous yet are also no longer considered "unprecedented." What, then, are the teaching activities and practices that might prove to care for students in radical and hospitable ways? A robust literature has emerged as faculty experiment with the ways that people have shifted to accommodate the unique lives of students—often dealing with systematic biases that will never go mentioned to or noticed by the faculty that teach them. How can we practice radical hospitality as classroom instructors in a way that delivers classroom content but also facilitates wellness?[4]

Adopting a trauma-informed pedagogy of radical hospitality in higher education involves understanding trauma while simultaneously considering how traumatized students might interact with systems of care within the university system (e.g., academic affairs, student affairs, housing, and student support services).[5] A robust literature lists six key points

3. Ernest Stromberg, "Introduction," in *Trauma-Informed Pedagogy in Higher Education: A Faculty Guide for Teaching and Learning*, ed. Ernest Stromberg (New York: Routledge, 2023), 2.

4. Stromberg, 3.

5. Christina Valdez, "Considerations for Developing a First-Year Seminar on Psychological Trauma," in *Trauma-Informed Pedagogy in Higher Education*, ed. Stromberg, 13.

that faculty should consider when deciding how best to facilitate a classroom experience for these traumatized students. These points include facilitating perceptions of safety within the classroom context, instructing with trustworthiness and transparency, allowing opportunities for peer support to emerge, developing assignments and activities that promote collaboration and mutuality among peers, empowering students with opportunities for choice, and responsibly addressing cultural/historical/gender/sexuality issues relevant to the student experience with the classroom content.[6] In doing so, faculty can help students better navigate not only their individual course experience but also the university system as a whole with the support of their instructors.

Impact of Trauma on University Life

Why might faculty be interested in reducing the impact of trauma and avoiding the possibility of retraumatization? Beyond the previously discussed introduction to and primary importance of the practice of radical hospitality, a number of impacts on student learning have been identified and discussed within the literature which could also impact course outcomes and classroom management experiences. For example, students struggling with trauma (including ongoing events such as harassment, discrimination, and even instances of systematic oppression) might have difficulty focusing in the classroom or even attending class in the first place.[7] Additionally, students struggling with past or present trauma are also more likely to have greater trouble than other students with learning new things, concentrating, and taking risks in the classroom.[8]

6. Joy Patton and Lauren Cortez, "How Trauma-Informed Care Principles Can Contribute to Academic Success for Students in Hispanic-Serving Institutions," in *Trauma-Informed Pedagogies: A Guide for Responding to Crisis and Inequality in Higher Education*, ed. Phyllis Thompson and Janice Carello (Cham, Switzerland: Springer International, 2022), 109.

7. Vanessa Lopez-Littleton and Dennis Kombe, "Racial Trauma: Dismantling Anti-Black Racism in Classrooms and Academia," in *Trauma-Informed Pedagogy in Higher Education*, ed. Stromberg, 44.

8. Rachel L. Gunderson, Carolline F. Mrozla-Toscano, and Dung M. Mao, "An Instructor's Guide for Implementing Trauma-Informed Pedagogy in Higher Education," *Journal of Faculty Development* 37, no. 2 (May 2023): 81.

These students might exhibit greater psychological arousal, experience defensive dissociation,[9] or feel helpless or out of control when triggered in the classroom environment.[10] Factors like these are problematic for students and faculty alike, not only in managing the classroom experience but also in facilitating new learning, particularly when students note that their peers do not seem to be learning either. These students are also likely to avoid or even fear normal classroom activities such as presenting/speaking, examinations, group work, or meeting expected course deadlines.[11] In all, traumatized students appear to experience a form of burnout because of the sense of helplessness or lack of agency that they feel over their own lives,[12] and this burnout has serious implications for the shared classroom experience.

Practical Trauma-Informed Strategies

What, then, are some practical ways to use our understanding of many students' lived and experienced traumas to create a more hospitable and transformative classroom? I share here some intentional course activities and policies that have helped address some of these needs in my own classroom. These are pedagogy-informed strategies from both scholarship and practical experience, and while they may need to be adapted to fit departmental or institutional needs, they are presented as generic enough to apply broadly. While not intended to be used as a form of virtue signaling, some of these activities or policies do indeed signal availability and inclusion to students in a significant and important way.

9. Neil Harrison, Jacqueline Burke, and Ivan Clarke, "Risky Teaching: Developing a Trauma-Informed Pedagogy for Higher Education," *Teaching in Higher Education* 28, no. 1 (2023): 1, 180.

10. Britt E. Rhodes, "Trauma-Informed Contemplative Pedagogy: Implications for Undergraduate Course Revision," *Journal of Baccalaureate Social Work* 24 (2019): 139.

11. Phyllis Thompson and Heidi Marsh, "Centering Equity: Trauma-Informed Principles and Feminist Practice," in *Trauma-Informed Pedagogies*, ed. Thompson and Carello, 19.

12. Janice Carello and Phyllis Thompson, "Developing a New Default in Higher Education: We Are Not Alone in This Work," in *Trauma-Informed Pedagogies*, ed. Thompson and Carello, 3.

Safety through Reflective Activities

Often, one of the best ways to remind students that they are in a safe space is to encourage them to remember the egalitarian character of the collaborative classroom environment. Given that reflection is a key strategy of trauma-informed pedagogy, using reflective activities can allow students to consider their own relation to any course material and also to center themselves. To be clear, we are not talking about asking students to reflect *upon traumatic course content.* Indeed, as scholars have highlighted, the majority of faculty are neither trained in therapy nor practicing as therapists in the classroom.[13] Rather, I accomplish reflection through three key activities.

First, I start the class with a moment of silence. If I'm in a well-equipped classroom, I might show a video of a flickering candle on the screen or dim the lights accordingly. Students are encouraged to think about their day and to leave behind any outside stressors or performance anxieties. Scholars note that it is important to encourage students that they may end their reflective meditation at any time for any reason.[14] I have often been surprised by how many retrospective comments I receive from students over the course of the semester about the importance of that silent moment.

Second, I incorporate written reflective experiences in the syllabus as related to class content, giving students four experiential activities to "accomplish" throughout the semester and then asking students to turn in a short one- to two-page reflection. Typically, each experiential activity involves an applied behavior related to a topic already discussed in detail in class (e.g., evaluating their own self-representation while engaging in small talk with an unknown other in a coffee shop) and then reflecting on how they might understand themselves differently as a result of the experience. Although the experiences themselves might seem relatively benign, these experiences are also structured in such a way that they are challenge-by-choice, in that students are welcome to drop any one reflective activity that seems uncomfortable with no grade repercussion.

13. Ernest Stromberg, "Trauma-Informed Mindfulness Meditation in the College Classroom," in *Trauma-Informed Pedagogy in Higher Education*, ed. Stromberg, 94.

14. Stromberg, 95.

Finally, I ask students to regularly process their written reflections (above) and to engage in low-stakes scaffolded discussions with a small subgroup of peers or—when appropriate—with the class as a whole. By setting community standards early in the semester, there are guardrails to make sure that people are discussing the concepts of the course, not one another.[15] It is through these communal reflections that students not only confront minor differences but also find that there are more similarities amongst their peers than they may have previously imagined.

Avoidance of Retraumatization

There is much discourse in contemporary society about the concept of "trigger warnings" (i.e., the explicit mention of themes that are sensitive in nature). Often, conversations wax and wane around two perspectives, either arguing that trigger warnings are wearing down the spontaneous resilience of American young people (a decidedly inhospitable perspective) or arguing that trigger warnings are essential ways to ensure that spaces are safe for all participants. Either way, scholars of trauma-informed pedagogies are quick to point out that these warnings are intended to give students the opportunity to be protected against retraumatization, not just to be used as a way for students to avoid discussing difficult course content.[16] In this chapter, we of course argue for the importance of trigger warnings, acknowledging that students who have been traumatized might generally exist in a baseline of low-level fear as adult learners, struggling to endure classrooms that discuss related difficult topics.[17] However, there are a couple of important caveats for the use of trigger warnings in order to make them effective.

First, it is important to acknowledge that all folks in the university community (e.g., students, faculty, and staff) have a diversity of experience, and that it is not unusual for them to have experienced negative life

15. Brynn Fitzsimmons, "Trauma Together: Rethinking Collaborative Learning," in *Trauma-Informed Pedagogy in Higher Education*, ed. Stromberg, 119.

16. Rose Gubele, "Trigger Warnings with Conscience: Presenting Texts about Sexual Assault with Respect," in *Trauma-Informed Pedagogy in Higher Education*, ed. Stromberg, 149; Carello and Butler, "Potentially Perilous Pedagogies," 155.

17. Jeanie Tietjen, "Naming the Urgency: The Importance of Trauma-Informed Practices in Community Colleges," in *Trauma-Informed Pedagogy in Higher Education*, ed. Stromberg, 118.

events that might cause trauma (i.e., not only situational events but also systemic trauma such as discrimination or other social inequalities).[18] Then, it is essential that people are given *sufficient time* to think about whether they will find a specific topic more than just uncomfortable. For example, mentioning a sensitive subject like interpersonal violence and then immediately launching into a survivor's narrative experience may seem to only weaken the implied concern for students in the course, taking them by surprise and not allowing for a meaningful response. Instead, I recommend that in those earliest days of the semester (either on "syllabus day" or very soon thereafter), faculty highlight when sensitive topics might emerge as related to specific topics. Teaching about infidelity and interpersonal violence is a core learning outcome of a specific relationship class that I teach, and I make sure to let students know on that first day that they have about nine weeks to consider their level of engagement with that more general topic of relational transgressions and the more specific instances of communicative aggression. I also give students a reminder during the class immediately preceding the one in which we broach the difficult topic, and I remind them once again at the beginning of the specific class. I am also careful to discuss available accommodations for affected students, mentioned later in this section.

Next, it is important to allow students to remove themselves from the classroom environment. While this seems obvious, what might not be so obvious is the impact upon students leaving mid-class should the topic ultimately prove too much for them to manage. Not only might this cause "othering" to occur for the specific student, exposing them to questions or assumptions made by other students, but also it might prove socially debilitating to the point that they would perhaps ultimately prefer to experience a more private, negative retraumatization rather the new, potentially traumatic experience of being outed and identified as a potential victim. Students should not *only* be allowed to leave should a topic become "too much." Instead, students should be given an alternative experience or assignment accommodations to substitute for attendance

18. Vanessa Lopez-Littleton and Dennis Kombe, "Dismantling Anti-Black Racism in Classrooms and Academia," in *Trauma-Informed Pedagogy in Higher Education*, ed. Stromberg, 50.

or activity-based points, *and be allowed to opt out of that particular class session in advance.*

Students who might have significant negative responses to specific course content must indeed be treated with respect and dignity and allowed to protect their own wellness, while also receiving alternate assignment options should any point-bearing activities take place.[19] These might include writing assignments, readings, annotated bibliographies, or other alternatives deemed appropriate by the course instructor. (It is important to note that these alternate assignments should be crafted in a way that they do not force students to recount their traumatic experiences in writing. Allowing a student to *not* talk about trauma but then *forcing* them to recount that same trauma through the written word is almost the exact opposite practice of radical hospitality.)

Healthy Interactions with Peers

Another way that the classroom experience can be more supportive for students who have experienced trauma is through healthy discussions with peers[20] and repeated collaborative interactions.[21] For example, I use a poster session on the final day of class where students display their summative thoughts on the semester and unpack their favorite topic or theory. Students are then encouraged to publicly share commonalities that they have noticed between their posters and others', or to highlight some new insight that they gained from a peer's poster. By keeping these conversations positive and reflective, students receive affirming feedback that increases perceptions of peer support in the classroom. (Some faculty use a constructive peer-review process to facilitate similar perceptions of support.) Using empathy and perspective-taking in such a positive context can actually alleviate fears of the unknown other within the classroom context, not only opening the student to that particular classroom but

19. Gubele, "Trigger Warnings with Conscience," in *Trauma-Informed Pedagogy in Higher Education*, ed. Stromberg, 148.

20. Ashley M. Hooper et al., "Re-Envisioning Learning Through a Trauma-Informed Lens: Empowering Students in Their Personal and Academic Growth," *Journal of the Scholarship of Teaching and Learning* 23, no. 3 (September 2023): 81.

21. Fitzsimmons, "Trauma Together: Rethinking Collaborative Learning," in *Trauma-Informed Pedagogy in Higher Education*, ed. Stromberg, 123.

also in other course contexts.[22] Such intentional classroom activities that involve peer support, collaboration, and mutual self-help[23] have been shown to similarly foster perceptions of trustworthiness and connection among students and their peers.[24]

Course Policies and Faculty Humility

The final set of recommendations is one I am currently navigating, a form of hospitality that seems alien to me in some ways. As someone who is deadline driven and timely, this author has often struggled with getting students to similarly agree on the importance of deadlines and timeliness. My interpersonal interactions with students tend to be invitational and supportive, but upon further reflection, my application of course deadlines was inflexible. One might imagine that popular instructors exhibit grace and compassion, but unfortunately that rarely happened with my reaction to a student's missed assignment deadline. Fortunately, after reflection and reading, I now understand how personal attitudes about time management need not be applied whole-cloth to all students, much less to students struggling in ways that I will never fully understand. The years spent experiencing various degrees of pandemic-related instability[25]—combined with the life uncertainty associated with a variety of family medical issues—educated me about how much one's life can be outside one's control. While my policies were already built to allow for some minor choice or life surprises in a student's experiences, I realize now that even those attempts at hospitality were still far too inflexible to accommodate the permanent sense of uncertainty that might exist in the life of any individual student recovering from traumatic experiences. It was in this moment that I was able to hear—through developmental self-reflection encouraged by scholarship on pedagogy—that an instructor

22. Robin A. Robinson, "The Whole Person in Front of Me: Toward a Pedagogy of Empathy and Compassion," in *Transforming Classroom Culture*, ed. Arlene Dallalfar, Esther Kingston-Mann, and Tim Sieber (New York: Palgrave Macmillan, 2011), 155.

23. Mays Imad, "Our Brains, Emotions, and Learning: Eight Principles of Trauma-Informed Teaching," in *Trauma-Informed Pedagogies*, ed. Thompson and Carello, 41.

24. Ibid., 42.

25. R. Kirk Anderson, Brendan Landy, and Victoria Sanchez, "Trauma-Informed Pedagogy in Higher Education: Considerations for the Future of Research and Practice," *Journal of Trauma Studies in Education* 2, no. 2 (2023): 125.

must indeed work to learn, to truly listen (rather than just hear), and to develop a humble sense of self.[26]

Hospitable Flexibility

This latter idea—the humble sense of self—can make it difficult when instructors get stuck on "well, that's the way that I had to do it . . ." as a justification for rigid or inflexible policy decisions. Formal policy flexibility in the syllabus removes any opportunity for a particularly ego-driven instructor to encourage student groveling and for the instructor to present as magnanimous. In fact, formal policy flexibility actually reduces workload and bias for the instructor, because they don't have to make case-by-case exceptions to benefit the student's well-being and sense of self-efficacy. I don't want a student to have to beg me for grace because they missed a class, nor do I care to look generous in a way that actually makes students question how far they can bend every course policy. Consider course attendance, for example. Some institutions don't require that faculty take attendance; many other institutions are required to do so by their funding sources, in part because tracked attendance is a prerequisite for financial aid eligibility.[27] That being said, attendance need not necessarily be a point-bearing exercise nor hold a corequisite status for passing a course. If a student has an excuse for why they didn't attend a course, don't require "proof." Imagine trying to track down a police report after an instance of interpersonal violence, or seeking a local obituary that proves the death of a loved one.[28]

Consider also whether due dates can be a bit more of a general guideline than a hard-and-fast rule. To be clear, I absolutely believe that students do themselves a disservice by delaying the due dates of work, but beyond group work or scaffolded assignments, perhaps instructors need not apply additional penalties beyond the difficulties of work accumulating. After all, personally, I have discovered that my own life gets harder with each granted extension for overdue work. At the same time, those

26. Hilistis Pauline Waterfall and Elodie Button, "Trauma-Informed Indigenous Adult Education," in *Trauma-Informed Pedagogies*, ed. Thompson and Carello, 153.

27. Janice Carello and Phyllis Thompson, "What Are We Centering? Developing a Trauma-Informed Syllabus," in *Trauma-Informed Pedagogies*, ed. Thompson and Carello, 214.

28. Ibid.

extensions are rarely *not* granted in the professional context should I need them. Scholars of trauma-informed pedagogies encourage us to extend the same grace to students that we might expect in our own professional lives.[29] I've discovered that when I tell students that the deadlines are there for them and their own successful progression to the end of the course (an inflexible grading date set by my institution at which point all graded material must be submitted), they often nod in agreement and work to meet the imposed deadline of their own volition.

Sacred Hospitality as an Extension of Vocation

Practicing hospitality as a sacred extension of one's academic vocation stems naturally from such a pursuit, and that calling also includes a radical rethinking of the classroom experience for those students who come in a posture of brokenness. By approaching folks with humility and in acknowledgment of individual experiences with trauma, the classroom can become not only a space of learning and growth but also of safety and reflection. I hope that each instructor is able to explore how best to engage trauma-informed pedagogical practices in their own personal practice of radical hospitality using belonging-based classroom practices. By acknowledging the tumult that might trigger not only those students struggling with more obvious markers of traumatic exclusion but also even the most seemingly-privileged students (whose biggest fear is often being "found out" as other), specific practices of trauma-informed pedagogy can simultaneously be *one way* to engage in radical hospitality—and even perhaps the *best way* to demonstrate the flourishing that can occur among students who feel fully supported by instructors practicing a trauma-informed pedagogical stance throughout their curriculum.

29. Ibid., 216.

Engaging Religious Diversity

Radical Hospitality in Catholic Universities for the Common Public Good

Hans Gustafson
University of St. Thomas

In the past decade, as student, staff, and faculty have become increasingly religiously diverse, Catholic universities in the United States have embraced this multireligious reality. Some have become leaders in higher education by recognizing the benefits of drawing on their cultural and religious heritage and leveraging their mission-driven dedication to radical hospitality. By engaging with religious diversity in the classroom and through co-curricular activities, these institutions align with Catholic principles while promoting the flourishing of all community members, including Catholics, non-Catholics, and non-Christians. This mutually beneficial approach enhances the universities' Catholic identity while fostering inclusive multifaith learning environments. This chapter explores theoretical and practical dimensions of how Catholic universities can engage religious diversity to transform their campuses into inclusive spaces where all perspectives are welcomed. By prioritizing radical hospitality and a culture of encounter, these institutions cultivate a resilient environment that supports personal and social flourishing, aligning their missions with the common good.

Theoretical Framework: Civic Religious Pluralism and Radical Hospitality

To analyze the ways Catholic universities in the United States can become robust multifaith communities requires a theoretical framework. In this case, I draw on the concepts of multifaith engagement as civic religious pluralism (CRP) and radical hospitality, while integrating Catholic social teaching (CST) principles into a Catholic institutional model for higher education. This approach does not shun, ignore, or dilute the Catholic religio-cultural heritage and identity of the institution; rather, it embraces, leans into, and draws on it to justify multireligious engagement. Furthermore, I examine the secular (some might say postsecular) Norwegian model of civic interreligious engagement (*det livssynsåpne samfunn*) as a way forward in creating religiously inclusive educational environments.

Multifaith Engagement draws on Diana Eck's civic religious pluralism (CRP)—not to be confused with *theological* pluralism[1]—which emphasizes energetic engagement with, rather than indifference to, religious diversity. Eck distinguishes pluralism from diversity by defining it as active participation and interaction with diverse religious groups. It goes beyond just tolerance, which can imply passive acceptance with no attempt to understand or sympathize. CRP involves a commitment to engagement (dialogue and understanding) across religious differences. Eck's framework is built on four key points. CRP is (1) not diversity alone, but the energetic engagement with diversity; (2) not just tolerance, but the active seeking of understanding across lines of difference; (3) not relativism, but the encounter of commitments; and (4) an ongoing process based on dialogue.[2] These principles aim to create a society where diverse religious beliefs and practices can coexist and interact constructively. In the context of the United States, Eck emphasizes the importance of the

1. Theological pluralism refers to a theological position about the accessibility of theological truth and the access to the ultimate end (*telos*) or ends (*teloi*). See Hans Gustafson, *Everyday Wisdom: Interreligious Studies in a Pluralistic World* (Minneapolis: Fortress Press, 2023), 261–64.

2. Diana L. Eck, *A New Religious America: How a "Christian Country" Has Become the World's Most Religiously Diverse Nation* (New York: HarperSanFrancisco, 2001), 70–73; Diana L. Eck, "About," Pluralism Project, https://pluralism.org/about. For a deeper analysis of CRP, see Gustafson, *Everyday Wisdom*, 247–54.

First Amendment's "no establishment" and "free exercise" clauses to lay common ground for CRP to support a secular society in which religious diversity is not only tolerated but also positively engaged. This engagement aspires to align with empathy and compassion, common values in many religious and secular ways of life. CRP encourages citizens to maintain their own religious commitments (religious, spiritual, secular, or otherwise) without necessarily being indifferent to the religious orientations of others. It promotes actively engaging with others to create a society where differences are respected and understood through not only dialogue but also energetic encounters and interactions.[3]

Hospitality, as described by Jennifer Kilps, within the Christian traditions, is "an act, or action, that is experienced as an interaction, involving more than one person; by definition hospitality is always relational. It is first and foremost an experience that can only be manifest in the concrete interactions between persons."[4] In other words, radical hospitality involves the act of welcoming the stranger in ways that anticipate and create a space for meaningful and reciprocal interaction. Unlike traditional hospitality, which often maintains an insider-outsider dynamic where the guest is welcomed but not fully at home, radical hospitality seeks to create a shared, co-created space where all individuals feel equally at home—empowered to rearrange the furniture and contribute to the environment. This extends beyond mere tolerance to actively engaging with others with an eye to nurturing a sense of belonging and honoring the dignity of every individual. Radical hospitality in this chapter rests on two sources: (1) hospitality as a core tenet of the Benedictine tradition; and (2) the work of Catholic comparative theologian Marianne Moyaert.

The Rule of St. Benedict, a set of guidelines for monastic life written by St. Benedict of Nursia in the sixth century, emphasizes hospitality as a chief principle. It states, "Let all guests who arrive be received like

3. Content from this section also appears in Hans Gustafson, "From Indifference to Engagement: A Secular Response to Religious Diversity," in *Beyond Dialogue: New Paradigms in Interfaith Discourse*, ed. Daniel Ross Goodman, Elaine Jean Lai, and Anthony A. Lee (Albany, NY: SUNY Press, 2025), forthcoming.

4. Jennifer Kilps, "Hospitality to the Stranger: The Experience of Christian Churches in the Resettlement of African Refugees to the United States" (PhD thesis, University of St. Andrews, 2007), 20.

Christ, for He is going to say, 'I came as a guest, and you received Me.' "[5] This hospitality is extended not only to pilgrim monks but also to the poor and the stranger, who are treated with honor and welcomed into the community. This Benedictine hospitality can be made radical by applying it to college campuses seeking to engage religiously diverse orientations by creating an environment of deep respect, inclusion, welcoming, and ultimately belonging. Benedict calls his monks to treat each individual, regardless of their religious orientation, with the same reverence and openness as Christ, who for Catholics is the personification of God in the strongest possible terms.

The title of Moyaert's important work, *Fragile Identities*, refers to the inherent vulnerability and dynamic nature of personal and religious identities, which are continually shaped and reshaped through openness and engagement with the other. This concept can be applied to the identity of the Catholic university, which involves recognizing that the university's religious identity is dynamic and open to transformation through interreligious engagement in ways that do not undermine or betray its Catholic religio-cultural heritage. Just as fragile identities require openness to be enriched by the other, radical hospitality embodies this openness as a fundamental aspect of engagement. Radical hospitality is, above all, an openness. This includes a theological and hermeneutical openness that, as in Eck's CRP model, extends beyond mere tolerance to actively engaging with the religious other. From Moyaert's Catholic perspective, "This openness does not undermine Christian identity. To the contrary: Christian identity takes shape precisely in its relationship to otherness."[6] Although hospitality can certainly include providing material aid, radical hospitality is also about welcoming and understanding the religious other in their full dignity and richness with an eye to fostering a sense of belonging beyond mere inclusion. Moyaert explains that radical hospitality requires a deep willingness to receive, to be interrupted, and to be transformed by encounters with others, particularly those with different religious and nonreligious orientations. As such, radical hospitality necessitates letting

5. Benedict of Nursia, *St. Benedict's Rule for Monasteries*, ed. Cuthbert Butler, trans. Leonard J. Doyle (Collegeville, MN: Liturgical Press, 1950), chap. 53.

6. Marianne Moyaert, *Fragile Identities: Towards a Theology of Interreligious Hospitality* (Amsterdam: Brill, 2011), 197.

go of one's own control and prejudices, as much as possible, to make space for the other's world and experiences. Moyaert bases her position in the biblical tradition, where hospitality to the stranger is seen as a virtue that involves a dialectic of expropriation and appropriation—losing oneself to find oneself through the other. However, this philosophy of radical hospitality, which promotes the personal journey from selfishness to selflessness, is not exclusively a biblical or Christian concept. It is found philosophically, both explicitly and implicitly, in many religious, spiritual, and secular traditions and ways of living.

Models for Successful Multifaith Engagement

The concept of *det livssynsåpne samfunn* (A Society Open to a Diversity of Worldviews), generated by Sturla J. Stålsett and the Stålsett Committee, commissioned in 2013 by the Norwegian Minister of Culture to recommend new approaches to state policies on religion, aligns with the spirit of radical hospitality within the context of state policy and offers a model for universities to consider.[7] It represents a shift from a position of neutrality (*livsynsnøytralt*) to a position of openness (*livssynsåpent*) by advocating for an actively supportive policy towards diverse religious worldviews. The committee's report set out eight fundamental principles for a coherent policy on religion and life stance in Norway: (1) Protect freedom of religion or life stance for everyone; (2) Religious manifestations must not violate others' rights; (3) Nondiscrimination: no disproportionate

7. The committee produced the report *Det Livssynsåpne Samfunn*, which reviewed Norwegian state policies on religion and recommended a secular approach distinct from both strict separation (e.g., French *laïcité*) and hegemonic church-state entanglement (Sturla J. Stålsett, *Det livssynsåpne samfunn: En helhetlig tros- og livssynspolitikk*, NOU 2013: 1 [Oslo: Kulturdepartementet, 2013]). This report underpins the 2021 Norwegian Act on Religion and Worldview Communities (*Lov om tros- og livssynsamfunn*), which defines the state-religion relationship. Rather than promoting assimilation of religious minorities and immigrants, this approach aligns with Eck's civic religious pluralism (CRP). As Stålsett notes, linking "full integration," "assimilation of values," and "secularization" casts immigrant religiosity negatively ("Fearing the Faith of Others? Government, Religion, and Integration in Norway," in *Religion in the European Refugee Crisis*, ed. Ulrich Schmiedel and Graeme Smith [Camden: Palgrave Macmillan, 2018], 118). Eck's CRP model highlights that tolerance alone perpetuates stereotypes and fears, failing to inspire genuine engagement.

treatment based on religion or life stance; (4) Active steps taken to enable all to practice their religion or life stance; (5) Equal treatment: ensure equal support for all religions or life stances; (6) Active policy pursued by the state to be evaluated by democracy, rule of law, human rights, nondiscrimination, and equality; (7) State-supported religious groups must be open and respect others; and (8) Everyone must tolerate manifestations of religions or life stances in the public sphere.[8] These principles resonate with the ethos of radical hospitality in welcoming and engaging with the religious other, extending beyond mere tolerance to active engagement to foster a greater sense of belonging to honor the dignity of every individual. Instead of monoreligious hegemonic or strictly neutral and indifferent secular models, this Norwegian model advocates for a spirit of openness by recommending policies in which authorities value and provide favorable conditions for the many different religions of all citizens and treat religious and life stance communities equally.[9] This concept is particularly relevant to a Catholic university embracing radical hospitality in multireligious contexts. Just as *det livssynsåpne samfunn* calls for the state to actively facilitate the practice of religion and life stances for all citizens, a Catholic university would create an environment that goes beyond mere tolerance to nurture a space where the religious identities of all students, staff, faculty, and community members are respected, engaged, and supported. This involves creating policies and practices that ensure all religious and nonreligious orientations are treated equally and given the resources needed to thrive. Similarly, a Catholic university practicing radical hospitality would actively facilitate interreligious engagement and understanding not just by accommodating but also by valuing the presence of diverse religious perspectives as a good unto itself that provides mutual benefit and reciprocal interactions. This approach moves beyond the minimal legal obligations of neutrality to a more proactive, constructive, and appreciative engagement with religious diversity to encourage a more inclusive campus community that honors the full dignity and richness of every individual.

8. Sturla J. Stålsett, *Det livssynsåpne samfunn* (Oslo: Cappelen Damm Akademisk, 2021), 44.

9. Stålsett, "Fearing the Faith of Others?," in *Religion in the European Refugee Crisis*, ed. Schmiedel and Smith, 116.

Catholic Social Teaching (CST)	Det livssynsåpne samfunn
1. Life and dignity of the human person	1. Protect freedom of religion or life stance for everyone
2. Call to family, community, and participation	4. Active steps taken to enable all to practice their religion or life stance
3. Rights and responsibilities	3. Nondiscrimination: no disproportionate treatment based on religion or life stance
4. Option for the poor and vulnerable	5. Equal treatment: ensure equal support for all religions or life stances
5. The dignity of work and the rights of workers	6. Active policy pursued by the state to be evaluated by democracy, rule of law, human rights, nondiscrimination, and equality
6. Solidarity	7. State-supported religious groups must be open and respect others
7. Care for God's creation	8. Everyone must tolerate manifestations of religions or life stances in the public sphere 2. Religious manifestations must not violate others' rights

Catholic social teaching (CST) is a tradition that guides the Catholic Church's approach to ordering society in responsible and ethical ways. Its roots can be traced back to the Hebrew prophets and Jesus' mission to bring good news to the poor and liberty to captives (see Luke 4:18-19). CST was formalized in the modern era with Pope Leo XIII's 1891 encyclical *Rerum Novarum*, which addressed the rights and duties of capital and labor. CST has significantly influenced various social policies and movements worldwide to promote a just society based on respect for human dignity and the common good. CST has seven core principles, all of which aim at advocating for an active engagement with societal issues and emphasizing the importance of each individual's dignity and the need for communal solidarity and responsibility in creating a just world: (1) Life and dignity of the human person, (2) Call to family, community, and participation, (3) Rights and responsibilities, (4) Option for the poor and vulnerable, (5) The dignity of work and the rights of workers, (6) Solidarity, and (7) Care for God's creation. For Catholic universities and colleges in the United States, CST provides a foundational framework that can influence mission, curricula, and co-curricular community engagement. Its principles are often incorporated directly into the missions, visions, convictions, and charisms of the institutions. In particular, CST's emphasis on human dignity, ethical responsibilities, and the common good helps shape university policies, student programs, and outreach initiatives to nurture an environment where ethical and moral considerations are paramount. CST is relevant for embracing the virtue of radical hospitality on Catholic college campuses as it strives for the welcoming and belonging of religiously diverse individuals and groups, and, as the chart above indicates, its principles provide an inviting framework for mapping the principles of *Det livssynsåpne samfunn* onto it for the creation of a formal framework for a coherent policy on religious diversity and life stances on college campuses.

In addition to CST, several other authoritative Catholic sources provide justification for embracing and engaging religious diversity at a Catholic university. The Second Vatican Council's declaration *Nostra Aetate* encourages members of the church to engage in dialogue and collaboration with followers of other religions by approaching them with care and compassion to recognize, preserve, and promote the positive aspects—both spiritual and moral—along with the sociocultural values found among these individuals.[10] Pope Francis, in his 2020 encyclical *Fratelli Tutti*, states, "[A]pproaching, speaking, listening, looking at, coming to know and understand one another, and to find common ground: all these things are summed up in the one word 'dialogue.' If we want to encounter and help one another, we have to dialogue."[11] Francis proclaims, "[I]n a pluralistic society, dialogue is the best way to realize what ought always be affirmed and respected apart from any ephemeral consensus."[12] Furthermore, Pope Francis also promotes a "culture of

10. Vatican Council II, *Nostra Aetate*: Declaration on the Relation of the Church to Non-Christian Religions, October 28, 1965, par. 2.

11. Pope Francis, *Fratelli Tutti*: Encyclical Letter on Fraternity and Social Friendship, October 3, 2020, par. 198, https://www.vatican.va/content/francesco/en/encyclicals/documents/papa-francesco_20201003_enciclica-fratelli-tutti.html.

12. Ibid., par. 211.

encounter, capable of transcending our differences and divisions,"[13] to which he calls Catholics to "be passionate about meeting others, seeking points of contact, building bridges, planning a project that includes everyone."[14] Here he is not calling everyone to join hands with the aim to arrive at some kumbaya consensus. Rather, he is encouraging the examination of obstacles that prevent bridge-building and, in their place, "create *processes* of encounter, processes that build a people that can accept differences."[15] Francis proclaims, "Let us arm our children with the weapons of dialogue! Let us teach them to fight the good fight of the culture of encounter!"[16] *Ex Corde Ecclesiae*, meaning "From the Heart of the Church," is a 1990 apostolic constitution issued by Pope John Paul II that defines and refines the Catholic identity of Catholic institutions of higher education. It articulates the norms of a Catholic university and was further contextualized for the United States by the United States Conference of Catholic Bishops in 2001 in the document *The Application for Ex Corde Ecclesiae for the United States*, which emphasizes the importance of Catholic institutions collaborating in ecumenical and interfaith efforts to address the spiritual and pastoral needs of students, faculty, and other university personnel who are not Catholic.[17] It further specifies that Catholic universities should "respect and encourage the religious liberty and the diverse religious traditions of the students."[18] This commitment reflects a broader culture of inclusivity and radical hospitality that ensures the religious and spiritual needs of the entire university community are

13. Ibid., par. 215.

14. Ibid., par. 216.

15. Ibid., par. 217, emphasis original. See community of disagreement (*Uenighetsfellesskap*), a concept from Lars Laird Iversen that values constructive engagement with differences and conflicts within a community. Rather than seeking uniformity or avoiding disagreements, this approach encourages respectful dialogue and the sharing of diverse perspectives as a means of fostering growth, understanding, and mutual respect.

16. Ibid.

17. It states, "With due regard for religious liberty and freedom of conscience, the university, in cooperation with the diocesan bishop, should collaborate in ecumenical and interfaith efforts to care for the pastoral needs of students, faculty, and other university personnel who are not Catholic." *The Application for Ex Corde Ecclesiae for the United States* (Washington, DC: United States Conference of Catholic Bishops, 2001), Part II, Article 6, sec. 4.

18. US Conference of Catholic Bishops, *Application for Ex Corde Ecclesiae for the United States*, 4.

met, regardless of their Catholic, non-Catholic, religious, or nonreligious orientation. All of these Catholic documents collectively support the practice of radical hospitality and the fostering of an inclusive environment that honors and engages religious diversity at Catholic universities and colleges in the United States.

Addressing Tensions in Multifaith Engagement

A primary tension for Catholic institutions, and a general concern (often misconception) among those who first engage with religious diversity, is the worry about losing something, watering down, diluting, downplaying, or compromising their religio-cultural identity and heritage. It may not be intuitive, but what happens more often when one engages with difference is that they not only do not water down their own identities and commitments, but they lean deeper into them and surface them in more authentic and committed ways. This is common in the comparative method, which offers valuable insights not only into other traditions but also, perhaps even more profoundly, into one's own self and home. For instance, an American Christian participant in an interfaith dialogue program captures this spirit by noting, "The amazing thing is, when you learn about others, it inevitably causes you to learn about yourself."[19] Max Müller, the nineteenth-century German scholar of religion, emphasized the importance of comparison, famously suggesting about religion: "He who knows one, knows none."[20] If an individual lacks knowledge of other traditions, then not only do they lack knowledge of those traditions, but they also lack full knowledge of their own tradition. In a similar vein, Marianne Moyaert observes,

> religious identity can no longer be formed and established in isolation from the "other." The permanent presence of the religious other brings about a new form of religious awareness, marked by contingency and relativity. The intimate presence of others and their vivid wisdom traditions undermines some of the certainties, non-negotiable con-

19. Pluralism Project, "America's Growing Interfaith Structure," 1.

20. Jon R. Stone, *The Essential Max Müller* (New York: Palgrave Macmillan, 2002), back cover.

> victions, and absolute truth claims that formed the building blocks of identity formation in the past.[21]

Contrary to diluting or negating one's religious identity, a comparative encounter with difference can actually illuminate and enhance it. This happens on the level of institutional identity as well.

The *Rooted and Open*[22] approach may serve as one model for Catholic universities wrestling with this tension to sustain their rich religio-cultural Catholic identity while actively engaging with religious diversity on their campuses. *Det livssynsåpne samfunn* parallels the "rooted and open" approach by being rooted in Norway's religio-cultural heritage, particularly in its historical ties to the Evangelical-Lutheran tradition, which has shaped the country's values and societal structures. At the same time, it is open to the evolving religious diversity of contemporary Norway by embracing an active approach that accommodates and respects the various religious identities and life stances present in the modern context to ensure inclusivity and equal treatment for all citizens regardless of their beliefs. The rooted and open model for Lutheran colleges and universities in the United States and articulated by the Evangelical Lutheran Church in America (ELCA) aims at maintaining a strong religious and cultural identity while also actively engaging with and being open to diverse religious traditions on their campuses. It draws on the distinctive values of Lutheran higher education, emphasizing commitment to academic excellence, service to the neighbor, and the flourishing of all people. It encourages Lutheran institutions to draw from deep theological roots while addressing contemporary challenges and opportunities. This approach is particularly relevant for Catholic universities as it provides a framework for maintaining a robust Catholic identity *rooted* in its religio-cultural heritage while actively *open* to and engaging with religious diversity on campus. It justifies the increasingly popular refrain that institutions are interreligiously open and inclusive "not *in spite* of but *because of*" their

21. Marianne Moyaert, *In Response to the Religious Other* (London: Lexington Books, 2014), 93–94; also cited in Gustafson, *Everyday Wisdom*, 265.

22. Evangelical Lutheran Church in America, "Rooted and Open: The Common Calling of the Network of ELCA Colleges and Universities," May 18, 2018, https://resources.elca.org/colleges-universities-and-seminaries/rooted-and-open/.

Catholic or Lutheran identity.[23] For Catholic universities, this model aligns well with CST principles, such as the dignity of the human person and the call to solidarity and the common good. Furthermore, it can enhance the mission of inclusivity and radical hospitality to ensure the mandate to care for the spiritual and religious needs of all members of the university, regardless of their orientation to Catholicism and religion.

Strategies for Multifaith Engagement in Catholic Higher Education

Catholic universities can maintain their robust Catholic religio-cultural heritage while engaging religious diversity by drawing on principles from Catholic social teaching (CST) and *det livssynsåpne samfunn* to cultivate a spirit of radical hospitality. The principle of *the dignity of the human person* aligns with the commitment to protect freedom of religion or life stance for everyone and to avoid discrimination based on religion or belief. Concrete steps could include establishing multifaith prayer and meditation rooms, as seen at Georgetown University and the University of St. Thomas. Additionally, offering courses not only in the study of religion but also in interreligious relations and leadership as part of the core curriculum can ensure basic religious literacy, as well as competency and skills for engaging with and appreciating religious diversity and difference in diverse democracies.[24] Universities can also ensure that dietary needs based on religious practices are met in campus dining services by offering halal and kosher options, especially for students living in university housing bound to expensive meal plans and during times of important religious holidays.[25] To address unique institutional contexts, universities

23. Martha E. Stortz, "Marked by Lutheran Higher Education," *Intersections* 49 (2019): 24–26. Janett I. Cordovés and Dawn Michele Whitehead, ed., *Interfaith Cooperation for Our Times: Educating Citizens for a Diverse Democracy* (Washington, DC: Association of American Colleges and Universities, 2022), x, 33, 51.

24. For more examples and a comprehensive map of academic programs focusing on interreligious and interfaith studies, see the resource curated by the Association for Interreligious/Interfaith Studies, "Map of Academic Programs," accessed July 24, 2023, https://www.aiistudies.org/map-of-academic-programs.

25. As tools and resources, see the IDEALS study (Interfaith Diversity Experiences and Attitudes Longitudinal Survey) and the INSPIRES Index (Interfaith, Spiritual, Religious,

and colleges will need to consider their specific culture, region, convictions, and charism when enhancing multifaith engagement. Popular strategies include forming interfaith student clubs, hiring religiously diverse chaplains, providing equal respect and financial support for all religious groups and interfaith initiatives, and creating leadership and research positions for students interested in interfaith work.

Opportunities for interfaith community engagement, such as service projects, internships, or community listening and dialogue sessions, alongside campus-wide events such as interfaith forums, art exhibits, or performances, can spark meaningful conversations and collaboration. Celebrating or acknowledging religious and cultural holidays fosters understanding and a sense of belonging. Peer mentorship programs pairing students from different religious backgrounds encourage mutual learning. Supporting faculty research through grants or fellowships and establishing alumni networks to connect graduates with current students further extend interfaith engagement. Virtual opportunities, such as webinars and global dialogues, can amplify these efforts. By embedding interreligious goals into institutional mission statements and fostering spaces where all voices are valued, universities can become models of radical hospitality and vibrant multifaith learning communities. The CST principles of *solidarity* and *the common good* emphasize the importance of unity and communal responsibility. These principles provide Catholic universities with a strong foundation to create an inclusive community by adopting policies that encourage openness and mutual respect among individuals and groups with diverse religious and belief practices. For example, the University of St. Thomas supports institutional resources including a center for interreligious studies, campus ministry interfaith dialogue programs, and academic initiatives that engage Judaism, Islam, and Orthodox Christianity. Providing resources and training for staff and faculty on religious diversity and inclusion can further support such

---

and Secular Campus Climate Index), which are research initiatives that assess how well higher education institutions in the United States foster a welcoming climate for students of diverse worldview identities by measuring students' interfaith experiences, attitudes, and perceptions over time. These studies aim to evaluate and represent an institution's commitment to inclusivity through longitudinal data on students' engagement with and respect for different religious and nonreligious perspectives.

efforts. Integrating these programs into the Offices for Mission and Diversity and Inclusion Services ensures that religious identity becomes a shared responsibility across the campus rather than being relegated solely to the chaplain's office or the theology department. Universities can establish interfaith councils or advisory boards that engage diverse stakeholders from across the campus in communication about the challenges, tensions, and opportunities that arise on a religiously diverse campus. By implementing these concrete measures, Catholic institutions not only transform their campuses into spaces where all members feel fully included and their voices and perspectives genuinely contribute to the flourishing of the campus and local community, but they also deepen their engagement with their Catholic identity, mission, and heritage.

The Future of Multifaith Engagement at Catholic Universities

Instituting these multireligious initiatives can enhance Catholic identity rather than diminish it, creating a sum greater than its parts. Shifting the approach from seeing religious diversity as something to mitigate and accommodate to something to support for its own inherent value is crucial. With this orientation, religious diversity can be recognized as a common social good alongside other public goods like education, health care, and environmental stewardship because it promotes the flourishing of all groups and individuals. It can begin with radical hospitality as the first step because it involves creating spaces for meaningful and reciprocal interaction with the aim of honoring the dignity of every individual. Radical hospitality extends beyond mere tolerance, accommodation, and welcoming to actively engage with others for the purpose of belonging, where all members feel fully included, with their voices and perspectives contributing to the flourishing of the campus and local community—a space where individuals are not just guests but truly at home, co-creating the community. The ultimate aim is not to dilute the Catholic identity of an institution at the expense of giving voice to religiously diverse identities, but rather to amplify and live into the Catholic identity of an institution precisely by actively supporting a multifaith environment where religious diversity is seen as an essential social good that serves the common good.

Growing Our Belonging with Nursing Students

Creating a Community of Care

Kala Mayer, Rachel Wheeler, and Karen E. Eifler

University of Portland

Even in Catholic institutions, it is not uncommon for college teachers to believe that some academic fields, such as those in the humanities, are more natural avenues for cultivating students' sacramental imaginations than others. STEM educators may feel more comfortable using the language of "awe" and "wonder" rather than "grace" or "beholding God's love through creation." Perhaps an analogy exists for the relative ease of weaving notions of a prophetic imagination, especially in criticizing harmful forces in existing social orders—and the concomitant call to returning to deeper ethical commitments—into pre-professional college programs such as health sciences, PK–12 education, and social work. These fields regularly expose learners to injustices and inequities of every kind, not just in curricular materials, but also in experiential learning directly in hospitals, schools, and social service agencies. Educator Kala Mayer, whose own expertise as a nurse is in public health and community health, sat with two of her colleagues to offer strategies she employs in all her courses to help student nurses develop the skills and dispositions they will need to serve effectively in the profession. It is clear in Kala's responses that she does not merely impart facts about the importance of compassion and understanding equity and belonging; she actively practices them in all interactions with and on behalf of students, from course design to classroom instruction to engaging with them outside the classroom. The examples she relates belong in every nurse's classroom, to be sure, but are eminently worthy of adding to *any* college teacher's repertoire.

RACHEL AND KAREN: What courses do you enjoy teaching?
KALA: Over the years, I've come to enjoy teaching a wide range of classes, including many that I never anticipated teaching. Like many academics, I initially assumed I would teach within my areas of expertise, and I do that extensively. However, some of my most surprising and rewarding teaching experiences have come from courses outside this specialization, such as NCLEX [national nurses' licensing exam] preparation and introductory courses for first-year students. Early in my career, I worked predominantly with senior-level students, but I have come to appreciate teaching first-year students. Guiding them at the very beginning of their nursing journey, helping shape their perceptions of what nursing can be, is a privilege. Foundational courses allow me to foster a sense of curiosity and purpose in students, setting the tone for their future learning and professional development.

In terms of pedagogical approaches, I design hands-on, experiential courses that integrate thoughtful and purposeful opportunities for reflection throughout the learning process. Additionally, I enjoy teaching conceptually challenging classes that demand systems-level thinking and navigating complex "gray" areas. Public health, in particular, provides rich opportunities for students to explore these complexities; it is exciting to witness how students' energy around these topics has grown in recent years, influenced by movements like Black Lives Matter and Me Too, as well as the impact of the COVID-19 pandemic.

RACHEL AND KAREN: What are some ways you practice radical hospitality in your classes?
KALA: So much of what constitutes good teaching goes unmentioned in our actual preparation to teach college students, and much of what I'm saying has been learned while in the teaching trenches. Early in my career, I focused heavily on the science of teaching. Over time, I have developed a deep appreciation for the art of teaching, including trauma-informed educational practices and community-based principles. Radical hospitality

has become a central element of my teaching philosophy, allowing me to create inclusive, compassionate, and empowering learning environments. Rooted in principles of social justice, equity, and moral imagination, radical hospitality is more than welcoming students; it is anticipating and meeting their needs in transformative ways. To create a radically hospitable classroom, I am guided by key values that foster inclusivity, compassion, and a deep sense of belonging for all students. The education of nurses requires an understanding of difficult realities, including child and elder abuse, as well as intimate partner violence. While images and simulations of severe injuries, burns, and surgical procedures are important for professional learning, they can be distressing or even (re) traumatizing for some students. In these situations, empathy is paramount as I strive to understand and address the diverse backgrounds and needs of my students. Modeling compassion and care, I aim to create a space where students feel heard and validated. Respect is equally important, honoring the diversity of each student's identity, perspective, and experiences. This means embracing cultural, racial, gender, and socioeconomic diversity, ensuring that all voices are valued and respected.

Equity and inclusion are foundational principles in my classroom. I work to provide the resources and support students need to succeed, regardless of their starting point. This involves accommodating individual needs and removing barriers to ensure that all students have equal opportunities to thrive. Inclusion goes beyond surface-level efforts, actively welcoming students who might otherwise feel marginalized or excluded. This extends to my willingness to learn from students and adapt my teaching practices. I recognize that I am always evolving as an educator, and I approach the classroom with humility and a readiness to accept feedback. Patience allows me to honor the unique learning paces and processes of my students, giving them the time and space to grow without judgment. Kindness fosters trust and meaningful connections, encouraging students to approach their learning and one another with compassion.

Creating a community of care is essential in my classrooms. I aim to provide a safe space where students feel comfortable sharing their thoughts and experiences. Trauma-based reactions to necessary material, such as discussions about patient deaths, inequitable resource allocation, and discrimination in health care, can be ameliorated by leaning into all that comprises a safe and supportive space for learning. Addressing bullying or exclusion promptly is a priority, as is building supportive relationships through one-on-one conversations and peer mentorship. Mindful listening allows me to effectively understand and address students' academic and personal concerns.

Empowering students is another cornerstone of my teaching approach. I encourage student agency by inviting them to shape their learning experiences through choices of topics, projects, and methods of assessment. Inclusive decision-making fosters a sense of ownership and pride, and celebrating the diverse contributions of students creates a culture of mutual appreciation and respect.

Finally, I extend hospitality beyond the classroom by being accessible to students through office hours and online channels. Organizing group activities and fostering collaboration help build a strong sense of community; advocating for students facing challenges ensures that they receive the support they need to succeed. Whether connecting students with resources or providing emotional support, I strive to be an advocate and ally. Whether working with first-year or advanced students, my quest is to extend radical hospitality to inspire curiosity, foster critical thinking, and prepare students to make meaningful contributions to the field of nursing and beyond.

RACHEL AND KAREN: Let's get even more specific. You've been a campus leader in designing and implementing trauma-informed educational practices. What inspired that work, and what have you learned in doing this?
KALA: Students were the inspiration for this work, and it has grown through the support and collaboration of my colleagues. I began working on trauma-informed educational practices (TIEP) seven years ago with my remarkable colleague, Dr. Sally Rothacker-Peyton. This journey has been profoundly educational, deepening my understanding of trauma and its impact on learning environments. Most importantly, I've learned that there is both a significant need for this work and a genuine openness among most faculty to engage with and implement trauma-informed approaches. This receptiveness underscores the importance of fostering supportive, inclusive educational spaces for all learners. Our work has produced several resources for faculty from all disciplines, such as LibGuides for interdisciplinary inclusive leadership (https://libguides.up.edu/inclusive-leadership) and TIEP (https://libguides.up.edu/tiep)

a leadership book club, and a diversity, equity, and inclusion (DEI) curriculum evaluation tool.

RACHEL AND KAREN: One of your projects has the wonderful title "growing our belonging." In your TIEP work, what's a significant activity, assignment, theme, or practice you include in your teaching to help students "grow their own belonging"?

KALA: Embedding trauma-informed pedagogy includes fostering small communities and group settings where students can connect meaningfully with one another and develop a sense of shared purpose. These small-group interactions provide a supportive space for students to find and amplify their voices, encouraging both individual expression and collective engagement. By prioritizing these practices, I aim to create a classroom culture where every student feels valued and included. From syllabus statements to classroom agreements that we revisit in nearly every session, students understand two things: (1) their safety and well-being is my top priority; and (2) they are ultimately responsible for learning all of the course content, not just that which feels comfortable. As nurses, they absolutely must stretch their comfort zones, but they do not need to do that on their own. In TIEP, I provide content notifications well in advance, and students have the right to remove themselves from the immediate session to attend to their well-being.

However, they are not off the hook for learning all the material they miss in a session. They employ their own agency to communicate professionally with me about their decision, and they must formulate a plan to acquire the knowledge they missed, whether that is visiting with me, checking in with colleagues from the course, or a combination of the two. They complete all assignments, take the exams, and meet the same standards as their peers. Being clear and consistent with expectations by having this spelled out in the syllabus, reinforcing the expectations regularly, and being a person of my word for all the agreements we craft creates a sense of safety and security and are all vital elements in creating a classroom of radical and inclusive hospitality. Students have responded very appreciatively to this way of cultivating a caring community that "grows their belonging," whether they are on the giving or receiving end of the care in a given moment. We are all responsible for one another's safety and capacity to flourish and learn together.

RACHEL AND KAREN: As a non-Catholic faculty member, how do you understand the Catholic character of our university as helpful to or hindering your work with students?

KALA: To address this question, I must first reflect on my own positionality. I was raised in the United Methodist tradition, coming from a family with a deep commitment to faith and service. My upbringing was profoundly shaped by my parents, who dedicated their lives to youth development and empowerment—my father as a high school history teacher and professional Scout leader and my mother as a Girl Scout professional and elementary school teacher. These experiences instilled my values of stewardship, service, and a commitment to holistic growth, which align closely with many principles emphasized in Catholic education.

While I don't identify with a specific religious label, I deeply respect and appreciate the role that spirituality and religion play in the lives of my students and patients. Many of my personal morals and professional ethics are rooted in Christian ideals, such as compassion, justice, and care for others. My work as a nurse and educator often involves navigating complex moral and ethical dilemmas, which requires drawing on principles of holistic care and moral reasoning—values that resonate with the Catholic intellectual and social tradition.

At the University of Portland, I see the Catholic character as an asset rather than a hindrance to my work with students. The integration of faith, reason, and service fosters a holistic approach to education, which is essential in health care and public health. The emphasis on social justice, ethical leadership, and the dignity of every individual aligns with my own commitment to inclusivity and equity. Moreover, the university's mission to welcome individuals of all backgrounds and to educate the whole person creates a supportive environment where students can grow not only academically but also spiritually and ethically.

Ultimately, the Catholic character of my university enriches my work by providing a framework that encourages thoughtful engagement with life's deeper questions and a commitment to serving others. This shared focus on community, justice, and holistic development complements my teaching philosophy and enhances my ability to support students in their growth as compassionate and capable professionals.

RACHEL AND KAREN: In what ways has learning about the prophetic imagination been a useful tool for understanding or enhancing the work you do?

KALA: The prophetic imagination has provided me with a new language and framework to critique existing systems while envisioning alternatives rooted in justice, equity, and compassion. This concept has allowed me to approach complex challenges—whether in trauma-informed education, DEI curriculum development, or community-based participatory research—with a lens that is both critical and hopeful. While I do not consider myself a content expert, I see my role as an organizer—a systems thinker who facilitates the work of others by building connections and creating space for meaningful collaboration. The prophetic imagination complements this skill set by encouraging me to critique harmful practices, envision alternative possibilities, and inspire action toward systemic change.

This lens deepens my understanding of trauma-informed systems. By applying the prophetic imagination to my work, I have been able to reimagine educational spaces as healing-centered environments where students feel safe, valued, and empowered to succeed. This perspective challenges traditional systems that often unintentionally perpetuate harm, advocating instead for flexibility within clear expectations, empathy, and relational teaching practices.

Additionally, the prophetic imagination aligns with my commitment to DEI efforts. It enables me to critique systemic inequities, such as the exclusion of marginalized voices in curricula, and work toward inclusive, equitable frameworks in higher education. It also provides a hopeful vision of what education can be—a transformative process that centers on justice, belonging, and the holistic development of all students.

This framework, combined with John Paul Lederach's concept of moral imagination,[1] has enriched my ability to engage in meaningful dialogue and foster collective action. Lederach's emphasis on relational healing and reconciliation complements the prophetic imagination's focus on systemic critique, offering practical tools for addressing conflict and fostering equity within institutions. Together, these approaches have

1. John Paul Lederach, *The Moral Imagination: The Art and Soul of Building Peace* (New York: Oxford University Press, 2005).

helped me expand my work at the intersection of DEI, trauma-informed teaching, and inclusive leadership, creating environments where growth, understanding, and community can flourish.

Ultimately, the prophetic imagination has enhanced my ability to envision and work toward a better, more inclusive future. It inspires me to embrace a growth mindset, value the power of relationships, and advocate for systemic change that uplifts the dignity of all individuals.

Saint Andrew's Abbey

An Experience of Radical Hospitality and Belonging in a Hybrid Graduate Leadership Education Course

Michael R. Carey and Dũng Q. Trần
Gonzaga University

We live and work in a society increasingly fragmented by multiple beliefs: political, religious, and social. Such diversity in thinking, feeling, and doing doesn't need to lead to fragmentation; it can also be the foundation of productive dialogue in the search for common meaning. But our experience of differences unfortunately often includes levels of individual and group rage and societal tumult. Such chaos undermines our ability to see clearly and produces dysfunctional and toxic communities and organizations, led by overwhelmed and confused leaders.

As teacher-scholar-advisors in a graduate program in leadership studies, we struggle to help students find ways to work beneath the roar and tumult of our times. One approach has been to give students an experience of radical hospitality and belonging that triggers creative thinking about how to effectively respond to the fragmentation they experience in their professional and personal lives. Since 2004, we have done this through a course that includes a weeklong immersive learning experience during which graduate students become participant-observers at a Benedictine monastery located in the upper Mojave Desert of California, joining the small community of monks at Saint Andrew's Abbey in Valyermo in the activities of their life there: chanting psalms at four daily services, using *lectio divina* to reflect on important readings, taking their meals in a contemplative and mindful fashion, and practicing long periods of silence. Most importantly, in this monastic community, students experience authentic hospitality, offered by a community whose hospitality has roots in nearly fifteen hundred years of practice by Benedictine monasteries throughout the world. As one graduate student said after completing the course: "Radical hospitality makes space for all voices to be welcomed and heard. It invites collaboration, which bolsters community. It creates a space for enhanced communication to unfold, which elevates engagement and retention. It emphasizes empathy and understanding, leading to both personal and professional growth."[1]

Certainly, we are fortunate to be able to offer this immersion in an active monastic community, as the program we teach in is primarily online-based and has committed to providing short, face-to-face experiences to our graduate and doctoral students who desire it and elect to spend additional resources of time and money to do so. That said, many of the insights about this approach to learning has lessons for campus-based classroom experiences in formal and informal educational contexts at contemporary Catholic colleges and universities.

Course Overview

The course, *Leadership and Community,* is offered primarily online over eight weeks, with the one-week field trip to Saint Andrew's Abbey occurring after four weeks of preparation online. To better understand how and why the monks of Valyermo work together to create their community, the graduate students in the course study principles of monastic culture through a variety of readings and by interviews with individual monks. Monastic practices such as *lectio divina*, the steps of humility, purity of heart, hospitality, stability, obedience, and *conversatio* (the key Benedictine vows) are examined. All of these are both the cause and the effect of the lived community of Saint Andrew's Abbey. Students learn that the founder of Benedictine monasticism—Saint Benedict of Nursia—understood that a life lived in community was essential to the spiritual growth of the individual, and that such community requires a radical hospitality that provides

1. Laura (alumna) in discussion with the authors, April 2024.

the individual with a diverse community of individuals who both support and challenge them towards growth and transformation.

The valuable gift that Benedict gave to the spiritual formation of those who desired to become agents of growth—and transformation—was his focus on the practical ways in which a community could be formed and maintained to nurture a balance between the freedom of the autonomous search for self and the responsibilities of a shared common life. For the early Christians and for Benedict, the true self was to be found, not through separation from the other, but through relationship with the other marked by love, compassion, and care. For Benedict, the false self was constructed upon fears, desires, resentments, and anger. The creation of a false self was also an attempt to hide from God, who called the individual to surrender their need to control—to die to selfishness—and to become an instrument of God's will in the world.

Students in the course learn that early hermits who struggled in their spiritual journey missed another person or community of persons to confront and question their oftentimes confused or self-centered thoughts. In the absence of mentors, counselors, and companions, even an individual with the purest intentions can unwittingly confuse delusional thinking for wisdom. The recognition of this danger to spiritual, emotional, and even physical health led to the development of informal communities centered around a spiritual mentor who acted as a guide to learning how to live life deliberately.

At least one contemporary writer thinks that Benedict's idea was to hide from a dysfunctional culture,[2] but Benedict was not trying to outwit, outlast, or overcome others: his written Rule was designed to assist others to live in real community to learn how to become a more perfect instrument of God's will for the entire world. Hospitality becomes the essential practice to allow the individuals in the monastic community to be supported and challenged as they do the inner work necessary to become an instrument of God's will.[3]

2. Rod Dreher, *The Benedict Option: A Strategy for Christians in a Post-Christian Nation* (New York: Sentinel, 2018).

3. Dũng Q. Trần and Michael R. Carey, "Cherishing the Wisdom of Community: A Benedictine Model of Leadership for Turbulent Times," in *The Palgrave Handbook of*

For graduate students in leadership studies, the insights of the desert monks from the third to the fifth centuries resonate with their understanding of demands of leaders to go beyond their own egos to become servant leaders who do what is best for individuals and organizations and to avoid rejecting someone who disagrees with the leader. Their preparation before entering into their experience at a monastery helps students internalize Benedict's insight that spiritual, emotional, and physical health are not only dependent on a wise man or woman—an abbot or abbess—but also on the day-to-day relationships that each monk has with others in the community. After their experience at the abbey, one graduate student in the course said: "The *Leadership and Community* course shaped my understanding and practice of leadership in professional and personal contexts, and it has given me a greater understanding of contemplative listening and thinking about the needs of others."[4]

Growth in humility is at the heart of the formation Benedict envisions for the individual entering the spiritual workshop of the monastic community. If the "why" of living under the Rule of Benedict is the attainment of purity of heart—that is, the ability to see clearly what is happening around you and to respond instinctively to what you are called to do — then the "how" of attaining purity of heart is through the cultivation of humility. For Benedict, humility has nothing to do with humiliation (although humiliation can be effectively responded to through humility). Humility means that one sees oneself as one is, strengths and shortcomings, gifts and limitations; it is through humility that the monk engages reality on reality's own terms and can then respond appropriately. One student said: "I think it is humility when you are in a conversation or at a meeting and you realize that everyone is there with their own good intentions and perspectives."[5]

Benedictine Sister Joan Chittister links the focus on relationships to the practice of hospitality:

Workplace Spirituality and Fulfillment, ed. Satinder K. Dhiman, Gary E. Roberts, and Joanna E. Crossman (New York: Palgrave, 2018), 883–900.

4. Lisa (alumna) in discussion with the authors, May 2024.

5. Julie (alumna) in discussion with the authors, May 2024.

> Real Benedictinism requires us to pour ourselves out for the other, to give ourselves away, to provide the staples of life, both material and spiritual, for one another. The question is not whether what we have to give is sufficient for the situation or not. The question is simply whether or not we have anything to give. That's what hospitality is all about. Not abundance and not totality. Just sharing. Real sharing.[6]

As one student said: "I've come at my work from a perspective of so much possibility and openness that I think it's energizing, and it allows everybody to hopefully feel and be able to accept all the other people's ideas and thoughts."[7]

The majority of students in the course have never experienced a monastery, whether that be a Catholic abbey, a Buddhist *vihara*, or a Hindu ashram. Although they have spent four weeks reading and discussing monastic culture, they arrive at Saint Andrew's Abbey with curious anticipation. This positive unease is important to their learning experience, as they try to make sense of the way that a unique community of monks puts into practice the theories of community and hospitality they have studied. The opening line of the Rule of Benedict is "Listen . . . with the ear of your heart" (RB Prologue) and the students enter their roles as participant observers with ears and eyes wide open as well.

Chittister continues to speak to the concept of hospitality:

> Benedictine spirituality says that we must continue to beg the stranger to come into our lives because in the stranger may come the only honesty and insight we can get in our plastic worlds. The abbot is instructed to listen to the criticism of the stranger because, the *Rule* teaches the community, "God may have sent that one for that very reason" (RB 61). The problem is that we may need to learn to practice hospitality of a different kind these days to get the same results. . . . Benedictine spirituality says that to become whole ourselves we must learn to let the other in, if for no other reason than to stretch our own vision, to take responsibility for the world

6. Joan Chittister, OSB, *The Rule of Benedict: A Spirituality for the 21st Century* (New York: Crossroad, 2014), 123.

7. Julie (alumna) in discussion with the authors, May 2024.

> by giving to it out of our own abundance, to make the world safe by guarding its peoples ourselves.[8]

As students live with the monks for a week, they see how hospitality affects their lives in ways both simple and profound. Students interview individual monks and learn of their struggles to live with others, to deal with conflict, to forgive others, and to ask forgiveness themselves. The students join the monks in their many services: contemplative chanting of the psalms and reflections on readings from the gospels, the epistles of Saint Paul and Saint James, and well-known Catholic philosophers, theologians, and saints. Students help clean up after dinner each night, washing and drying dishes, putting away leftover food, and setting up the tables for the next day's breakfast. In all these experiences, students understand that hospitality happens through daily reminders and practice of support and challenge.

One student thought that their experience during the course helped them understand their experience at work better:

> In the monastic community, there are certain things that need to be done every day and different monks step in at different times to do those things: for example, setting up the chapel, ringing the bell, reading at services, serving at meals, or cleaning up afterwards. This is just the same in the warehouse I manage because certain things need to be done, and sometimes people are on vacation, sick, or whatever. Everyone still knows that there is a job to do, and so it's not going to stop.[9]

Students in the course prepare for their immersion by learning how the Benedictine tradition consciously emphasizes the hospitality that forms community through authentic relationships. For example, students learn that the vows that each individual makes as they join the monastery are grounded in this openness to relationship: stability, obedience, and

8. Joan Chittister, OSB, *Wisdom Distilled from the Daily: Living the Rule of St. Benedict Today* (New York: HarperCollins, 2009), 125.

9. Jim (alumnus) in discussion with the authors, May 2024.

conversatio, a Latin term that can refer to a "conversion of manners"[10] but can also be defined as "constant conversion."[11] If the ultimate goal of each monk's living in community is to attain purity of heart—i.e., a clearer understanding of God's will in their life—then stability, obedience, and *conversatio* define not only who the monk should be, but also what the community within which they live and learn should be.

Regarding the first vow of stability, a superficial understanding limits it to the concept that a monk remains in one monastery for life. In fact, the concept of stability goes beyond physical location—and therefore the monastery. Stability is about the minimum conditions for the development and continuance of relationship. Vowing stability, the monk makes a commitment to stay in relationship even when it is difficult. Stability embraces the precept that everything involves relationships. If autonomy or individualism is the operating logic of a group of people living together, then relationship is difficult and real community almost impossible. Stability, therefore, is the foundation of both relationship and community. Still, it is important to note that one needs to develop a certain amount of personal autonomy (healthy independence as opposed to being embedded) to be able to contribute to an authentic, healthy, and life-giving relationship.

Because the students in the *Leadership and Community* course are studying leadership, they understand that stability means that leaders and followers trust one another to want the same things because they are motivated by the same needs and values; it means that they make the best possible interpretation of each other's actions. Stability requires and produces patience, allowing things and people to have the time they need to process events and situations and be productive. Further, stability implies forgiveness and the belief that no past mistake is unredeemable. In all this, stability says to both leader and follower that whatever problems exist must be dealt with here and now. Assuming as an exception a dysfunctional community where withdrawal is required to maintain one's mental or emotional health, the insight of stability is that the individuals

10. Thomas Merton, *The Life of the Vows: Initiation into the Monastic Tradition* 6, ed. Patrick F. O'Connell (Collegeville, MN: Liturgical Press, 2012), 278.

11. Judith Valente, *Atchison Blue: A Search for Silence, A Spiritual Home, and a Living Faith* (Notre Dame, IN: Sorin Books, 2013), 131.

who run away from organizational problems will find that the problems run after them.

The fragmented world in which we live now can drive us away from relationships: i.e., it is too difficult to maintain them; we would just prefer to be by ourselves anyway; we don't like some of the communities we are a part of, so this is our way out. This is aggravated by a society that seems to be spinning out, with polarization, and even hatred, among members of one half the country for those in the other half. The temptation to say, "OK, deal me out," is great at this moment in all our lives, regardless of our political persuasions. This is where the dynamic of stability becomes important.

One of the students who spent a week with the monks said:

> The helpful part for me is when we're talking with them and getting to know them even personally through the kitchen work and through other things—just being there!—that they're just regular people and they have conflicts, and they have things that they don't like, and they're tired or you know, irritated with the way this is going or, you know, something like that.[12]

The second vow made by monks entering the life guided by the Rule of Benedict is obedience. Obedience has often been characterized as a relinquishment of individual will in favor of mindless submission to a superior. For Benedict, however, obedience means obedience to the truth; as Parker Palmer noted, the Latin root for the word obedience is *audire*, meaning "to hear" and, interestingly, the Latin root for the word absurd, or meaninglessness, is "to hear nothing."[13] Benedict urges the members of the community "to hear"—to listen carefully for the truth as it is present in each situation. Toward the end of the Rule, monks are exhorted to mutual obedience; like stability, this is both cause and effect for healthy relationship and community. By opening themselves to hear how the Truth is present in other members of the community, the monks

12. Julie (alumna) in discussion with the authors, May 2024.

13. Parker Palmer, *To Know as We Are Known: Education as a Spiritual Journey* (San Francisco: Harper, 1993), 43.

learn how it is present in them. Benedict sees this mutual obedience as essential to purity of heart.

If stability keeps individuals from abandoning each other and the community, obedience builds upon that commitment to determine what the individual and community response should be. The leadership studies students understand that obedience is not a ploy to maintain authoritarian leadership, attempting to control (or indoctrinate) the consciousness of followers; obedience actually demands more from the leader, requiring the leader to go beyond their agendas, biases, and fears to become open to what is best for all. Similarly, obedience demands that followers move past a "stimulus-response approach to decisions"[14] and become open to hear what truth there may be in community policies or plans.

So, the monastic dynamic of obedience helps remind students that in the end, each of them needs other people to hear what God is calling them to do in the myriad decisions that comprise their lives. In community, other people support us and challenge us to hear better, to distinguish more accurately between the noise of our own ego, biases, and fears, and the authentic voice of God. Communities and relationships can become dysfunctional—each of us probably has personal experience with that reality—and when they do become dysfunctional, leaving can be an act of obedience. But the experience of dysfunction in relationships or in a community should not create confusion about what it is we are leaving: we are leaving the dysfunction, not the fundamental need we have for community and relationship.

Community is necessary for each of us as individuals because it is only through relationships that support and challenge us that are we able to authentically question ourselves and our thinking and feelings, to learn and change for the better. Support without challenge is co-dependence; challenge without support is oppression. Support *and* challenge are what we need to grow. For the monks, the support and challenge of living in community with other monks is what they need to obtain purity of

14. Victoria Hochreiter, Cynthia Benedetto, and Marc Loesch, "Review and Analysis of the Stimulus Response in Consumer Behavior, Organizational Culture, and Leadership Theory," *International Journal of Management, Marketing, and Decision Sciences* 3, no. 1 (Winter 2023): 25–36.

heart—i.e., the ability to see clearly what is happening around them and to respond instinctively to what they are being called to do by God.

One student saw how the monks understood community as a lesson for leadership: "I believe that thinking of others in the community, creating trust with each other, being intentional, finding ways to encourage each other and lift each other up, and ways to serve, are ways we can positively help contemporary organizations."[15]

The final monastic vow of *conversatio* has been loosely translated as "constant conversion."[16] If stability sets up the preconditions necessary for relationship to flourish and community to exist, and obedience defines the attitude of openness that allows members of the community to mutually engage each other, *conversatio* demands that this entire process go beyond occasional acts of friendship or collaboration to become a way of life. *Conversatio* is essential to complete what stability and obedience begin—the realization of mutual and respectful interdependence: through it, relationship and community become ways of being, rather than of doing.

Going back to the experience of the early desert monks, and even in the Rule of Benedict, a monk can leave the specific monastic community to become a hermit if the monk is able to see all of humanity as their community; then the Spirit speaks to the monk through the support and challenge provided by everything in the world.

One student said that they "really enjoyed it when the different monks would just talk and share their day-to-day realities."[17] From another student:

> This course showed me how the dynamics of community shift when deliberately imbued with hospitality and belonging. Community, in this way, morphs into a psychologically safe space where dialogue has permission to flow, disagreements transcend into possibilities, and deeper connections are forged.[18]

15. Lisa (alumna) in discussion with the authors, May 2024.
16. Valente, *Atchison Blue*, 131.
17. Julie (alumna) in discussion with the authors, May 2024.
18. Laura (alumna) in discussion with the authors, April 2024.

During their immersion at the abbey, students experience firsthand the hospitality offered to them by the monks. Pervading the history of Benedictine monasticism is the offering of hospitality to the stranger, formalized in the Rule as "to receive guests as Christ" (RB 53). If the guest coming to the community is to be treated as Christ, more is demanded than simple acceptance of the guest's presence in their lives; serving the guest—who may be a complete stranger—is a way to operationalize what each individual has learned about who they are before God. One graduate student underscored this by saying:

> In my workplace, when I hold an event or train a new employee, I remember my time at the Abbey, how the monks received each guest as Christ and "see" Christ in each person they serve. I try to find ways to make guests or new employees feel welcome and a part of the community.[19]

The Rule adjusts the normal rhythm of life in the monastery to provide for the needs of the guest. The assignment of a porter or gatekeeper who is always available and the provision of special kitchen and dining facilities and lodging areas allow meeting the needs of guests on their schedules, rather than on the monastic schedule. If the guest is to be seen as Christ, extraordinary effort must be made to make the guest feel welcomed. Given that strangers can also be threats to the well-being of the monastery, Benedict requires that the guests enter the authentic relationships of the community as well, thus showing their desire—even for a short time—to join the community in its mission and add fresh challenges and support to community life through their interactions.

The lesson of Benedictine hospitality for us is that we must work against the fundamentalism that excludes those who are different than we are, or the nationalism that seeks to protect the borders from the entry of anyone not of a particular race, religion, and/or ideology.

Benedict understood from his reflection on the first letter of Paul to the Corinthians that charity—what we now call love—was the greatest of the three virtues of faith, hope, and charity. The classic definition of charity skirts the concept of love, usually describing it as a feeling of benevolence

19. Lisa (alumna) in discussion with the authors, May 2024.

or being well-meaning to others. It is from that meaning that charity is defined as giving to others in need.

More than fifteen hundred years of monastic communities living under the Rule of Benedict attests to their concern with providing for the poor who come to their doors. But the real wisdom of the Rule goes beyond charity as donations to charity as love. Benedict constantly urges that the other deserves charity not because the monk is a Christian, but because the other is Christ. For Benedict, each person the monk encounters—whether a poor person living outside of the monastery, a pilgrim knocking on the monastery door, or another monk sleeping in the same dormitory room—is Christ in the here and now.

By asking that they see the other as Christ in the here and now, Benedict makes every encounter sacred for the monks. Making every encounter an engagement with Christ is directed to the ancient goal of the monastic life: the attainment of purity of heart. If the monk understands that God is present in the other, then the monk is more alert, more open, more willing to respond fully to what they are being called to do in each present moment.

Spending a week living with Benedictine monks in the upper Mojave Desert might seem an odd way to teach leadership, or for that matter to try to understand how to engage effectively, and live and work in a society increasingly fragmented by multiple beliefs. Yet at the end of this course, graduate leadership students write papers on how their various experiences at the monastery have made them more interested in and able to inculcate radical hospitality and community into their own organizations. One student reflected:

> I noticed that once I got into the rhythm of life in the monastery, I better experienced what I was doing there. And the silence became very important to me: silence from after compline until after breakfast. Eating breakfast with everyone in silence—Just sitting and being in silence but being there with everybody with whom you've been talking during the day. You're all just sitting there and it's quiet and you're eating good food and you're looking out to the beautiful environment through the large window in the refectory.[20]

20. Jim (alumnus) in discussion with the authors, May 2024.

While at the monastery, students use the ancient monastic method of reading called *lectio divina* each morning to reflect on one of the readings from the course. *Lectio divina* is composed of four stages of engaging a text, whether the written work or the text of one's life: *lectio* (what does it say?), *meditatio* (what does it say to me?), *oratio* (how must I respond?) and *contemplatio* ("let go and let God"). While living with the monks at their Abbey, students find *lectio divina* a productive way to gain deeper insights into the authors they read before coming to their week at the monastery. And as one student noted:

> Pretty amazing being able to look at something through the lens of what does it say, what does it say to me? Bringing my own self, my own journey, my own experience into this passage that I'm reading . . . . What does it mean to me? You read something. Whether it be the news, whether it be a research essay, a poem, the Bible. What does it mean to me now? What do I do with this? How do I put this into action? But am I really sure I'm going to put that into action?[21]

Concluding Thoughts and Recommendations

Education can broaden our awareness of the world in which we live and work, but how can it prepare us to do so authentically and effectively beneath the roar and tumult of our times? To apply the insights gained from this particular graduate course to other learning experiences in other levels of education, we offer three recommendations:

1. Learning experiences should creatively include methods of meditation, contemplation, and discernment to equip students to be proactive rather than reactive to what is happening in their lives. This course uses the tools of a monastic community—*lectio divina*, silence, and collective reflection on readings and psalmody—but every academic discipline has tools of reflection that are complementary to critical thinking skills that learning demands. These tools can be used for learning that is constrained to a campus-based classroom environment as well as those flexible enough to spend time in an active monastic community.

21. Katie (alumna) in discussion with the authors, April 2024.

2. Learning experiences should include the study of historic examples of collaboration and community that illustrate how past societies, cultures, and people dealt with the roar and tumult of their times. This course examined the wisdom of the third-century desert hermits and the sixth-century institutional monks who lived during the fall of the Roman Empire. But every age in diverse cultures throughout the world offers historic examples through which students can learn how to live and work to heal and mend rage and fragmentation.

3. Learning experiences should immerse students in spaces and communities that remain hopeful and hospitable despite the individual and group rage and societal tumult around them. This course went to a hopeful Benedictine men's monastery in the Mojave Desert, but it could just as easily have been a Buddhist monastery, a Hindu ashram, a L'Arche or Catholic Worker community, or any number of groups that devote their energies to serve marginalized populations, all of which provide practical experience in radical hospitality.

The story of this learning experience in a Benedictine monastery that has worked for fifteen hundred years to positively engage the world provides a helpful metaphor for the hospitality that is needed against the roar and tumult of these times: healing our fragmented world requires patience and a long-term vision of what's possible. The story of this learning experience began twenty years ago, and hundreds of graduate students have been positively affected in their personal and professional lives by understanding community more deeply. The faculty involved in learning with students at the monastery have been equally positively affected, both in understanding community better and in experiencing how students leave the course with more patience and hope for the future.

Managing the Chaos

Tapping the Jesuit Gifts to Form Novice Teachers

Thomas Knestrict
Xavier University

The spiritual aspects of my life were always kept separate from my academic work. Much like the traditional research insistence that we do not use personal pronouns in academic writing, we are taught to keep our personal biases and, more specifically, our faith-based ideas clear of any work deemed to be objective social science. Of course, this is impossible. Houck noted an intimate connection between what she called "scholarly knowledge" and "self-knowledge."[1] My personal journey has greatly affected my perspective on my work, my research, and most powerfully on my relationships with young students who enter our teacher preparation program. I have discovered that allowing this part of my life into my work has made me aware of the students' needs to allow their personal life experiences and, yes, their spirituality into their teaching as well. I have found that this fact provides the students with a resiliency to support them through their journey through the roar and tumult of teaching young children. I have also learned that the Ignatian perspective is not a fad or a marketing ploy. St. Ignatius knew the value of a good model. If

1. Anita Houck, "You Are Here: Engagement, Spirituality and Slow Teaching," in *Becoming Beholders: Cultivating Sacramental Imagination and Actions in College Classrooms*, ed. Karen E. Eifler and Thomas M. Landy (Collegeville, MN: Liturgical Press, 2014).

we don't provide models for our students, they will seek models on social media or elsewhere. It is what makes a Jesuit university different from other universities and it is why some families send their students to us.

Noticing these facts freed me to create ways of providing these resiliency skills to all our students regardless of their faith path. The Gifts of Our Ignatian Heritage are faith-derived concepts; however, a spiritual faith is not required to access them and apply them to their young lives. The Gifts were conceptualized by a group of professors on our campus. These concepts capture some of the teachings of St. Ignatius of Loyola and translate into skills that can support student resilience and cultivate happier, more secure adult human beings. These Ignatian concepts are used as teachable skills that are embedded within our liberal arts core curriculum and the professional program in education. They have been modified somewhat to make them accessible to all faith traditions and even to someone who is without the traditional notion of faith.

The Journey Begins

In my forty-plus years as an educator, I have noticed that schools of education are rarely consulted when issues of instruction are discussed in the larger institution. Why might that be? Several years ago, our university made a considerable investment in creating a Center for Teaching Excellence. The quality of teaching across campus was a concern, and this was the intervention developed. The School of Education was not consulted, and the center was developed without any input from the resident pedagogues. I was pleased and not surprised at all when our Center for Mission and Identity, whose mission is to find the best ways to promote our Ignatian mission, encouraged me to investigate ways we could better understand and teach the Gifts of Our Ignatian Heritage.[2]

The Gifts are a summation of fundamental Ignatian values that are applicable not only to a faith journey but also towards a healthy human journey. They are often applied by the university in hiring, program changes, and university-wide decision-making processes. However, it

2. Jesuit Resource, "Gifts of Our Ignatian Heritage," Xavier University, 2009, https://www.xavier.edu/jesuitresource/understanding-our-heritage/jesuit-tradition/ignatian-gifts.

is the practical, everyday use of these ways of thinking that makes a significant difference in the lives of our students, faculty, and staff. They are phrased and intentionally constructed to reflect the Jesuit values at the core of our institution and make them accessible to nonbelievers or followers of other faiths.

The Gifts are expressed as charges to all educators:

- The Gift of mission—a personal mission is the DNA of all other decisions; your personal mission is an expression of your innermost values and directions. It becomes your constitution, the solid expression of your vision and values.
- The Gift of reflection—being able to look back on your day, week, year, life, or even just one lesson, to evaluate and adjust. Reflection is among a teacher's most valuable skills. It has also been shown as beneficial for general mental health in all humans. It is a major chunk of Ignatian pedagogy which is, essentially, "experience, reflect, and act."
- The Gift of solidarity and kinship—walking with and empathizing with the people you are serving. Knowing and creating relationships with students, parents, and colleagues have long been seen as essential pieces of inspired teaching.
- The Gift of service rooted in justice and love—always serving others and considering the needs of those who have the least in our society. This commitment to serving others includes everyone in our lives and is an essential piece of our social justice mindset.
- The Gift of discernment—intentional decision-making on an impactful subject, considering not only the rational but also the realms of feelings, emotions, and desires. Discerning is different from simple decision-making. If we are deciding what to eat for dinner, we decide. When we are thinking about what profession we want to pursue, we discern. It takes longer and should include not just the facts but also feelings and can often include a choice between two goods.
- *Magis*—Latin for "more." When discerning, one must consider the more universal good. We like to teach that "the needs of the many

never outweigh the needs of the few, or the one," or "the needs of the one never outweigh the needs of the many." Cultivating the gift of *magis* allows one to strike a balance between the two.

- *Cura personalis*—care for the whole person: their physical, social/emotional, and spiritual selves. Instructing the whole student has long been a core idea in all age groups in education.

It was a goal to use these seven Gifts as a shared frame of reference and common language to discuss the complexities of the teaching experience, to provide the means among faculty and students to discuss the issues that arise when teaching. Allowing us to talk across contexts was a goal as well. While there is considerable difference in the experiences of primary and secondary pre-service teaching experiences, the Gifts provide a common contextual lens to discuss these different experiences.

While our teachers in training and their faculty were generally aware of the Gifts when we began this initiative, most teachers in training were not consistently taught these concepts beyond the initial shared experience during their first days on campus. We observed that the introduction of Jesuit spirituality and the Gifts was so intense it was a fire hose of information. We also found that this was too often the last the students heard about the Gifts until graduation. Likewise, faculty were not always aware of the Gifts or, if they were, they did not embed them within coursework. In education, we observed the value of these concepts and the natural way they fit within our existing curriculum and felt that these concepts were best understood within the context of courses for majors. In the School of Education, it made sense that discussions about developing a sense of mission or reflection would take place within introduction to education courses. Many of the Gifts were already being taught as part of introductory methods courses, but operationalizing these ideas provided words to discuss the contextualized meanings in a deeper, more integrated way. For example, one pre-service teacher returned to class after a challenging observation she experienced in the field. A student became physically and verbally out of control, and staff had to physically restrain the student. When we began to unpack this experience in class, the student, clearly upset, began by asking the class the question, "Why did they have to wrestle him to the ground like an animal? That does not look like serving in justice and love or *cura personalis*. In fact, it seems the opposite." It was evident that the student clearly understood the concept of *cura personalis* and service rooted in justice and love. Through our discussions, we all had access to the language of the Gifts. Explaining that the teachers have an obligation to keep all students safe, including the out-of-control student: that is *cura personalis* in action. I also asked the question, "While restraining a student is difficult to watch, can it still reflect 'service rooted in justice and love'?" The pre-service teacher would process and interpret the event through the lens of *cura personalis* and service rooted in justice and love. Their conclusions would be their own, but they were employing the Gifts to reach those conclusions.

Existing Pedagogical Models

Because educational research is based on understanding how people learn best, there were many ways the education faculty's expertise could be used to design a curriculum that was engaging, effective, and allowed for the development of resiliency skills such as reflection and discernment. It became clear that to teach these concepts effectively, they needed to be embedded in coursework so that each concept would be introduced to first-year students with ever-increasing complexity and application as the students continued their higher education experience. This is what Jerome Brunner called a "spiral curriculum" in the 1960s and has been a mainstay of teaching theory since then.[3] As the complexity and depth of the concepts increased, so would the generalization of the information. Specifically, if we are initially teaching the concept of mission, we would define it and then increase its connectivity to related concepts like solidarity and kinship, or reflection. Within the context of discussions related to teaching and learning, one pre-service teacher was able to identify an instance in her observation where she saw a mentor teacher greeting a parent as they dropped off a student at school. She took several minutes to ask the mom how she was doing and how her mother and the other kids in the family were. She also took the time to tell her how well the son (her student) was doing in reading. The college student observed that the

3. Tim J. Dowding, "The Application of a Spiral Curriculum Model to Technical Training Curricula," *Educational Technology* 33, no. 7 (1993): 18–28.

mom was completely at ease and enjoyed the interaction, and this pre-service teacher observed that this connection was related to solidarity as well as justice and love, and that both would ultimately serve to benefit the student. That integration and deep, almost reflexive, understanding, reflected in the use of the common language of the Gifts, showed the value of using the Gifts as a conduit to understand the subtleties of teaching. In fact, by the end of four years, our students understand how all the Gifts are related to one another and that when they understand one, they understand its connection to the others.

This generalization is what Jean Piaget posits with his concepts of assimilation and accommodation of novel information, concepts crucial not just in teachers' professional contexts, but also for their own learning. Using the familiar language of the Gifts helped our students understand the crucial professional notion that all learners construct an understanding of the relationship between concepts and related experiences. Although defining and identifying the definitions of the Gifts is important, it is only the first step in deeply learning and internalizing the full meaning of each.

A New Teaching Tool: Podcasts

As professors who teach teachers-in-training how to teach, we acknowledge the value of observing examples of good teaching. Often, pre-service teachers come to understand what good teaching looks like by watching veteran teachers. This makes modeling best teaching practices—such as understanding their own lived experiences—with our own students imperative. In recent years, we noticed that many of our students learn best using tools such as podcasts and videos in conjunction with written material. In 2023, a colleague and I began producing a podcast called "The Gifts."[4] Our goal was to provide an audio resource filled with authentic examples of people using the Gifts in their personal and professional lives. Each episode contains a twenty- to forty-minute interview with a person who has incorporated a particular Ignatian Gift into their life. We invite guests on the show to articulate their understanding of a particular Gift

4. Thomas Knestrict and Teresa T. Young, https://www.xavier.edu/jesuitresource/online-resources/podcast-resources/index.

and how it is applied daily. These examples were used in our classroom discussions and embedded within many courses in the School of Education as assignments, along with questions designed to facilitate making meaning of the podcasts' information. To illustrate, in my required human development survey course, I assign as an introductory assignment the initial podcast that defined each of the Gifts. The students listen to the podcast and respond to prompts. These responses are then used as discussion points in class.

This assignment served as informational; they were simply made aware of the Gifts. The assignment was then followed by an in-class discussion about the podcast and the possible value of the information. Students were then required to think about the possible ways the Gifts might be applied to the field observations they were completing for class. They were also asked to teach someone else about the Gifts. The teaching of the concepts to others allows them to construct a deeper understanding of the Gifts, how they can be used as a common vocabulary for discussing the events observed in their field placements, and how they might apply to their lives outside of school.[5]

Some illustrative student responses:

"Having solidarity with the students we are working with helps me understand what issues they might be bringing into the classroom." (Alec, First-Year)

"Teaching is a service. I can see how, even though you don't make a lot of money doing it, it would still be cool to serve this way." (Cora, Sophomore)

"There was a kid in my observation who needed a lot of help. The teacher really went out of her way to help him and figured out a way to give him that help. But I looked around and the other students were working hard so, no one missed out on anything. That's *Magis.*" (Meghan, Sophomore)

These reflections provide evidence that our novice teachers are beginning to think about how these concepts are related to teaching. The goal at this level was to provide these first-years and sophomores examples of the Gifts being applied so that, as they move into the classroom, they

5. Jyrki Reunamo and Marja Nurmilaakso, "Vygotsky and Agency in Language Development," *European Early Childhood Education Research Journal* 15, no. 3 (2007): 313–27.

can begin to see exactly how these ways of thinking might be beneficial to both their teaching and their personal lives as well. It also gives evidence that the Gifts provided a common language to discuss these events in class.

Advanced Students Take It Higher and Deeper

As pre-service teachers move into their junior and senior years in the teacher preparation program, they gradually take on more teaching responsibility. By the end of their senior year, they are teaching full days for fifteen weeks. During this time, we want them to apply relevant Gifts to their classroom practice. Periodic discussions about the value of reflection when planning and implementing a lesson is a focal point during this time. Rarely do even veteran teachers teach a perfect lesson. It is often a matter of teaching, identifying mistakes, adjusting, and trying again. This embodies the Jesuit Gift of reflection.

There is a phrase we use in the Xavier School of Education attributed to James Comer, the great urban educator: "There is no significant learning without significant relationships."[6] Much of his work deals with the development of what he calls "human capital." Human capital consists of the human connections teachers develop with students and the impact those relationships have on learning. Developing a sense of solidarity and kinship with the students one serves and the families they live with is a value the Gifts speak directly to. Not coincidentally, these are also values communicated to teachers in the varied professional organizations to which teachers belong throughout their careers. This leads to fruitful discussions of solidarity and kinship, *cura personalis*, and service rooted in justice and love. Previously, without practicing the common language of the Gifts, these were difficult topics to discuss, as they remained theoretical. The podcast and subsequent assignments referring to solidarity and kinship move our students toward the concrete, as they stress the importance of teachers knowing their students, their students' families, and the circumstances they are living in. The following are reflections that students shared in class during this time in their program.

6. James P. Comer, "Educating Poor Minority Children," *Scientific American* 259, no. 5 (1988): 42–49.

Observations on Solidarity and Kinship

"Bobby would come late to school almost every day. He got free breakfast and lunch but because he was late, he often did not get to eat. They tried to save some cereal and milk for him, but it was often warm milk by then and he chose not to eat. How is he supposed to care about learning when he is hungry?" (Morgan, Junior)

"I sat in on an I.E.P. [Individualized Educational Program] meeting last week. They were discussing all of the assessments they had done on this student. The psychologist and principal were using all sorts of big words that I knew from class but I could see the mom had no clue. She simply sat there quietly, said nothing, signed the papers, and left. I think she felt kind of stupid because she didn't understand what they were saying. I thought that was terrible." (Janae, Junior)

"I watched as the parents dropped off their kids at school. This one mom was walking, had four small children and her son, seven years old, whom she was dropping off at school. One kid was running away, another was crying, the seven-year-old dropped his lunch, mom bent over to pick it up, and her purse emptied out. This was every day for her. No wonder she doesn't want to come into school for meetings or to volunteer. I felt for this mom." (Teresa, Senior)

Becoming a Reflective Practitioner

"My first lesson was a disaster. I planned way too much and was so focused on getting through the material I was not checking for learning at all. I reflected on the plan and decided to rewrite the lesson plan with about half as much information. I also planned in moments of assessment to make sure that I was checking for understanding. The next day it went much more smoothly. I am thinking that not fearing a lesson going [badly] and knowing you can improve it for the next time is what this block class is about." (Isabelle, Junior)

"As I look back on my first methods class, I feel like I was so nervous about making mistakes that I didn't think about my teaching. I don't remember big chunks of the lessons I taught. While I did OK, I was not able to reflect on the lesson because I pushed it out of my mind. I would love to do those lessons again and be more aware." (Angela, Junior)

Examen and Vocation

During the second year of implementing this curriculum, our campus Center for Faith and Justice contacted me and asked if I would be interested partnering with a Jesuit priest to begin talking to students about vocation. They felt that adding a discussion about discerning vocation (in the sense of career, not necessarily religious life) would benefit the students. Believing it related to discernment and mission, I agreed to participate. It would include adding the Examen to discern what profession they might be called to. The Examen is a daily prayer technique that involves reflecting on the events of the day to help people detect God's presence and discern God's direction. It's based on Ignatian spirituality and was developed by St. Ignatius of Loyola, the founder of the Jesuits, five hundred years ago.[7] Father Eric, the head of our Faith and Justice division on campus, agreed to come into my Multicultural Child Development class three times to teach the students how to use the Examen prayer to help them discern their possible vocation and to have another model for discerning other deeply personal and complex issues in their personal and professional lives.

Father Eric instructed the students to pray the Examen as a mindfulness activity, every day for three weeks. Then the students reflected on the benefits of the Examen and discussed any insights. Father Eric spent time defining discernment and using it as a meaningful way to work through important life decisions such as one's vocation.

Discernment, mission, and service rooted in justice and love came up during these discussions, deepening the students' understanding of these concepts. For example, when talking about the benefits students sensed when using the Examen, many pre-service teachers noted the reflective qualities of recalling the day. It allowed them to notice when what they were doing had purpose and aligned with what they saw as their mission in teaching and in their life in general. The written reflections below show the impact the Examen had on pre-service teachers in this three-week period:

7. Thomas G. Plante, "Using the Examen, a Jesuit Prayer, in Spiritually Integrated and Secular Psychotherapy," *Pastoral Psychology* 71, no. 1 (2022): 119–25.

"The Examen gave me a structure to follow. Praying has always been difficult for me. This gives me a kind of recipe to follow. After I did it for a while, I found that I stuck to it and also followed through with things I was praying about." (Josephine, Sophomore)

"I noticed that when I was working with children during the day, I would reflect on that during my Examen and I would be reminded of why I want to teach. It's that connection I feel when working with a student. It just feels like exactly what I need to be doing." (Morgan, Sophomore)

"Discernment has always been hard for me to understand. But on the podcast when Father Murphy told us that 'choosing what sandwich to order at McDonald's is a decision, but figuring out what vocation I am called to is discernment' made me understand the difference. Deciding what to do with my life is heavier; it will take longer. It's more important." (Sophia, Sophomore)

The addition of Father Eric, the Examen, and the discussions that occurred in class resulted in an extraordinarily rich and contextualized experience for the students. It was evident that their understanding of the Gifts had soared. Through discussion, reflection, and discernment, they seem to develop a reverence for these ways of thinking, to see their value in shaping their practice as educators. In the end, it is the action taken because of discernment and reflection that is most important. We see this as the highest level of learning: when students apply previous understandings and create something new. This is exactly what happens employing the Ignatian Gifts. As you move from definitions to active practice, learning the Gifts ceases being a solely academic endeavor. It becomes more. With the increase in depth of understanding, there is a simultaneous change in the type of experience one has. As the meaning deepens, so does one's connection to the information.

Throughout life, we experience these concepts in different contexts and circumstances and find that they apply in those situations as well. Ignatius knew this intuitively and, because of the Jesuits' commitment to living in solidarity, he also knew that the experiences of his followers would be deepened because of their connections to others and their living within and as part of these diverse contexts. Teachers live this reality daily too. Truly gifted teachers bond with students and make the information relevant, engaging, and connected to prior learning. This is often what differentiates inspired teaching from adequate teaching.

Inspired teachers give reason and purpose to the new learning. If you can make the students care about the learning, they will engage. If we afford students the opportunity to experience this perspective and expose them to other cultures, they begin to apply these previously intellectual concepts practically. Relationships and solidarity with others become windows into the deeper complexities of their meaning. The Gifts become the common language to discuss and process these complex and contextual experiences.

Over the years, I have learned that students hunger for meaning and purpose. On the wall of one of our large residence halls is a large poster with the Xavier Promise printed for all to see. The promise is recited by students the first day they are on campus and several more times after that. Students are drawn to the line that speaks of purpose and righteous passion: "And together we will succeed at changing the world." This excites many students and faculty and provides the energy to learn more, serve more, and come together as men and women for and with others, a key element in Jesuit education. The Gifts provide the habits, language, and context to turn this sentiment into action. Many of my students report that when they serve others, the Gifts provide a way to think about and the language to describe how they are changing the world for the better. This righteous purpose and mission fit perfectly into a teacher preparation program and produce teachers who are not just practically ready to teach but spiritually ready as well.

Our experience tells us that it feels good to serve others. It provides personal and spiritual satisfaction that often develops into habits that students carry into their lives after college. Tools like the Examen can be helpful when discerning life choices and when working with their own students and families.

Measuring Impact

Data collected in the first three years of embedding the Gifts into the entire education curriculum indicated that there was something notable occurring in student cohorts. They were using the language of the Gifts. They were talking about reflecting daily on their practice and their life. They seemed to be applying the concepts of the Gifts intentionally. Inspired by the anecdotal evidence, we have started a longitudinal study that will examine the Gifts' impact at one year, five years, and ten years post-graduation. These time frames are intended to reflect whether the student recalled the Gifts after starting a new job or during graduate school at the one-year mark. Five years out reflects the adjustment to adult life, including life changes such as getting married and having children. Ten years is when the students may have fully entered into their adult lives. We expect to see the quantitative data support what we have observed.

Conclusion

It is evident that presenting the Gifts of Our Ignatian Heritage to our students helps them understand what they are doing and why. The idea of a spiral curriculum—beginning with a simple understanding of the concepts and building complexity sequentially—has been a valuable structure for developing this embedded curriculum. The vivid connections between the spiritual Gifts and the secular professional habits that students must acquire provided a pathway for professors to grasp and adapt the scope and depth that they should target when teaching the Gifts in their classes.

The Gifts also provide students and faculty with a common language with which to teach important concepts such as having a mission or vision of the purpose of your career, building relationships with parents and students, and approaching teaching as a vocation, not merely a job. The Gifts gave words to students and their faculty to think through and express these feelings.

What turned out to be an unexpected grace to me as the person who envisioned using the Gifts as a teaching tool was how the Gifts allow students and faculty to see God in what we do. While not everyone chooses this spiritual angle, the Gifts are situated to legitimate that option, offering a spiritual metaphor for the pedagogical model of the spiral curriculum. Instead of simply spiraling to a deeper understanding of an intellectual concept, it allows a potentially transformational way of understanding one's faith and its application to what we do in the classroom, ultimately allowing us to view our jobs as teachers as a calling linked to our faith or spiritual beliefs.

Finally, the Gifts provide a practical framework for managing the inevitable complexities of teaching in a diverse world, complexities that often burn out people quickly and foster a hopeless outlook on teaching and student learning. The Gifts of solidarity, service rooted in justice and love, and mission undergird teachers. These ideas prepare people to form meaningful relationships that will benefit both the student and the teacher. When we form these communities, based upon a mutual understanding of the importance of respect and caring, we are all stronger. Research suggests this also creates a more supportive, effective, and engaging educational environment. Being intentional in providing meaningful, practical, and often spiritually beneficial models helps students to manage the roar and tumult of teaching in a diverse society.

PART III

THE CHOICE

TO SPEAK OR NOT TO SPEAK

Generating creative imagination, ethical discernment, active hope, and meaningful action

Learning to Serve

A Neuroscience-Informed Scaffold to Develop Students as Community Leaders

Nancy A. Michael and T. M. Vanessa Chan-Devaere
University of Notre Dame

Neuroscience is one of the fastest-growing disciplines in higher education. Although the interdisciplinary field of study was formally founded only in 1969,[1] in this short period, neuroscience has become ever-present in contemporary culture. A Google Ngram search for the word "neuroscience" shows a steady rise of the word in English books since the early 1960s. However, this cultural presence also comes along with what some call the rise of "neurohype," or claims that are attributed to neuroscience but not substantiated by the available evidence.[2] As a result, we are inundated with neuroscientific references, but often without the knowledge to meaningfully discern their trustworthiness.

This growing cultural awareness is matched by a growth in undergraduates enrolling in neuroscience curricula across the United States. A recent analysis of college programs in the United States indicates a 40.7 percent increase in the number of "neuro" programs being offered

1. Society for Neuroscience, "About SfN," accessed December 12, 2024, https://www.sfn.org/About.

2. Scott O. Lilienfeld et al., "Neurohype: A Field Guide to Exaggerated Brain-Based Claims," in *The Routledge Handbook of Neuroethics* (New York: Routledge, 2017), 241–61.

at colleges between 2013 and 2017.[3] Our home institution, the University of Notre Dame, has seen rapid growth in enrollment in its Neuroscience and Behavior major in the ten years since its inception. All in all, the language of neuroscience—of wiring and rewiring, networks and systems, chemicals and synapses—speaks to the sensibility of people today in a privileged way.

While some might hold that the rise of neuroscience coincides with an increased secularization of culture and a disavowal of the sacred, we offer that neuroscience offers a mechanistic account of how people learn, and that this can and ought to provide a material basis for how we face the challenges of the world today. However, *knowledge* of the mechanisms alone does not provide us the skills or motivation to face those challenges; this is where Catholic social teaching (CST) about our obligations to the broader human community will inform the skill-building in support of such knowledge. Our goal, as educators of a neuroscience curriculum in a Catholic institute of higher education, is not only to pass on knowledge of neuroscience, but also to form individuals with habits of skillfully using their knowledge at the service of their communities. In this way, we can affirm the church's consistent calls to action in the context of our classrooms and beyond, moving our students from a disposition of merely "knowing" toward one of "doing."

The premise that "knowing" is not the same as "doing" is not a novel one. Jesus famously calls out the Pharisees consistently in the gospels as those who know what to do but do not act on their knowledge. Blessed Fr. Basil Moreau, the founder of the Congregation of Holy Cross (the founding order of our institution), said that "the mind will not be cultivated at the expense of the heart,"[4] taking the "heart" to be the deepest, most essential part of ourselves. As is articulated in Christian spirituality, the heart informs our daily actions in a habitual manner, beyond our conscious acts of knowing. Moreau also believed that "education is the

3. Christopher Rochon et al., "Quantitative Indicators of Continued Growth in Undergraduate Neuroscience Education in the US," *Journal of Undergraduate Neuroscience Education* 18, no. 1 (2019): 52.

4. Ave Maria Press, "Bl. Basil Moreau Quotes," accessed December 13, 2024, https://www.avemariapress.com/basil-moreau-quotes.

art of helping young people to completeness,"[5] compelling us to create an embodied education that offers students new life through their study.

These sayings of Blessed Fr. Moreau's often animate discussions on our campus around the mission and character of our university. Indeed, there are many opportunities for service, formation, and fellowship all over campus, but this formation tends to be extracurricular in nature, outside disciplinary study. As such, by drawing on the integrated and scaffolded nature of brain function and learning, we maintain that the act of bringing together mind and heart must also be done in the context of intellectual formation, such that the regular matching of "knowing" and "doing" is intentionally integrated in disciplinary education. Partnering acts of "knowing" and "doing" through the principles of CST invokes the prophetic imagination in the context of the discipline of neuroscience.

Human Learning and Memory: Not Just "Knowing," but "Doing" Too

In his *Confessions*, St. Augustine wrote extensively on memory in the formation of self. He articulates that we experience the world from the outside, and those external experiences are necessarily interpreted through the constructions of the internal self. As such, humans are self-reflexive, born out of the capacity of the mind and memory. However, in the seventeenth century, Western philosophers like René Descartes diminished earlier, more accurate descriptions of human knowledge and behavior by separating the functions of mind, body, and self as discrete entities. The recognizable phrase "I think, therefore I am" reduces the value of human capacity from the fullness of self so accurately articulated by Augustine to a human capacity in which all that is valued is the "thinking" or "knowing."

It's time to return to the fullness of being described by St. Augustine. If we ever want what we "know" to be expressed as active dispositions in our students, we must embrace the functional integration of knowledge, skill, and behavior as neurobiological necessities of educational practice.

Learning, broadly speaking, is the process by which one integrates experiences across the nervous system, and "memory" is the ability to

5. Ibid.

draw on these experiences for future use. In this way, when we assess learning, we are really assessing *memory*. Assessment strategies in most classroom settings, however, dismiss the multiple ways nervous systems express memory in their function and disproportionately assess a narrow component of memory called *declarative memory*: one's ability to *declare* previously stored information.

If information recall is sufficient, then this is where learning could stop. However, we posit that education's disproportionate focus on recalling information has reduced the likelihood that "knowing" will result in "doing." The supposition of this chapter, and the work of this volume as a whole, is a call to intentionally construct learning environments that cultivate prophetic imagination and action. Therefore, learning must go deeper: we must intentionally engage pedagogical strategies that develop the brain's ability to communicate across neural systems, explicitly integrating the neural systems of "knowing" with neural systems of *sensing* and *feeling*.

Active learning is a pedagogical strategy that focuses not only on *what* students learn, but also on *how* students learn, offering opportunities to engage *sensing* and *feeling* as part of an explicit pedagogical strategy. A large body of interdisciplinary literature demonstrates significant increases in learning gains when active strategies are incorporated into the learning environment.[6] As all human behavior is situated within a broader context beyond the self, active learning strategies simultaneously engage social and emotional neural networks, further enhancing arousal and novelty in a learning context.[7]

When we consider educational practice and the holistic formation of the human being in the context of integrated brain function, we are able to recognize that no matter how well-intentioned the pedagogical strategies are that engage the neural circuits of "knowing," this "knowing" will never result in the integrated learning that is required to develop dispositions of heart that lead to habitual expressions of dignity and solidarity. If we

6. Janet M. Dubinsky and Arif A. Hamid, "The Neuroscience of Active Learning and Direct Instruction," *Neuroscience & Biobehavioral Reviews* (2024): 105737, https://doi.org/10.1016/j.neubiorev.2024.105737.

7. Ryan T. LaLumiere, James L. McGaugh, and Christa K. McIntyre, "Emotional Modulation of Learning and Memory: Pharmacological Implications," *Pharmacological Reviews* 69, no. 3 (2017), https://doi.org/10.1124/pr.116.013474.

are ever to do differently because of what we know, we must intentionally scaffold active learning practices that integrate memory formation across neural circuits of "knowing," sensing, and feeling.

Community-engaged learning environments are one kind of active learning environment that offers an extraordinary opportunity to develop a prophetic imagination and a disposition of heart towards the common good. By explicitly weaving classroom content into real-life settings, with real-life people, these immersive active learning experiences necessarily engage knowing, sensing, and feeling neural circuits in the context of real-life situations. Through contextual activation, learners can work towards developing robust memory networks for curiosity, problem-solving, and future learning.[8] This perspective offers a beautiful opportunity to begin to consider how we can expand our view of higher education to include intentionally scaffolded experiences that are not only integrated in a singular course, but that also are scaffolded with continuity and depth across a curricular and community experience.

Curricular Implementation

The undergraduate Neuroscience and Behavior program at the University of Notre Dame is attempting such an undertaking. Faculty designing the curriculum identified disciplinary core competencies for knowledge, skill, and attitudes representative of the field of neuroscience and behavior, taking additional steps to identify competencies that would reflect engagement with CST and the mission work of service to justice set by the university. Syllabi were collected from all instructors who contributed to programmatic instruction and evaluated to determine which core competencies of knowledge, skill, attitudes, and/or dispositions were present in each course and at what depth. Following this analysis, the requirements for the major were reorganized not only to provide the learning experiences that would help students develop core disciplinary competencies, but also to scaffold opportunities of disposition development in the context of disciplinary understanding. In doing so, we have attempted to arrange the student's learning sequence such that

8. Dubinsky and Hamid, "Neuroscience of Active Learning."

the curricular and co-curricular experiences are no longer random and elective but instead support a cohesive path of disciplinary *and* human development from beginning to end.

Our particular philosophy of curriculum construction is guided by our understanding of neuroscience, human development, learning and behavior, and Blessed Fr. Moreau's call to help young people to completeness. To support the development of a mental model of the reader, we have articulated specific examples for early, mid-level, and advanced level coursework. These examples are far from the only way to develop such a learning arc and are still in their early stages of development. We will close with guidance for other programs, regardless of discipline, to begin to explore and build such an experiential educational framework.

Early Coursework Example

Through a one-credit seminar during the first year on campus, students are introduced to opportunities within the major, as well as how these disciplinary opportunities intersect with the Catholic character of the university and mission-engaged undergraduate education. Students are invited to participate in co-curricular activities that encourage "translation" of neuroscience directly into community action. By introducing ideas of content, community engagement, responsibility to communicate disciplinary information directly to the public, and a "normalcy" of engaged co-curricular experience early on in a student's matriculation, our program is able to "seed" ideas of a neuroscience-informed common good in our students shortly after their arrival on campus.

Our goal of the "early seeding" is to spark an internal desire that motivates intrinsic curiosity for students to discover intersections among their disciplinary course of study and the lives of individuals and community members, as well as how their education can and should be used to support the tenets of CST. By intentionally crafting engaged opportunities that mature with a student's disciplinary knowledge and sense of self, we invite students to consider the "problem of trust" in the context of scholarly communication and community-based action. Put simply, elements of trust are prerequisite for any scholarly work to penetrate the world around us. Throughout their curriculum, students revisit this "problem of trust" with increasing complexity during their formation on campus.

Mid-Level Coursework Example

To foster development in the middle stages of matriculation, we introduce assignments in large classrooms (i.e., greater than fifty students) that promote communicating scientific knowledge to the public. One such example is Vanessa's Media Project, used in classes for sophomores and juniors like Cognitive Psychology and Introduction to Cognitive Neuroscience. This project involves reading a recently published article (within five years), determining the key points of the article, writing it as a five-hundred-word press release, and finally imagining where the research would show up in the public sphere by making a brochure, pamphlet, news clip, podcast, or other media.

During several semesters of assessing this project, student feedback has fallen into three general categories: (1) knowledge of the scientific media process, such as identifying the newsworthy points and how to write a press release; (2) techniques of communicating succinctly, in plain language that does not assume prior knowledge; and (3) taking the perspective of another who would see the science differently. An example of how these show up together can be seen in these students' responses to the question, "What is one skill you think you gained through the process of doing this project?":

> A skill I definitely gained by doing this project is being able to articulate scientific information to the less scientifically literate. I didn't realize how difficult this was, but learning to do this effectively drastically improves my own understanding of scientific topics such that I'm able to translate in an understandable way.
>
> I gain the skill of retraining my brain to view things through a different [person's] experience. When reading the press release over and over I tried to think about how my mom or roommate in business would understand and then adjusted the wording from there.

Certainly, while most students focused on the knowledge and skill aspects of the question in identifying their newfound confidence in reading and communicating about science, some responses showed an explicit articulation of their own development of perspective taking, as well as an awareness of not just the "how," but the "why" of such an endeavor.

One student commented that a skill used was "[d]iscovering the purpose/influence that research might have for others." Another noted how this project " . . . made me think about how much these studies really do have to teach people and how awesome it would be if more people utilized sources that would help them understand new scientific findings."

Advanced Coursework Example

As students mature, so do courses that increase both their depth of experience and opportunities for collaboration. Advanced coursework focuses on integrating university-community partnerships into broader community capacity-building strategies, all in the context of nervous system development. In these advanced elective courses, students work with community partner organizations who have relationships with different instructors. Organizational interest in a particular course's content determines what entities are available for student partnerships any given semester. Course instructors ensure that disciplinary knowledge is accurate, and partner organizations determine the needs and direct the outcomes of the students' projects. The goal of these partnerships is the development of sustainable community resources that are not only scientifically accurate but also promote individual and community well-being based on the principles that govern healthy nervous system function.

For students seeking deeper intersections between neuroscience and society, we have developed additional opportunities that include academic-year internships or summer NEAR (Neuroscience, Epigenetics, Adverse Childhood Experiences, Resilience) Science fellowships. These students work intensively with a regional nonprofit, Self-Healing Communities of Michiana, whose primary mission is to nurture personal and community well-being through the neuroscience of human resilience.

As students matriculate, they engage different aspects of the same world—aspects previously unknown or invisible prior to this new learning. Students have offered the following reflections after participating in community-based partnerships:

> To be sure, I learned a lot about neuroscience and neurodevelopmental principles. I grew as a scientist, and I learned how to better analyze information and to communicate. Yet, the most important thing that I learned, in my opinion, is how to see others as individ-

> uals. This is the lesson that will influence me the most as a human being.
>
> I think this knowledge can and should affect the way each of us interacts with other people in the future in the way of public policy. . . . Also, in keeping with the principles of Catholic Social Teaching, there is a natural correlation of rights and responsibility that we should follow. In this class and at this university, we have been blessed with an abundance of opportunities to learn and grow as scholars and as human beings. By employing that right, we also realize a responsibility to [ensure] others have the same right. Using our scientific knowledge to better inform policy is one of many ways we can achieve that.

More generally, students are excited by the opportunity to enact meaningful change in the community through these partnerships. Sometimes, this is because it aligns with their professional goals:

> I sensed greater responsibility and interest in this project because the idea of community engagement aligned with my intention to become a doctor, as of which I would be able to directly translate my effort and knowledge to help others.
>
> Music has always interested me and when I finally got into the class and saw that the final group project was going to make a difference to those in hospice, I was so excited. . . . I volunteered at a hospice in the area and now being able to apply what we have learned in class to create something that could help those at [an adult hospice care center] is special to me..

For others, the proximity and immediacy of the experience made it a more impactful experience:

> . . . knowing that the work we do could actually have an impact on someone and improve their life. Even if it helps just one person, it is so fulfilling to know that our work might have made a difference and was not submitted just for a grade.
>
> This group project has been unlike any other I have done during my college experience. . . . All group work in my other classes seem

> to be based [on] fake scenarios; however, I think it is really cool that we were able to take what we have learned all semester about music and its effects and apply them to a real-life scenario.

When reflecting specifically on how scientific knowledge can serve the common good, students saw how their experiences informed their viewpoints. For these students, they felt as though the things they learned in class mattered beyond just memorizing for a test; this was now knowledge meant to be shared with the community, so that this information can help others.

End-of-semester assessments tell us about the immediate impact of such activities but cannot inform us of changes in disposition of heart that persist after any course or initiative is over. As such, we can gain confidence about the long-term impact on human development once our students are no longer restricted to the confines of our classroom walls and campus norms. Through formal and informal surveys, we have found that alumni are pleased with their overall experience, but those who engaged directly in (co)curricular learning experiences similar to those articulated above appear to have been particularly changed, as exemplified by this witness from a student five years after graduation:

> I'm now a second year pediatric resident, so I spend a lot of time communicating with children and families. [. . .] Many of my co-residents have shared that they've had limited formal training on translating information effectively [. . .] so I'm grateful for the practice I had in your courses. [. . .] My heart is definitely in primary care, and I love how neuroscience grounds much of the anticipatory guidance I share in well checks. [. . .] I recently had an experience where secondary trauma unfortunately was relevant to my team, and I immediately turned to my Developmental Neuroscience project with the [Family Justice Center], which was developing a staff curriculum on exactly that.

Doing the Work in Your Own Places and Spaces

Although we have presented our community engagement opportunities in a scaffolded fashion, we did not begin their development in this bottom-up manner. We are lucky to work with a small group of educators who have a personal disposition towards education of the whole person. The importance of having a team whose personal charism is aligned with works of justice cannot be understated. Building outward, we have also been fortunate to work with students who are highly motivated towards social change and to be at an institution that encourages and reinforces the importance of formation for the common good. Thus, we started with the resources at our disposal: a core group of faculty motivated to action, an engaged student base, and institutional support for community relationships.

As part of a continuous learning cycle across educators, students, community, and institution, these opportunities have evolved with our program over the years. Every campus community is unique in their people, place, and purpose, so there is not a "one size fits all" strategy. Therefore, for those curious about creating an engaged curriculum at their home institution, in this last section, we outline several points of consideration. From curriculum to community to assignment-making, we invite you to consider your own curriculum questions of thinking, sensing, and feeling in a classroom setting. We offer some key questions at each stage so readers can evaluate the stage that most strongly speaks to their work and strengths and build from there.

Curriculum Design

At the disciplinary level, it is critical to identify and articulate not just the content you want for your learners, but also the *attitudes* and *skills* that demonstrate the development of a prophetic imagination and a bias toward action. These explicit "core competencies" will help guide the way you evaluate current coursework and co-curricular opportunities and organize your scaffolding of curriculum in support of building these attitudes and skills as learners matriculate. With the help of the campus center for teaching excellence, we recently completed a curricular review executing such a process of internal curricular development and evaluation. Core faculty members identified that the ability to communicate science, translate knowledge for local communities, and build trusting relationships with community partners were key elements of the student formation we sought. We reviewed syllabi of all faculty across campus whose coursework contributed to our curriculum and conducted focus groups with these faculty to gain a deeper understanding of course content and assignments needed to accurately gauge knowledge, skill, and attitude development. Using those data, we reenvisioned our curriculum to prioritize courses that embedded these holistic elements of student formation.

Key Questions:

- What is/are the common goal(s) of the learning experience across the curriculum that will guide student development, not just in content but in skills and attitudes?
- What strengths or starting points might already exist in your curricular courses that support these goals?
  - How do you learn from the individuals who may already be impactful in this space?

Institutional Support

As a Catholic institution, the University of Notre Dame not only commits to service to justice through our mission but also supports this sentiment by building and sustaining infrastructure support. The existing infrastructure on our campus afforded us easier access to embed community-facing projects and partnerships in our courses and curriculum. This institutional commitment increased the confidence of instructors to know that students had multifaceted support in partnering with local organizations, and that we had the means to invite speakers and develop projects.

We suggest evaluating institutional mission and existing campus offices. Regarding the mission, this is important for two reasons. First, if the mission of the institution matches well with the outlined curricular goals, it is easier to find alignment between campus-wide initiatives and the objectives of your program to secure support. Second, alignment allows you to draw from other places where the mission is prominent to appeal to students' experiences. If the goal is to bring such character-forming experiences within the spaces of intellectual formation, this can help students make those connections in their own experience of campus life.

Some campuses may already have centers for community outreach and engagement or initiatives that support community-based learning. These are excellent places to begin, not only for potential community partners but also for ideas of how these relationships can be implemented into a course or curriculum.

Key Questions:

- How does your institution's mission support common good engagement?
- How does your institution actively engage or sustainably support those mission values?
- What resources or networks are already available on campus or within your core faculty? What are some gaps that need to be addressed?

Community-Building

Building trusted and sustainable relationships with the local community is perhaps the most important element of successful community-engaged learning. From our partnership experiences, we have learned that "the Academy" has a poor reputation in our community, particularly among the most vulnerable; an entity that comes in with an idea, takes what it needs (i.e., collects their data), and leaves at the end of a grant without ever reporting back or continuing in relationship.[9] Cultivating sustainable relationships with community partners is a foundational component of trust building. Sustainable partnership takes the most time and is the most personal. That said, trusting relationships with community partners are also the most foundational component to the success of transformational learning. This type of engaged learning requires that faculty "practice what they preach." We must reconcile the notion that often we have the privilege of "telling people how it is" without the responsibility of *participating* in service to justice.

We have found great success in forming individual relationships with others in our local community through common interests discovered via meetings at various community events. Campus colleagues in different units become critical assets in this work, as friends across campus have put us in contact with local churches, charities, and nonprofit organizations after hearing about our work. Never underestimate the power of relationships.

9. W. Marcus Lambert et al., "Ending 'Domestic Helicopter Research,'" *Cell* 187, no. 8 (2024): 1823–27, https://doi.org/10.1016/j.cell.2024.02.027.

If you are new to your community, you can start by identifying institutional programs or people who are already working with the local community. Those who already have established relationships are often willing to lend their "social capital" to others with sincere intentions, and new partnerships grow from there. This is exactly the history of the two authors writing this chapter. When Vanessa first arrived in South Bend, COVID precluded any in-person events from happening, but through Nancy's network and the help of the Center for Social Concerns, she was able to meet and collaborate virtually with multiple groups. Once these initial introductions and connections have been established, it cannot be overstated that the success, durability, and sustainability of these new partnerships then relies on the dependability and transparency of the "new" instructor. In other words, move only at the speed of trust; how much the community trusts the individual instructor and the strength of their relationship is the moderator of progress and collective impact, so expect these partnerships to take time to develop and to be sacred to protect once earned.

Key Questions:

- What "wicked problems" does your discipline speak to? Whom do you know in that space outside "the Academy"?
- What organizations in the area already might be working on the same issues within the community?
- How can you thoughtfully and earnestly offer connection and collaboration that offers mutual benefit?

Classroom-Community Partnerships

As mentioned above, a common challenge of campus-community partnerships is the perception (and unfortunate historic reality) that the "partnership" proposed is one-sided and only benefits the academic entity.[10] It is important to be intentional about working with a prospective partner to ensure that they are involved in the decision-making about what can be useful in a class-based deliverable. A related challenge is

10. Lambert et al., "Ending 'Domestic Helicopter Research.' "

the degree to which a community partner can commit to the success of a project. Because so many of these organizations are strapped for time and funding, they may be limited in their ability to welcome students into their day-to-day workings.

Our most successful partnerships have been those in which the community partner has been an active agent with a vested interest in learning from the students, and where the deliverables are determined by input from the partner on what would be effective in their community or organizational settings. Faculty ensure accuracy of "translation," and community partners determine project format.

Key Questions:

- What synergies exist between opportunities of course/curriculum/student development and community needs?
- How can these partnerships become sustainable in supporting the needs of both community and student?

Conclusion

The process of establishing, building, and integrating community partnerships into curricula is an extended process requiring long-term commitment. It does not come without professional (and in many cases, personal) burdens, as it is often undervalued by academic institutions even as they express their support (see Bell and Lewis for some proposals as to why).[11] Despite this, we have been driven to teach our students and model for them the use of their college education for the common good, motivated by both our disciplinary knowledge of how people learn and our commitment to formation of both mind and heart.

If our charge as educators at Catholic institutions is to prepare our students not only to see but also to *act* on the societal challenges of the day, the neuroscience of learning suggests that, in addition to disciplinary content, these attitudes and behaviors must be modeled, and learners

11. Marissa Bell and Neil Lewis Jr., "Universities Claim to Value Community-Engaged Scholarship: So Why Do They Discourage It?," *Public Understanding of Science* 32, no. 3 (2022), https://doi.org/10.1177/09636625221118779.

must *engage* early and often for attitudes and behaviors to stick. We hope that this account of our motivations, efforts, and recommendations for action will inspire readers to do the same in their own classrooms and institutions. In this way, students not just of neuroscience, but in all academic disciplines, will be both motivated and formed on how to use their knowledge to build God's kingdom on earth.

"Is This Class About Religion?"

Examen-ing Imaginings in Interdisciplinary Courses

Aaron Van Dyke and Elizabeth Boquet
Fairfield University

When the call for this collection was circulated, the two of us were deep in a semester of team-teaching the course we describe in this chapter. We were also deep in the midst of caregiving journeys for our elderly parents. Our course was an introductory team-taught honors seminar centered on enduring questions, with the specific questions shaped by the faculty of record. We designed our course around questions of illness and healing, which reflect Aaron's expertise in biochemistry and Beth's in health humanities. On the first day of class, we asked students to contribute to a Blackboard discussion forum, responding to the following prompt: "Think about any text you've read in which disease and/or illness plays an important role in the story. Summarize what you remember about this story and post this writing to the discussion board thread. Why do you think this was a memorable piece of writing for you?"

We begin with this quick-write because students can accomplish it quickly, with no problem. They can always remember one character, one book, one poem that meets this criterion. These themes are central to humanistic inquiry and Ignatian contemplation. What is wellness? What is illness? Who accompanies us on the journey? What systems support (or hinder) our full human flourishing? In *Illness as Metaphor*, Susan Sontag writes, "Everyone who is born holds dual citizenship, in the kingdom of the well and the kingdom of the sick."[1]

Exploring the implications of this dual citizenry is a difficult task, so we designed this course to support students' engagement of both sacramental and prophetic imaginings throughout the semester. In this chapter, we share our course design, activities, and rationales, including *lectio divina*, an on-campus retreat experience, and variations of the Examen (a foundation of Ignatian spirituality). In this chapter, we hope to offer you—the reader—practical strategies to promote student flourishing.

Slowing Down, Going Deeper: *Lectio Divina*

Nearly all the participants in this seminar were first-semester, first-year students, just beginning their college journeys. As we developed this course, we tried especially to counter the feeling of being overwhelmed that first-year students experience. In our course framing and initial class meetings, we intentionally invited students to experience the full range of activities: in-class writing; small- and large-group discussions; a variety of texts; and co-curricular events. Our introductory course section, then, introduced students to *lectio divina* through an integrated unit featuring a video on this topic by Father James Martin, SJ,[2] a reading from *The New York Times* echoing these contemplative reading practices, and a genre-bending poem reimagining the writer's medical history. Individually and together, we read and reread the poem, applying the steps of *lectio divina* and considering the ways repetition allows us to draw deeper meaning from the text.

Human flourishing is less the result of a highly optimized algorithm and more the result of productive deceleration, giving the imagination time to breathe. If our goal as Ignatian educators is to cultivate students' sacramental and prophetic imaginations, then we must intentionally create space and time. We began by assigning a reading that invites students to read and reread poetry. Holt writes,

1. Susan Sontag, *Illness as Metaphor* (Toronto: McGraw-Hill Ryerson, 1978), 3.

2. "James Martin, S.J. on 'Lectio Divina,'" *America—The Jesuit Review*, August 20, 2014, video, https://www.youtube.com/watch?v=i27FqIyk2qY.

> When I read the same poem every day, I'm training myself to 'look without looking.' By circling back again and again, guided by sound patterns, I let my subconscious do some of the noticing. Rather than consciously analyzing the poem, I focus on listening as the lines on the page release their music and their meaning. Repetition cultivates a deeper kind of attention, one that pushes past facile understanding to intimacy with the work.[3]

We paired Holt's article with Nicole Sealey's "Poem: Medical History"[4] and, following thoughtful discussions of the creativity involved in reframing that most practical of genres into poetic form, we asked students to write their own medical history poems, submitting as an assigned journal entry either their own versions or their reflections on the process of composing it.

Too often, students are positioned as receivers of composed knowledge, positioning them most frequently as critics of prepackaged wisdom. While we value critique, we wanted to engage students as knowledge-makers, as rhetorical imagineers. We wanted them to climb inside their assignments and look out with what Holt describes as a "practice of sustained concentration [that] can also nurture human connection by encouraging the intimacy of attention." Combined with more traditional assigned texts and reflective responses, we view this approach as eliciting an "intuitive, multidimensional concentration"[5] that helps to foster a sacramental worldview.

Creating Space: The Campus Retreat

A centuries-old strategy for shifting one's worldview is the practice of retreat. To retreat is to withdraw from the familiar. By exploring a new space on campus through a retreat, first-year students settle more deeply into their new home and find some respite from their increasing busyness.

3. Elliott Holt, "My Secret Weapon Against the Attention Economy," *New York Times Magazine*, August 17, 2021, https://www.nytimes.com/2021/08/17/magazine/poetry-repetition.html.

4. Nicole Sealey, "Poem: Medical History," *New York Times Magazine*, August 19, 2021, https://www.nytimes.com/2021/08/19/magazine/poem-medical-history.html.

5. Holt, "My Secret Weapon."

Offering a retreat within the first quartile of the term builds on our momentum in the classroom while capitalizing on the newness of the college experience. When thinking about a retreat at your institution, consider what spaces are not in students' daily routines. These might include a conference or retreat center, a museum or creative arts gallery, or some other less-frequented space on your campus. Off-campus locations can also be potent retreat venues, but logistics (including costs) can be prohibitive. At Fairfield, we partnered with the Murphy Center for Ignatian Spirituality, benefiting from staff excited to support our retreat ambitions in its lovely location, an architecturally rich, nineteenth-century French country house.

We designed the day so that all participants, including us, would first have time to explore. We urged students to find a space that spoke to them. "Where does the spirit call you?" we asked. "Are you someone who enjoys a window with a view for writing? Perhaps a comfy chair to reflect?" We enlivened the spaces with art supplies (colored pencils, markers, paper, and sticky notes) to help prime students' prophetic imaginations. We asked everyone to write one hope for the retreat on a sticky note and affix it to a whiteboard as they entered the Murphy Center. Collecting our hopes is a reminder that in the Catholic tradition, as in others, we learn and live in community. We resisted the teacherly urge to read aloud or formally analyze these contributions in any way. For us, the symbolism of this low-stakes exercise was sufficient. As course leaders, we continually reflected on our own positionalities on this day, and, while we recognized that we could not entirely escape our professor roles (nor could students shed their assigned identities), we could examine them, intentionally choosing the most invitational, most welcoming, most contemplative of our available pedagogical practices.

We used the initial structured activity to set the tone and theme of the retreat. We desired to dive deeply with students into the unity of head and heart, a principle of the Catholic intellectual tradition,[6] recognizing how difficult it can be. Retreatants often attempt to straddle the head and heart, keeping one foot in each. This is understandable, especially in an

6. Monika K. Hellwig, "The Catholic Intellectual Tradition in the Catholic University," in *Examining the Catholic Intellectual Tradition*, ed. Anthony J. Cernera and Oliver J. Morgan (Fairfield, CT: Sacred Heart University Press, 2000), 1–18.

academic setting, where so much time is spent on intellectual, rather than spiritual, formation. It takes tremendous courage, including vulnerability (another form of courage), to engage matters of the heart. Yet this is the precise purpose and gift of Catholic education: to awaken in students a healthy attention to their internal affect.

The humanities focus of our course helped to bridge this head-heart distance. As we called students to our first collective experience, we read aloud the opening line of Namwali Serpell's book *The Furrows*: "I don't wanna tell you what happened, I wanna tell you how it felt."[7] We then asked students to write briefly in response to this prompt: "How are you feeling as you arrive at our retreat today?" After briefly sharing these written reflections, we followed with a body scan exercise, underscoring the call to *feel* and *name the feelings* happening during this retreat experience.

While the retreat is an opportunity to withdraw, we strive to avoid a sense of disconnect. This is why, in retreat planning discussions, Beth suggested we return to the technique of *lectio divina* (as introduced by Father James Martin). Over the next thirty minutes, students could work with *any* text from the course so far. We asked them to ground themselves in the retreat by going deeper into the text and offered several writing prompts:

- How does the text connect to your (and others') hopes for our retreat?
- How does it connect to the feelings you arrived with, or the feelings you're trying to let go of? Or the feelings you're trying to access?
- What happens when you try to stay with those feelings? Where does that lead you?

"Students, in the course of their formation, must let the gritty reality of this world into their lives, so they can learn to feel it, think about it critically, respond to its suffering, and engage it constructively."[8] Father

7. Namwali Serpell, *The Furrows* (New York: Hogarth, 2022), 2.

8. Father Peter-Hans Kolvenbach, SJ, "The Service of Faith and the Promotion of Justice in American Jesuit Higher Education," Ignatian Center for Jesuit Education, Santa Clara University, October 6, 2000, https://www.scu.edu/ic/programs/ignatian-worldview/kolvenbach/.

Peter-Hans Kolvenbach, SJ, former superior general of the Society of Jesus, offered these enduring words nearly a quarter-century ago. A fully engaged head requires a fully engaged heart; these are prerequisites to developing students' sacramental and prophetic imaginations.

Two hours into the retreat, we broke for lunch. The cooperative weather and outdoor benches were ideal for students to stretch their legs, boost their vitamin D levels, and informally chat with one another about their experiences. We did not offer specific prompts or activities to avoid the appearance of a "working lunch." Rather, we trusted that the simple foods (wraps, chips, fresh fruit, water), the inviting physical space, and proximity would encourage human connections. A cost-effective option would be to invite students to bring their own food.

The culminating experience of the retreat was an adaptation of the Ignatian Examination of Consciousness (Examen), incorporating the following five steps: (1) gratitude, (2) context (what do I bring?), (3) consolation, (4) desolation, (5) upcoming (what do I desire?).[9] This structured method of reflection asks a person to identify movements of *consolation* (a lasting sense of freedom and fulfillment) as well as *desolation* (an ongoing unfreedom and depletion). While typically the Examen is a short (seven- to ten-minute) stationary prayer, we asked the students to incarnate the five steps into a personalized walking Examen. Over the course of thirty minutes, students identified unique sacred spaces on campus that embodied these five steps. Students placed a symbolic "trailhead" at each of these five places using intentional journaling, movement, photography, or music. This walking Examen provided another opportunity for first-year students to explore their new home.

The "trailheads" marked by students give them an opportunity to discover the transcendent in the immanent. Later in the course, we returned to the walking Examen as a capstone experience, trusting that not all connections between the retreat and the classroom needed to be immediate. Some experiences benefit from the gift of time.

To close the retreat, we gathered as a group around the sticky notes of hope from our opening and offered the following prompts:

9. George Aschenbrenner, "Consciousness Examen," in *Notes on the Spiritual Exercises of St. Ignatius of Loyola* (St. Louis: Review for Religious, 1981), 175–85.

- Where do you feel like we've made a tiny bit of movement toward these hopes?
- Where have we not yet made any movement?
- How can we bring these hopes forward for the remainder of the semester, in and out of class?
- What feels important to remember as we prepare to return to the classroom and our more "academic" work?

After journaling, students were invited to share a few words with the larger group. This kind of "reporting out" might be difficult to stimulate if it is not already a part of the classroom culture. We inculcate this practice in the course through giving low-stakes writing assignments and then asking students to share their thoughts. Students can share with a peer or a small group of peers; sharing need not be solely with the whole class. Feedback is also not a requirement of sharing. Listening attentively and receiving someone's words with gratitude can create powerful sharing experiences and build students' confidence to share again. We were fortunate that all students could attend our day-long retreat (held on a Saturday), but we acknowledge that this may not always be possible for students with external commitments. Because of this, the retreat is not a component of the course grade.

Sacramental Engagements: The Sensory Examens

Sacramentality, according to Andrew Greeley, is akin to the smile of the vanishing Cheshire cat in *Alice in Wonderland*; after catching a view of the transcendent, it gleefully disappears.[10] In the previous section we invited students to a walking Examen to discover what in nature stirs up such a smile. In this section, we take another approach to discover the transcendent through the immanent by integrating the Examen with the Ignatian Composition of Place meditation. The resulting sensory Examen asks students to explore their sacramental imagination through one (or more) physical senses.

10. Andrew Greeley, *The Catholic Imagination* (Oakland: University of California Press, 2001).

Ignatius believes that God is found in our internal, affective movements. These movements are mediated through our physical senses: smell, touch, taste, sound, sight. Composition of Place is a form of contemplation imaginatively engaging the senses. It begins by entering into a Scripture passage using *lectio divina*: a slow, intentional reading. Next, the reader is brought more fully into the experience by composing the scene—using every physical sense—as an artistic director would compose the stage of a play. For example, in the gospel feeding of the five thousand (see Matt 14:13-21): What is the weather? How does it feel on your skin? How do the fish and bread taste? Finally, these sensory details are directed back to the reader's internal movements. What deeper desire has been awakened in you? Is there a curiosity to follow a detail further? Is there an aversion that made you step back?

Because the sensorial element of the Composition of Place draws spiritual pilgrims deeper into Scripture, we explored how, when applied to the Examen, it might draw students deeper into their sacramental imaginations. Students were provided a three-step framework to develop their sensory Examen. In part 1, they explored variations of the Examen to recognize that traditions are kept alive as each person infuses their own lived experience, geographical context, and historical circumstance.[11,12] In part 2, students were asked to appropriate each of the five steps of the Examen using language that articulated their lived experience and context. In part 3, students layered on a sensory element that best expressed—and drew the audience into—the steps of their Examen. A class period was set aside for a peer exchange of sensory Examens. Peers were given the freedom to encounter as many Examens as the class period would meaningfully allow. Students presented their work as downloadable slide shows, curated playlists, or tactile experiences with objects representing the five Examen steps.

The most effective sensory Examens authentically communicated students' life experiences. For example, an undergraduate climate researcher focused his sensory Examen on weather and touch. Through

11. DotMagis editor, "Reimagining the Examen App," IgnatianSpirituality.com, January 1, 2015, https://www.ignatianspirituality.com/reimagining-examen-app/.

12. "Resources for The Daily Examen," Xavier University, accessed December 1, 2024, https://www.xavier.edu/jesuitresource/resources-by-theme/daily-examen-resources.

a campus journey, his Examen asked students to consider their body, clothing, and tactile engagement with the landscape in each of the five steps. One student creatively explored the Examen through taste in the campus dining hall, writing "a meal is the communion of people." Many students explored sound. While several students curated Spotify playlists, these Examens were not nearly as effective as the ones that represented students' own original sonic observations. For example, a flutist played her instrument in different campus spaces, the changing acoustics reflecting each step of the Examen.

Cura Personalis as Health Care

As we moved deeper into the semester, we grappled with longer, more complex texts, most notably Ricardo Nuila's book *The People's Hospital*, which chronicles his experiences as a physician at Ben Taub, a public hospital in Houston, Texas.[13] Ben Taub is, as Nuila describes it, a hospital of firsts: the first successful heart bypass, the first artificial heart transplant, and the first stop for the city's most medically and financially vulnerable. In telling the story of his patients at Ben Taub, Nuila tells the larger, more complex story of health care in America. Jesuit educated, Dr. Nuila brings a sacramental sensibility to his healing and his writing, witnessing the irreducible human dignity in his patients and fellow health care providers. Nuila expects readers to engage their prophetic imaginations to hold both the hope and the peril of health care in the complicated circumstances faced by medical providers, patients, and families at Ben Taub. Working together, we unpacked the book's most powerful movements, examining the assumptions underlying America's health care system: Who has access? What does it provide? How does it promote human healing?

As part of our collective work in this section, we posted the Fairfield University Student Medical Benefits Plan in a shared document and asked students to annotate it. Most were surprised to discover eligibility requirements and limits on certain kinds of coverage. They worried whether mental health services utilized at the campus counseling center would accrue towards their annual coverage limit. They asked, "Who decides if a procedure is medically necessary?" and "How do I get a second opinion?"

13. Ricardo Nuila, *The People's Hospital* (New York: Scribner, 2023).

Finally, they bristled at exclusions for reproductive health care, gender-affirming care, and "art/dance-based therapies," all of which seemed obviously necessary and beneficial.

To support students' engagement with this more complex reading, we added sections of Ellen Carillo's book *A Writer's Guide to Mindful Reading* to the *lectio divina* approaches we worked with earlier in the semester. Specifically, students applied a reading strategy of their choice from Carillo's chapter on "Developing a Repertoire of Reading Strategies" to Nuila's *The People's Hospital*.[14] Students journaled about a reading strategy they used to complete Nuila's text, as well as a character whose health care journey resonated with them. As we look forward to teaching this course again, we realize this section developed implicitly as a unit of the course focused on *cura personalis*, even though we never directly introduced this principle, an oversight on our part and one we intend to revise before the next course offering.

Concluding Encounters

During the final unit, we focused on encountering our collective imaginations and connecting them to the prophetic imaginations circulating through much of our course material. We didn't introduce much new material during this unit, which comprised the final weeks of the semester. Instead, students worked on their three final projects: (1) a multimedia project (composed using Adobe Express), illuminating a self-selected challenging area of illness or disease; (2) a sensory Examen; and (3) a final reflection. The first two projects were peer-facing, designed to engage with the whole class; the third project was intended for and submitted only to course instructors.

For the multimedia project, students arrived independently at their ideas by responding to a series of prompts during the semester in small groups with peers whose topics were thematically related. (For example, one group all had topics related to mental health.) Peer groups met both in class and outside of class, providing brainstorming, composing, and editing support. Course instructors met individually with students and

14. Ellen C. Carillo, "Developing a Repertoire of Reading Strategies," in *A Writer's Guide to Mindful Reading* (WAC Clearinghouse; University Press of Colorado, 2017).

also facilitated a late-stage group meeting as work on these projects drew to a close. The projects were due prior to the final class meeting. All were posted to the course discussion board for shared viewing. During the last class, students spent time navigating each other's projects and responding to them on the project discussion threads. We chose this approach (rather than an oral presentation) to reduce pressure and anxiety in favor of quieter reflective engagement. Following this period of independent viewing and response to these multimedia projects, students then shared their sensory Examens for peer engagement. The sensory Examens (described in detail in the "Sacramental Engagements" section of this chapter) added an intentional, creative dimension of peer engagement beyond what was required by the multimedia projects.

During one of our first class meetings, a student posed the question highlighted in our title: "Is this class about religion?" Aaron thoughtfully replied, "The question of religion is one of the most enduring of all questions." The two of us have returned to this exchange frequently. And we agree, still, that it is a provocative, productive one. Could we design a course on "enduring questions" without touching on the moral, spiritual, and cultural systems that together comprise a religion, or many religions? Explicitly, yes; implicitly, probably not. Together, we traveled great distances over the course of that semester—emotionally, spiritually, physically. Aaron pursued his spiritual direction certification and racked up frequent flyer miles traveling cross-country to support his elderly parents. Beth suffered the illness and death of her father just after midsemester and spent weekends clearing out his apartment and closing out his life. The semester calendar is unforgiving, not made for pauses. In designing a course on enduring questions, we hoped our course would guide students in enduring life's inevitable challenges. We could not have anticipated how well this course, as designed and in companionship with our students and with each other, would prepare us as course instructors for the same, or how much we would need it to do so.

Empowering Students to Integrate Disciplinary and Religious Wisdom to Help Improve the World

Rodger Narloch
College of Saint Benedict and Saint John's University

"What real difference can I make?"
"It's pointless. It won't actually change things."[1]

Students often utter such phrases in exasperation when confronted with important issues of our time. We live in a world with many needs; the depth and scope of these needs can overwhelm and paralyze students from doing anything about them.

"It's academic."

Here is another common phrase, often tied to academia in negative ways. It implies that information learned in higher education is irrelevant or of little practical value. In academia, however, we are called to be much more than "academic." Not only must we help our students to find their education relevant and practical, but we also ought to empower them to put their education to use for the betterment of the world.

1. Students' examples were used with their permission and pseudonyms have been substituted for all names.

In this chapter, I describe pedagogies I utilize in my psychology capstone course, entitled *Guidance for Life: Psychological and Benedictine Wisdom*.[2] This course guides students to answer the question:

> What practices, strategies,
> or actions . . .
> supported by psychological
> and Benedictine wisdom . . .
> will YOU choose to enact . . .
> to help improve the world?

The course prompts students to integrate the wisdom of their academic disciplines and of their institution's religious traditions and then determine how to use this knowledge to positively impact some issue in the world that is especially important to them. Thus, this course provides a template for one way that the academy can be more than just "academic."

While my course focuses on the spiritual tradition of my institution (Benedictine) and my discipline (psychology), the essence of the course is transferable to any spiritual tradition and many academic disciplines. All spiritual traditions have a core set of principles. They could be universal Catholic principles (e.g., respecting human dignity) or more specific instantiations of Catholic principles within a particular charism such as the Benedictine (e.g., listening with the ear of the heart) or Jesuit (e.g., caring for the whole person). With an understanding of these principles, students can use them as a lens for identifying complementary ideas within their disciplinary research. Students discover wisdom emanating from the juncture of two different epistemological methods, their discipline and the institution's religious tradition.

Within psychology, for example, one might use the principle of respecting human dignity to identify research on psychological topics such as empathy and open-mindedness, which could point to concrete strategies for how to cultivate a respect for others. Thereby, the spiritual principle guides the selection of research, which, in turn, can help effectively put

2. Many thanks to Michael Rubbelke, Jessie Bazan, Karlyn Forner, Derek Larson, Julie Lynch, Garrett Miller, and Parker Wheatley, with whom I consulted when writing this chapter.

the principle into practice. This could occur in other disciplines as well. In economics, there is convergence between the Catholic emphasis on community[3] and economic research indicating that we prefer to cooperatively pursue common goals, provided we can trust that the partner will reciprocate.[4] In the discipline of communication, the Benedictine practice of "listening with the ear of your heart"[5] connects with communication research on the affective dimension of listening, which involves empathy, acceptance of the other for who they are, and support for the person's development.[6] In environmental studies, ideas from both a Catholic perspective[7] and a disciplinary perspective[8] support the importance of shared responsibility for the care of the earth. From these examples, it is evident that one can identify junctures between the wisdom of spiritual traditions and academic disciplines. The following sections describe how my course prompts students to explore this kind of integrated wisdom, from which they derive specific strategies they can use to make a difference for a world in need. As I describe my course, I encourage you to reflect on the principles of your institution's own spiritual tradition as well as your own discipline's research and theory.

Course Unit #1: Orientation to the School's Spiritual Wisdom Tradition AND Discerning One's Vocation

My course begins with a two-week overview of Benedictine principles. Although this capstone course enrolls exclusively junior and senior undergraduates, this overview of our spiritual tradition is essential,

3. Bernard F. Evans, *Lazarus at the Table: Catholics and Social Justice* (Collegeville, MN: Liturgical Press, 2006).

4. Jon Elster, "On Seeing and Being Seen," *Social Choice and Welfare* 49, nos. 3–4 (2017): 721–34, https://doi.org/10.1007/s00355-017-1029-9.

5. Joan Chittister, *Wisdom Distilled from the Daily* (New York: HarperCollins, 1990), 14–26.

6. Liora Lipetz, Avraham N. Kluger, and Graham D. Brodie, "Listening Is Listening Is Listening: Employees' Perception of Listening as a Holistic Phenomenon," *International Journal of Listening* 34 (2020): 72, https://doi.org/10.1080/10904018.2018.1497489.

7. Pope Francis, *Laudato Si'*: Encyclical Letter on Care for Our Common Home, May 24, 2015, https://www.vatican.va/content/francesco/en/encyclicals/documents/papa-francesco_20150524_enciclica-laudato-si.html.

8. Aldo Leopold, *A Sand County Almanac* (New York: Oxford University Press, 1949).

as students' knowledge of our Benedictine ethos is often superficial; a deeper understanding is necessary for them to engage in the sophisticated integration required in the course.

We begin this unit with a discussion of Michael Himes's description of the sacramental worldview[9] of Catholicism, which emphasizes seeing the divine in all things, a concept at the heart of a Benedictine way of seeing the world. Next, students experience Benedictine prayer practices such as *lectio divina* and the Liturgy of the Hours, and we discuss how such practices strengthen a sacramental vision. Finally, we review articles[10] and videos[11] that help students understand how a Benedictine worldview can be applied by all people, not just those in a monastic community.

The other major goal of this first unit is helping students discern their "vocation project issue," the particular societal/world issue on which they desire to make an impact. I stress that it must be: (1) personally meaningful, (2) practical (i.e., narrow enough that they can legitimately make a difference), and (3) immediate (i.e., to be enacted within one to two years). The first of these dimensions, being personally meaningful, is essential. To keep this course from being "academic" (i.e., irrelevant), I ask students to choose a particular societal/world issue that matters to them . . . something about which they are passionately concerned, something they feel called or compelled to try to improve. Their issue could be part of their anticipated career; alternatively, it could be manifested in their non-work life through volunteering or simply living an intentional pattern of day-to-day life.

9. Michael J. Himes, "Finding God in All Things: A Sacramental Worldview and Its Effects," in *Becoming Beholders: Cultivating Sacramental Imagination and Actions in College Classrooms*, ed. Karen E. Eifler and Thomas M. Landy (Collegeville, MN: Liturgical Press, 2014), 3–17.

10. Rodger Narloch, "Cultivating Sacramentality through Administrative Work: Guidance from St. Benedict on Being a Catholic Department Chair," *Journal of Catholic Higher Education* 33, no. 1 (2014): 21–31.

11. Kathleen Norris, "Lunch and Learn: How Hospitality Makes Life Better and Easier," November 9, 2018, Quad 170, Collegeville, MN, USA, MPEG-4, 38:53, https://www.csbsju.edu/benedictine-institute/lunch-learned-archived-videos/, and Nicholas Tangen, "Benedictine Perspectives on Diversity, Equity, Inclusion, and Justice: DEIJ as Spiritual and Communal Practice," April 4, 2022, Quad 262, Collegeville, MN, USA, MPEG-4, 59:22, https://www.csbsju.edu/benedictine-institute/diversity-equity-inclusion-and-justice/.

Many students' thoughts about their future are focused on career issues, rather than on the more holistic, deeply personal ways they can make a difference in the world. To prime their vocational thinking, we discuss *Let Your Life Speak* by Parker Palmer. Palmer emphasizes choosing activities in life that are authentic to our innermost passions. A key passage that helps guide students' reflections about their vocations is:

> Our deepest calling is to grow into authentic self-hood, whether or not it conforms to some image of who we ought to be. As we do so, we will not only find the joy that every human being seeks—we will also find our path of authentic service in the world. True vocation joins self and service, as Frederick Buechner asserts when he defines vocation as "the place where your deep gladness meets the world's deep need."
>
> Buechner's definition starts with the self and moves toward the needs of the world: it begins, wisely, where vocation begins—not in what the world needs (which is everything), but in the nature of the human self, in what brings the self joy, the deep joy of knowing that we are here on earth to be the gifts that God created.[12]

Through discussion of this passage, students begin to understand the deeper kind of vocation issue I am asking them to identify within themselves. This passage also helps liberate them from feeling responsible for helping to alleviate *all* societal ills. It allows them to enter a space where they can reflect on who they are, what they care deeply about, and which aspect of our broken world that *they* are most passionate about attempting to heal.

One could characterize the Buechner-Palmer reflection on vocation as employing a sacramental imagination. To contrast, I weave in another approach to vocational discernment that enlists the prophetic imagination. Authors such as Deanna Thompson[13] and Kathleen Cahalan[14] argue

12. Parker Palmer, *Let Your Life Speak* (San Francisco: Jossey-Bass, 2000), 16–17.

13. Deanna A. Thompson, "A Vocation I Didn't Choose," *Christian Century* 139, no. 14 (2022): 10–11, https://www.proquest.com/magazines/vocation-i-didnt-choose/docview/2686230375/se-2.

14. Kathleen A. Cahalan, *The Stories We Live* (Grand Rapids, MI: Eerdmans, 2017), 89–106.

that it is not only from places of deep joy that our vocation springs. Often, vocation is guided and motivated by feelings of sadness, trauma, and grief from sources of hurt or injustice. Through our experience of (or identification with) profound suffering, we discover passion for a cause that compels us to act. Indeed, the vocation issues my students adopt seem to come more from a place of hurt than a place of joy. Students who choose vocational issues related to diffusing mental health stigma or reducing the negative effects of bullying, as examples, are often propelled by painful personal experiences with those issues. Joy, however, remains present; devoting themselves to remedying a cause of sadness or suffering in the world becomes a source of joy.

Care must be taken to provide students with the safe space to look within themselves, authentically identify, and ultimately publicly express their vocation issues. Below are ways I attempt to foster conditions for this kind of personal reflection and self-disclosure. First, I allow time for students to get comfortable with their vocation issue. I introduce this concept in the third week of the semester and ask them to submit initial vague ideas. While these are typically a distant approximation of the vocation issues they ultimately articulate, they contain essential, compelling nuggets of their ultimate issue. This begins a series of exchanges, either written or in-person, with each student as they refine their issue. Second, I gradually increase the degree to which I ask them to publicly express their vocation issue. At first it is just with me, then they share with their classmates in pairs, and then in groups of three or four. It is only during the last month of the semester when they share it with the entire class, and by that time they are comfortable talking about it; they have truly claimed the issue and identify with it. Third, I never ask them to share what motivates them toward their vocation issue. As I mentioned earlier, many vocation issues come from places of deep pain; sharing such personal information is not something I require. While these pedagogical strategies are helpful in creating a classroom environment for exploration and expression of students' vocation issues, I believe a successful environment has less to do with pedagogical technique and more to do with the instructor genuinely expressing care and empathy for their students at every phase of the process. When a trusting and caring relationship is established, students will wholeheartedly contemplate their deepest vocation because they understand its realness in their lives, and they understand its importance for them to live a meaningful life. They find this compelling—far from "academic."

In addition to helping students identify vocation issues that are personally meaningful, I simultaneously help them hone their issues to be both practical and immediate. Through this project, I want students to develop an action plan they can begin implementing upon graduation. This is important so we do not fall into the trap of thinking we need more education, experience, influence, or connections to make a difference. The problem, of course, is we often use our time and energy acquiring more and more of those instrumental things, always putting off tackling the issue. I want students to recognize that they can always do *something* to make a difference at some level. Toward this end, I help students see multiple ways of framing their issue:

> There are two different ways to frame your vocation project issue, one that is more societal and one that is more individual. Let's use the issue of racism as an example. You could use a societal frame by focusing on how to use Benedictine and psychological wisdom to help reduce racism in society or your local community. Or you could use a more individualistic frame by focusing on how to use Benedictine and psychological wisdom to help you yourself be more deeply antiracist. Either of these ways of framing the issue is appropriate for this course. Choose whichever way is going to be more real, more meaningful for you.

These framing options help students think in more practical, concrete ways about actions they can take. Initially opting for a narrow frame does not mean it needs to stay that way as one accumulates more education, experience, influence, and connections. Ultimately, the most profound and sustainable change comes from transforming the societal structures which cause the issues of need; however, this may be impractical for some students and on some issues. Therefore, I want students to create a pattern of life where they are focused on helping alleviate a problem in whatever way is practical. Vocation issues can evolve, but they ought not be delayed.

The following are examples of vocational issues students have identified:

- Combating systemic racism in my workplace by challenging the English-only policy that prohibits employees from speaking their own language in front of customers
- Improving the lives and acceptance of people with intellectual disabilities

- Empowering and supporting people in prioritizing their mental health despite obstacles they face
- Fostering a social norm of authenticity within a social media world that promotes inauthenticity

Course Unit #2: Mining the Wisdom of the Spiritual Tradition and the Academic Discipline

The objective of this unit is for students to learn in-depth information about both their institution's spiritual tradition and their academic discipline. Unlike the first unit's basic orientation to the institution's spiritual tradition, this unit helps students delve into specific spiritual practices. Students now take responsibility for learning about and educating one another on these practices. To do this, I set up an exercise in which pairs of students read about different facets of Benedictine spirituality and then teach their classmates about their topic through a series of small-group discussions. For example, one pair is assigned the Benedictine principle of hospitality. This pair reads several short chapters from *Monastic Heart*, in which author Sister Joan Chittister, OSB, identifies specific elements or practices of the Benedictine monastic tradition that foster hospitality.[15] After reading these chapters, this pair of students meets for twenty minutes with another pair who read chapters relating to a different Benedictine principle. During their discussion, they teach each other about their respective topics. This process is repeated multiple times across three consecutive class days, so students ultimately become well versed in a dozen foundational principles of the tradition. This structure, of course, could be adapted to other spiritual traditions, using different sets of readings focused on your institution's foundational spiritual principles.

Next, students interweave this wisdom of the spiritual tradition with knowledge of their academic discipline. They do this by using the spiritual wisdom to guide their search for research and theory within their academic discipline. In the above example, a pair of students assigned to teach about the Benedictine principle of hospitality now examines the research and theory within psychology that dovetails with Benedictine hospitality. To clarify, they do not select only psychological research

15. Joan Chittister, *The Monastic Heart* (New York: Convergent, 2021).

which examines explicitly spiritual topics. Rather, they use a Benedictine lens to scour the research literature for empirical validation of ideas that are consistent with our spiritual tradition, even if that research does not emanate from a spiritual tradition.

This is a highly creative exercise because a spiritual tradition may use terms that are simply not found within nontheological academic disciplines. For example, *conversatio morum*, a Benedictine concept referring to ongoing life transformation,[16] is not going to be found within the psychological literature. Therefore, students must search topics which get at similar concepts but use different terms. Additionally, sometimes disciplines do use the same terms as a spiritual tradition, but in a way that is wholly incomplete compared to its spiritual conceptions. For example, there is empirical psychological literature on the topic of listening; however, careful discretion is needed to select only those sources that are consistent with the holistic, other-affirming sense of "listening with the ear of the heart" foundational to Benedictine spirituality.[17] Therefore, students must have a relatively deep understanding of the spiritual wisdom to properly use it as a lens for finding relevant research in their discipline.

As students conduct this literature review, they post sources to a collective database accessible to their classmates. They also deliver two twenty- to twenty-five-minute presentations to the class. Each presentation describes some of the key research studies, explains how the studies connect with particular Benedictine principles, and gives suggestions on how their classmates might use the research ideas to inform strategies for making a difference on Vocation Project issues. By the end of the presentations, all students have access to a rich database of disciplinary research sources that tie to the institution's spiritual wisdom tradition.

Course Unit #3: Vocation Project—Using Integrated Wisdom to Make the World Better

In a crescendo that brings together all prior aspects of the course, students reflect on the integrated spiritual and disciplinary wisdom to create

16. Paul Wilkes, *Beyond the Walls: Monastic Wisdom for Everyday Life* (New York: Doubleday, 1999), 41–62.

17. Chittister, *Wisdom Distilled*, 14–26.

specific concrete strategies that each of them, personally, will use to make a difference on their vocation project issue. One difficulty students face during this phase is thinking about specific applications. For example, students often articulate strategies about fostering empathy for individuals different from themselves. In doing this, they cite research showing that empathy is important. However, I need to nudge them a step further. Students must go beyond simply showing THAT empathy is important for their vocation project issue; instead, they must indicate HOW it can be fostered. What are *they* going to *do* to help create more empathy?

A second challenge is to keep students focused on the immediacy of this task. As discussed earlier, students may lapse into complacency because they do not feel they have attained an occupation or accumulated the social or financial capital to make a difference. As a result, students' initial strategies tend to be future-oriented to a point that limits immediate implementation. For example, if one wishes to make our health care system more patient-centered, I do not allow them to put forth strategies reliant upon their first becoming a physician or reaching upper levels of hospital administration before implementation. Too many circumstances could subvert those long-term plans. Rather, I want students to create strategies they can implement within the next one to two years. They learn that there is always something a person can do to help improve the world, at least within some scope, and that they have the requisite wisdom to know what to do.

Below are a few examples of students' vocation project issues and the strategies they identified based on their integrated spiritual and disciplinary wisdom. Please note that these are only brief summaries; in a final double-spaced ten- to twelve-page paper and oral presentation, students fully articulate their vocation project issue, the strategies they plan to employ, and how those strategies are informed by the integrated spiritual and disciplinary wisdom. Much of the final paper is devoted to a fuller exposition of how the strategies they generate are grounded in the empirical research they discovered in the second unit of the course.

There are a few things to notice within the examples below. First, one can see the prophetic imagination at play. Each describes a place of hurt or need in the world that motivates the student toward action. Sofia's example especially illustrates this as she generated her vocation project issue from direct experiences of racism within her part-time job. Second, the examples show how one can take expansive issues such as racism, mental health stigma, or climate change and narrow them to a point where personal, meaningful action can occur. Third, all examples show how changing a societal ill can begin with individual persons; there may be limits on how much we can prompt others to change, but that need not inhibit us from striving for personal change, with the hope that our personal change has a ripple effect within society.

> Sofia: The focus of my vocational issue is the presence of systemic racism in the workplace, specifically regarding the English-only policy that prohibits employees from speaking their own language in front of customers. . . . My goal is to challenge and combat racism through my own actions and interactions with others: How can I avoid conforming to this racist policy? How do I handle microaggressions and biased expressions? How do I prevent myself from eliciting biased responses?
>
> Strategies to Apply:
>
> - Avoid conformity through value-affirmation
> - Utilize effective confrontation actions
> - Prevent myself from engaging in biased expression

> Elizabeth: I want to promote conversation about mental health to diminish the stigma by deepening my internal understanding of self, my external understanding of the world, becoming a better listener, and having genuine interactions with the people I encounter in my daily life. My hope is this will make mental illness a more approachable topic and will inspire others to have similar conversations and further end the stigma.
>
> Strategies to Apply:
>
> - Enable a deeper understanding of myself and how my thoughts and biases influence my behaviors towards mental health
> - Have a greater understanding of other people by being more open to outside ideas and having a better sense of respect for all people
> - Listen mindfully and carefully to fully understand the issue and the speaker's point of view while making them feel heard and respected
> - Foster genuine interactions with others to build trust, respect, and honesty among myself and those I speak with

> Christine: The focus of my vocation project is on addressing climate change and specifically the ways that consumerism habits contribute to climate change. . . . The more resources we consume through various activities, such as buying things, the more of a strain we are putting on our planet. . . . I plan on approaching this issue from an individualistic frame where I focus on helping myself become less consumerist.
>
> Strategies to Apply:
>
> - Addressing my desire by cultivating contentment with what I have through
>   - Practicing gratitude
>   - Taking breaks in consumption
> - Addressing the way I think through
>   - Practicing mindful awareness
>   - Engaging in creative problem-solving
> - Putting my strategies into action through habit formation

Whereas the above examples focus on strategic actions students could apply to their day-to-day lives, some students target strategies that apply to the career they will be entering immediately after graduation. You can see this below with Brendan, who will begin a career in human resources, and with Regan, who will be working in special education with autistic children.

> Brendan: My vocation project is aimed at minimizing toxic relationships and their harmful effects, whether that is in romantic relationships, friendships, familial relationships, or professional relationships like those seen in the workplace. I see it possible to raise awareness about toxic relationships and foster both work and personal social environments to reduce the chances of toxic relationships at both a broader societal level as well as at a specific organizational level.
>
> Strategies to Apply:
>
> - Foster empathy for victims of toxic relationships through social media story-sharing support group
> - Initiate a gratitude intervention in the workplace
> - Exhibit humility in leadership

> Regan: My vocation project is to make a positive impact on the lives of individuals with autism. My first goal is to create safe spaces for individuals with autism and their families to give and receive support

to one another. My second goal is to spread autism awareness and work to break down the stigma that surrounds autism.

Strategies to Apply:

- Create in-person and online support groups
- Provide first-hand experiences for neurotypical individuals to interact with individuals with autism through Peer Mentorship programs and Unified Sports programs
- Create a brief educational video to increase the knowledge of autism in the general public

Assessment and Next Steps

This course has been well received by students as reflected in strong student course survey responses. Additionally, I ask students to write a paragraph about the most profound insight they gained from the course. This could be a specific course concept or research finding but it could be broader, such as a change in the way they think or see the world, a personal realization, or an insight about others. Students generate many kinds of responses to this prompt, but one consistent theme is how this course helped frame their vocation. This is illustrated in the two student reflections below.

> I think the most profound insight I have had through this class is my vocation. At the beginning of this class, I had no idea what I wanted to do by the time I graduated. The vocation project allowed me to really sit with myself and find out what was most important to me and how I can best help others.

> The most profound insight has been the reorientation of my understanding behind vocation. The idea of vocation does not solely refer to a static moment that we strive to reach. Although it does refer to this notion, it can be expanded to include the here and now. What we do day by day constitutes our vocation, so long as it pushes us forward in a positive direction.

My hope is that students thoughtfully reflect about their vocation and create concrete strategies in this course that will empower them to employ a prophetic imagination, thereby channeling their hurt and dismay into tangible change in the world. However, there is no way of ensuring they will implement their strategies after this capstone course ends. To provide incentive, my department is pursuing the creation of an annual award targeting alumnae/alumni three to five years after graduation. This award would be issued to a young alumna/alumnus who has applied their disciplinary wisdom to positively impact a societal need. In addition to recognition and a monetary award, the honoree would be brought to campus as the keynote speaker at a banquet for our senior majors. The honoree would serve as a role model who could inspire the next cohort of graduates. Through this, graduates would see that the accumulated wisdom of their education is far from being simply "academic." Rather, it is the key to creating the kind of change the world needs.

Enriching Education through Interdisciplinary Integration of the Catholic Intellectual Tradition

Reflections on a Faculty Professional Development Project

Sandra L. Guzman-Foster
University of the Incarnate Word

It is no secret that higher education is quickly evolving and continues to evolve. As a result, teaching methodologies must change. This is especially true for not only liberal arts institutions, but liberal arts institutions that have a Catholic identity. As faculty at Catholic higher education iinstitutions, we must engage students on intellectual, moral, and spiritual levels to ensure that they receive a transformative, holistic, and values-based education. The Catholic intellectual tradition (CIT) offers a foundational framework for such an approach, with its emphasis on the integration of faith and reason, the dignity of each individual, and a commitment to social justice. This framework is uniquely positioned to meet the challenges of Catholic higher education today by fostering a sense of belonging, empathy, and critical inquiry among students.

Teaching reflective writing is one of my favorite things to do. Hence, I reflect daily as a way to decompress from a long day and to document challenges, wins, and new learnings. I will share my personal reflection on a three-day faculty retreat that was held in June 2024. The retreat was meant to empower my colleagues at my university with the tools and knowledge necessary to draw on the rich insights of CIT to nurture both intellectual and spiritual growth among ourselves and our students. This is critical and relevant in the world today. Therefore, we must critically reflect on our pedagogy and the social implications of our teaching relevant to social justice and these evolving changes in our educational system and in the world.

Overview of the Retreat

The idea for this retreat was a result of my participation in Collegium in June 2022. It was here that I realized an internal struggle was present. I know there are many of my colleagues doing wonderful things in their classrooms related to our mission, but I also fear what I hear from some of my peers—the mission is being lost. When I inquire about their reasons for this thinking, they reply that it is because our numbers of sisters have decreased and there are not many colleagues left who worked with the sisters. The Sisters of Charity at our university are dedicated to education, health care, and social justice. They established and continue to uphold our mission of academic excellence, faith-based service, and community engagement, rooted in commitment to compassionate care and social responsibility. Their legacy at UIW is reflected in our university's emphasis on holistic education, ethical leadership, and service to marginalized communities. Reflecting on this history as well as in the present, my colleagues have a point. I see very few glimpses of our mission compared to the last five years. I vividly remember the day I came for a campus visit and I could not only see the mission, but I could also feel it when I interacted with my future colleagues. Many of us, including me, come to work here because of the school's diverse student body and because we love the mission and work of the sisters. Granted, the pandemic placed us all in emergency teaching mode; we are still trying to recover and emerge from reflection to action when it comes to mission.

The primary goal of this retreat was to help my colleagues see themselves as champions of change and to use CIT to enrich their pedagogy. My hope was that with a selected group of faculty, seeds could be planted and perhaps the mission would bloom once again and be more visible. We are living in times of uncertainty and divisiveness, and this kind of workshop was urgently needed. Little did I know that this retreat would have a transformative impact on my own pedagogy and understanding of CIT and the prophetic imagination.

When I think of CIT, I think of how we envision our roles not just as facilitators of learning, but also as mentors, advocates, and role models for one another and for our students. Additionally, we tend to approach our work of teaching, service, and scholarship through a mission-driven and mission-focused lens. I often wonder how faculty could be encouraged to approach their pedagogy with a vision that goes beyond the present day and to encourage our students to question existing societal structures. If we approach our pedagogy with this vision, our students can imagine a world transformed by justice and compassion. This can happen only if we help our students view themselves as having agency to effect change.

By integrating faith, reason, and culture into our curriculum and pedagogical strategies, our multidimensional approach to knowledge enriches our students' academic experiences. This is a unique feature of CIT and one I hoped would help us see its necessity if we want to be the kind of Catholic institution we all hoped we could be. Bringing in CIT's principles of ethical inquiry into the classroom leads to intellectual pursuit and fosters a deeper, more holistic engagement with course content. Who would argue that this is not relevant in today's world?

In my pedagogical approaches, I do my best to foster hope and to critically engage my students so they can recognize the impact of their contributions in the world. By using the prophetic imagination, we create spaces in which our students are seen, heard, and empowered to make changes. This is done by engaging in transformative dialogue. It is in these spaces where our students are co-creators of a hopeful and shared future, not passive recipients of knowledge. When we connect CIT to the prophetic imagination, we empower our students to see themselves with agency and to envision possibilities for a more just and compassionate society that fosters human dignity for the common good. This connection enriches their educational journey at our institution, providing them with a sense of purpose, ethical responsibility, and hope.

Identity, Call, and the Mission

On the first day of the retreat, we started with an opening prayer and a quick overview of the schedule for the next three days. Before we could dive deeper into CIT, we first had to understand who we are as a Catholic university. It is important to note that my colleagues are part of various religious traditions; we do not all practice the Catholic faith. However, the Catholic identity is what makes us unique as an institution. Coming together to learn more about CIT despite our differences in religious beliefs has brought us all to this university. What a profound insight of who we are as an institution and how we perceive and understand our mission!

After our opening prayer, we were immediately challenged to think about our beliefs, values, and our identity as an institution. "*What is one word you would use to describe the culture of the university?*" was the question posed to all of us. As colleagues shared their words, I took notes. "Friendly," "Accompaniment," "Belonging," "Love," "and "Conflict" were common words shared by the group. Some of these words resonated with me while others did not. It depends on the day and the context. There have been times when I felt all of these at the university, while there have been times when friendly, accompaniment, belonging, and love seemed invisible. We get caught up in the politics that are embedded in university life. We let them overwhelm us and, in some cases, the needs of our students take a back seat. I get it, but I also know what impacts me will impact my students. It is my responsibility to teach, engage, empower, and help my students see themselves as agents of change so that they can imagine and live in a world that is just. Therefore, I must do my best to leave any baggage I may be bringing to that space on that day at the door. This doesn't mean I forget what was bothering me, but instead it means I must put aside some time to discern about the challenging or difficult incident that occurred prior to teaching on that day.

Next, we read Jeremiah 1:4-8 and were asked to reflect on the following questions: "How have you experienced God's calling in your life?" and "When you had this experience, what happened to you?" As I pondered on these questions, other questions came to mind, such as: "Am I doing God's work?" "How am I serving others?" "How am I being of service?" "Do I find joy in this journey?" As I reflected on my own experiences, I came to realize that it is my faith that gives me the energy, confidence, and joy to serve others. However, there are times when I feel depleted and wonder, "Now what am I supposed to do?"

Following this reflection, we read Micah 6:8 and 1 Corinthians 12:4-13. These readings were followed by sharing this statement from Pope Paul VI: "People listen more readily to witnesses than to teachers, and if they listen to teachers, it is because they are witnesses."[1] To me, a "witness" in this context refers to people who exemplify or embody the values, knowledge, or truths they speak about. It is people who "walk the talk." Too often we "talk the talk," but don't "walk the talk." This is a major shortcoming that exists, and one that I shared with my colleagues when I was a full-time faculty member. Before I was the director of the Center for Teaching and Learning, I was a full-time faculty member in the Dreeben School of Education, where I worked with graduate students. This is where I witnessed firsthand that students are naturally drawn to those faculty who "walk the talk" because their credibility comes from lived experiences and personal integrity.

We were then invited to reflect on the following questions: "What is my unique contribution to the whole?" "How have I experienced working for the common good?" And "What is God asking us to do today?" Identifying weak spots when it comes to policies; being present and available to help with knowledge and knowledge gaps; and my ability to dialogue about diversity, equity, inclusion, justice, and belonging with others (DEIJB)—these are my contributions to the common good and our community. These are some of my gifts in how I approach, relate to, and collaborate with others. Granted, it is not always a positive experience when I identify weak spots or when I dialogue about DEIJB. These topics can be challenging because no one wants to hear about gaps and because of the anti–DEI rhetoric we are seeing at the state and national levels. After some quiet time, we concluded that we are the embodiment of many gifts and, as a result, we have the ability to flourish as a community. "How do we do this?" and "How do we do this with love, compassion, and grace?" lingered in my thoughts.

After we explored our individual and communal identities and calling, we turned to our university mission. We read a short passage about the sisters and the mission and were asked to reflect on the following questions: "How does my calling reflect my choice to serve at the university?" "How does the university promote the many gifts and charisms present in its midst and utilize them to create communities of love and hope?"

1. Quoted in (and adapted from) Pope Paul VI, *Evangelii Nuntiandi*, December 8, 1975, par. 41, https://www.vatican.va/content/paul-vi/en/apost_exhortations/documents/hf_p-vi_exh_19751208_evangelii-nuntiandi.html.

And "How does the university apply the spirit and essential values of its founders to the most pressing issues we face today, e.g., the COVID pandemic, systemic racism, the worldwide migration phenomenon, the climate crisis, etc.?" It was not easy to answer these questions. These are the kinds of questions that need more mulling, and I needed more time.

The first question, "How does my calling reflect my choice to serve at the university?" brought up a distinct memory. My calling is a spiritual and deeply personal element. It is connected to my sense of purpose and aligns with my identity, passions, and beliefs. For the longest time, I have always felt I was called to serve others and seek justice. For example, I can remember coming home from school when I was in kindergarten and sharing with my mom about an incident that occurred on the playground. I had noticed a classmate being picked on in the corner of the playground. I could hear the taunting and see the pushing against the fence. I wanted to know why this happened. In my young mind, I thought it was different from when my siblings took my things without my permission. I knew what I saw on the playground was wrong. This was my first lesson on bullying. Once my mom explained to me what it meant to be bullied, I shared more details with her, such as the one being bullied was smaller than the bullies, his hair was never combed, his clothes were always dirty, and he had holes in his shoes. From that day on, I made sure that I stuck up for him even if it meant that I, too, was bullied. My teacher finally noticed what was happening on the playground and put a stop to it. For the remainder of the year, we were both left alone.

This experience connects to where I am today. Many of our students are members of structurally marginalized communities. Additionally, many are first-generation college students. Their transition from high school to college is not as seamless as it would be for someone whose parents graduated from college. It is especially difficult for these students if they are living away from home, where family is a critical part of their lives. For the first time, they are on their own. I see myself in many of these students because I was one of those students. So, when I am asked, "How does my calling reflect my choice to serve at the university?," my calling is grounded in a commitment to social justice and fostering educational access for students who are members of historically underrepresented and structurally marginalized communities. As a first-generation Mexican American scholar, I understand firsthand the challenges that many of our students face. The university's mission as a Hispanic-serving institution aligns with my purpose to empower students academically and personally. Through mentoring, developing inclusive pedagogical practices, and contributing to institutional equity initiatives, I aim to create opportunities for students to thrive. Serving at this university is not just a professional choice but also a reflection of my calling to make a lasting impact in higher education.

Before I could get to the other questions, we were asked, "What are God's gifts to us?" The first thing that came to mind was that our students are God's gifts to us. We serve a unique population of students by choice and because of our mission. However, the higher education system today is badly designed, and a liberal arts Catholic institution is not immune from this design. We are overworked, overwhelmed, and spread too thin. We don't do enough when it comes to truth and transparency. In fact, we are fragmented. However, there are small pockets of hope, and many faculty *are* mission-focused and mission-driven and doing great things in their classrooms. These are the faculty that are contributing to the faith formation of our students. Some of those faculty were present in this retreat. "It is important to pay attention to what is around us" was shared. What a profound statement! We can get stuck and remain stuck in the fragmentation, but those simple words of "pay attention to what is around us" provides a perspective that we should all heed.

Before we moved on, we were asked to take fifteen minutes to deepen our reflection and contemplation by taking a walk outside. Having quiet time to reflect on all that we shared on the first day was a blessing. Walking outside among the beautiful grounds was a reminder to pay attention to what is around us. God's creation is everywhere, and reflecting on what I learned about myself and seeing what my colleagues took away as they learned more about themselves was profound. Engaging our voices in a space without judgment was what was needed.

Comprehensive Understanding of CIT

After our walk, we welcomed our keynote speaker, Rachel (pseudonym), a scholar and practitioner of the Catholic intellectual tradition (CIT), who guided us through a deep, introspective exploration of its principles via an interactive lecture. The session began with a reflective call to prayer and singing of the hymn: "Come by here, my Lord, come by here. Someone's prayin', Lord, come by here. O Lord, come by here." This moment set the tone for a journey of inquiry, truth, and prophetic imagination, calling us to embrace discernment rather than conformity.

Rachel's lecture invited us to embody what Walter Brueggemann[2] describes as the prophetic imagination; the capacity to envision and work toward an alternative reality rooted in justice, compassion, and hope. She framed CIT as a tradition that demands not only theological reflection but also action, urging us to challenge oppressive structures and imagine a world where all voices are valued. For the first time in a very long time, I felt validated in the way I approach my teaching and the kind of spaces I provide for my students. I have been honest and transparent with not only my teaching, but also my policies. As a result of this transparency, I have received fewer invitations to be part of university committees, initiatives, and meetings. I believe it is because I name the oppressive structures that exist, and I amplify the voices of those in the shadows. I always think of what could be if only we did x, y, and z. The prophetic imagination! In my mind, we must always humanize the work that we do. This is critical when planning for the work that needs to be done for a more humane, just, and better future.

Her questioning continued. "Who are we?" "Where are we going?" And "Who is God?" These questions called us to reflect on our identity and purpose in a way that disrupts the status quo. CIT, she emphasized, is not a static tradition but one that evolves through dialogue, critique, and engagement. By highlighting the diverse cultural and historical roots of the church—such as its foundations in Alexandria, Antioch, and Ethiopia—Rachel reminded us that CIT itself is born of the prophetic imagination. These early communities sought to understand their faith in context, shaping theology through the lens of their lived experiences and their longing for liberation. Personally, when I think of the word "liberation" and how it fits into my pedagogy and spaces, I reflect on Paulo Freire's work and his connection to liberation theology.[3] It feels as though he was living out the prophetic imagination in a way that resonates deeply with

2. Walter Brueggemann, *The Prophetic Imagination: 40th Anniversary Edition* (Minneapolis: Fortress Press, 2018).

3. Paulo Freire, "Education, Liberation, and the Church," *Religious Education* 79, no. 4 (1984): 524–45, https://doi.org/10.1080/0034408400790405.

CIT. Freire wasn't just a thinker—he was a doer. He didn't ask others to step into political activism unless he was already there himself.

Freire challenged us to think about the church—not just as an institution, but as something alive and evolving. He contrasted what he saw as the traditional church, the modern church, and the prophetic church. For Freire, the prophetic church was where it was needed to be. It's the church that stands with the poor, the oppressed, the exploited—the church that risks everything for the sake of human dignity. This prophetic stance, this refusal to accept the way things are, is what drives the search for justice that Freire believed in so deeply.

It's also about dialogue—real, authentic dialogue that forces us to face the contradictions in our society. Freire saw how ignoring those contradictions, such as turning our backs on immigrants, refugees, migrant workers, and the forgotten poverty-stricken areas of the world, was counter to what the church calls us to do. His work reminds us that the prophetic imagination isn't passive. It's an invitation to enter the hard, messy work of justice.

Even today, those of us, me included, who carry forward his ideas are finding ourselves under attack by forces that fear dialogue, change, and loss of our power and privilege. And that's the thing about the prophetic imagination: it's disruptive. It doesn't let us stay comfortable. It pushes us to act, to speak, and to stand with those whom the world often overlooks. And in that, Freire's legacy is profoundly Catholic, rooted in hope, justice, and the belief that, through dialogue and action, we can imagine and build something better. I have used Freire's work in my pedagogy and in some of my research. It makes sense why I feel a strong connection to his work.

Rachel's statement, "There are no white people in the Bible," served as a powerful example of prophetic critique. It dismantles dominant narratives that marginalize the contributions of non-European voices in sacred history and intellectual traditions. I felt as if my mind was being read. For me, it is important that my students learn to dismantle the dominant narrative about educational policies and how they impact students who are structurally marginalized in a system that was not designed with people of color in mind. This critique aligns with Brueggemann's call to challenge "royal consciousness"—the systems of thought and power that suppress the radical inclusivity and justice central to prophetic faith.[4]

4. Brueggemann, *Prophetic Imagination*, 76.

In this spirit, Rachel asked us to consider how we can integrate CIT into our teaching as an act of prophetic imagination. By creating brave spaces for dialogue and reflection, we can help students confront biases, question assumptions, and seek truth. This process, she explained, involves engaging art, beauty, and reason to teach what it means to be human. It calls for an honest reckoning with our intellectual heritage, including the exclusion of voices from diverse backgrounds, genders, and faith traditions. This part of the retreat reminded me of a class I taught the semester when some of us returned to the classroom from the pandemic. We were still allowing students to join via Zoom, but they could also attend class in person. It was in this class and through practices such as reflective writing, poetry, creating a *cajita*, ongoing dialectical circles, and developing an action plan for social issues, we shared our experiences as members of a dialogic learning community. As a result, we all experienced transformative teaching and learning. In fact, I learned as much from my students as I believe my students learned from me. Most importantly, we envisioned the possibilities of a different world. We learned that we need to constantly ask ourselves about the consequences of our practices (both private and public), even when we feel that they are well intentioned. A call for us, both professors and students, is to question our surroundings and to examine ourselves and our community's intentions as a way of increasing our awareness to stand up for desired change.

The prophetic imagination also invites us to critique our own practices. Rachel posed questions that disrupted our tendencies toward convenience: "Am I planning and preparing for ease, or am I teaching with intention?" and "Do I guard and protect the possibilities of profound conversation?" The first question sparked my attention. I wondered how many times any of us have planned or prepared out of convenience and why we did so. When things come up, why is this the first thing we do without realizing it is counter to what we want for our students? What are the alternatives? We need to find alternatives that do not veer us off course. She urged us to make room in our schedules and our classrooms for the kind of transformative dialogue that fosters wholeness—both for ourselves and our students. She's right. Even when we are overwhelmed, we must stop and make room so that we can continue providing transformative educational experiences for our students. The second question is something I think we should not do. In fact, I welcome profound conversation. I borrowed the following statement from a colleague and put it in my course syllabus:

> *This course is meant to be provocative. You will likely read and hear things that you disagree with or find troubling. Depending on your social position (e.g., gender, race/ethnicity, nationality), you may also have strong responses to discussions of social inequality. Instead of focusing on the intentions and actions of individuals (i.e., reading the texts as a personal attack on individuals belonging to dominant groups), focus on the systems of oppression that maintain social inequalities. All students should be willing to discuss the causes of social inequalities and ways of mitigating them without becoming defensive or accusatory or expecting others to speak for the groups to which they belong. I hope we will create an atmosphere in which dissenting and differing viewpoints are welcome and in which we aim toward a deeper understanding of the authors' perspectives as well as our own and those of others, as opposed to seeking consensus or engaging in combative discussions. I encourage you to share insights from your professional and personal experiences. These experiences can be most educational when they are brought back to the text to make an argument, to illustrate or critique a broader concept, to make connections between one's situation and broader social processes. Since each of us has a limited set of experiences, we need to use sources in addition to personal experience to make and assess scholarly arguments. In particular, this means providing evidence to support claims and assertions. Remember to speak from your own experiences, "I" or "My," instead of speaking for others in your group.*[5]

I believe a course that welcomes profound conversations offers learning beyond the surface level for both the professor and the student. Students can practice critical thinking and analysis with one another and broaden their perspectives.

Incorporating prophetic imagination means reimagining the academy as a place where disciplines intersect, where fractured knowledge becomes whole, and where faith and reason coalesce to address the deep questions of existence. This approach is not merely theoretical; it is profoundly practical. Rachel highlighted figures such as W. E. B. Du Bois, Frederick Douglass, and Martin Luther King Jr., whose lives exemplify the prophetic call to justice and equity. Their contributions remind us that the prophetic

5. Sherry Herbers, email, Summer 2021.

imagination requires courage to confront systems of oppression and faith to envision a better future. Additionally, she emphasized the need to amplify voices of women, people of color, and other faith traditions in our intellectual heritage.

By engaging us in song, reflective dialogue, and vulnerability, Rachel modeled the prophetic imagination in action. Her lecture encouraged us to reimagine our roles as educators, asking: "How can we help our students and ourselves become whole?" "How can we guide them to grow into who God calls them to be?" She empathized that this work requires attentiveness to the voices we exclude, the traditions we neglect, and the spaces we fail to create.

Ultimately, Rachel demonstrated that CIT, infused with the prophetic imagination, is a call to search for wholeness and holiness. It challenges us to see education as a vehicle for justice, empowering students to explore, question, and act. Through CIT, we are invited to imagine a world where faith, reason, and compassion intersect, leading us toward a more inclusive and humanistic vision of the common good. Rachel's lecture illuminated how CIT's principles call us to imagine a more compassionate and just world. By weaving inclusivity, justice, and faith into teaching practices, we can inspire our students to engage in ethical inquiry, critical thinking, and authentic learning experiences. The session concluded with an invitation to work a little harder—to guard this tradition, ask who is missing from the conversation, and commit to creating a community where everyone, especially those living in the shadows, can flourish.

Final Thoughts

Reflection is central to CIT, which values the ongoing alignment of personal actions with spiritual and ethical commitments. The prophetic imagination calls for a constant reevaluation of one's actions and beliefs, pushing educators to model continuous self-awareness and moral accountability for their students. Although we were able to gather a lot of information during these three days, reflection was the overarching strategy used when questions were posed to us.

What kind of strategies did I leave with to help me infuse what we learned into my own practices? One takeaway was to promote reflective practice through journaling and storytelling. During the retreat, we engaged in storytelling and journaling as methods of reflection. This was especially prominent during our individual reflections, in which we wrote about our challenges, insights, and successes in integrating CIT. By framing our experiences as stories, we can refine key lessons that align with CIT's values.

Having some of our colleagues share their examples was very similar to using case studies, another reflective tool. Four of our colleagues shared their experiences of infusing CIT into their courses. They highlighted and illustrated how they have transformed challenging moments into meaningful CIT-aligned experiences in their courses. Through personal anecdotes, we witnessed how reflective practice can foster personal and professional growth, as well as deepen connections to CIT principles.

CIT inspires faculty to think creatively about pedagogy, aligning with the prophetic imagination's call for innovation and transformation. The retreat encouraged all of us to experiment with new teaching strategies and foster environments where students can engage in ethical and intellectual exploration. We were encouraged to create and share our stories, metaphors, and parables inspired by the retreat. By building narratives around words and themes encountered during the three-day experience, we fostered a shared CIT-inspired vision. The retreat showcased CIT-inspired innovations, such as service learning projects, interdisciplinary case studies, and reflective assignments. Faculty testimonials underscore the impact of these methods on student engagement, demonstrating how CIT's values can inspire creativity in the classroom.

The enduring values of CIT—wisdom, compassion, and the pursuit of justice—are timelessly relevant. By embracing these principles, we can transform our classrooms into spaces where students feel respected, valued, and empowered. The prophetic imagination embedded within CIT calls educators to continually strive for a world shaped by justice, inclusion, and ethical inquiry, setting a standard for future generations.

Living Ethically in an Unethical World

Teaching Psychology Ethics through a Jesuit and Catholic Lens

Thomas G. Plante
Santa Clara University

The world is a mess on so many levels and in so many ways. Violence, extreme political polarization, cancel culture, climate change, racism and discrimination, incivility, widening economic disparity, misinformation, the damaging impact of social media, and so forth dominate the daily news and it all seems to be getting worse by the day. College campuses are fraught with fallout from these issues, while students of today experience increasing fragility with exploding mental health problems associated with anxiety, depression, suicidality, and substance abuse. In fact, recently the United States Surgeon General released an unprecedented advisory regarding the increasing crisis of mental health challenges, most especially among youth.[1]

All of our societal troubles can be attributed at their core to human behavior and, in particular, challenges with poor ethical decision-making. A fundamental ethical conflict between egoism and the common good exists, where the common good seems to get lost in the overwhelming tide

1. Office of the Surgeon General, *Protecting Youth Mental Health: The U.S. Surgeon General's Advisory*, 2021, https://www.hhs.gov/sites/default/files/surgeon-general-youth-mental-health-advisory.pdf.

of self-serving egoism. It seems that most people are much more invested in their individual needs and desires than in what might be in the interest of all. While there are no simple answers to turn these disturbing trends around, thoughtful consideration and reflection of best practices in ethical decision-making may help. Doing so through a Jesuit and Catholic lens can perhaps help us even more. The Catholic tradition, including the long history of Catholic social teachings and their emphasis on morality, can be put to good use to discuss contemporary ethical difficulties and conflicts even in a secular manner with non-Catholic audiences. College students of today need helpful tools to assist them in navigating the overwhelming ethical challenges in our unfolding contemporary society and world. Ethical decision-making, assisted through an understanding of moral philosophy and enhanced through a Jesuit and Catholic lens, can help our students increase their chances of living more ethically in an often-unethical world. Although a Jesuit and Catholic approach is highlighted in this chapter, the principles and examples that are discussed can be utilized and adapted for any faith-based or even secular college environment. At least this type of education may make students more aware of ethical challenges and introduce them to important moral philosophy and faith-based tools for their ethical problem-solving life toolbox.

Catholic and Faith-Based Universities Can Help

Catholic and other faith-based universities are uniquely positioned to offer thoughtful classes that can address the many problems in society through a careful understanding of ethics, as well as applying tried-and-true ethical decision-making strategies to any academic discipline. Faith-based colleges and universities often offer required core classes that address topics such as religious studies and theology, ethics, and community engagement as examples that might be either ignored, optional, or designed only for a narrow range of academic majors at secular colleges and universities. For example, I have taught a professional ethics seminar for clinical psychology doctoral interns and postdoctoral fellows in the department of psychiatry and behavioral sciences at Stanford University School of Medicine for over thirty years. I always ask these students if they ever have had an undergraduate course in general ethics or in moral philosophy in particular. Rarely do these students state that they had one of these classes as a college student. In fact, I typically get many blank stares. However, when the occasional student does report that they had an ethics or moral philosophy course in college, they typically state that they were enrolled at a faith-based, often a Catholic, college or university for their undergraduate studies. Graduate students in psychology and other health care disciplines (e.g., social work, counseling, medicine, nursing) often are required to take an ethics course during graduate or professional studies. However, these courses are usually focused on the profession's code of ethics and typically are presented in a more legalistic manner about adhering to these codes and standards to avoid malpractice and other negative career consequences. They typically study their profession's ethics code and then apply the code to various case studies. This approach differs greatly from a more aspirational approach to ethical decision-making and behavior that is found in moral philosophy as well as Catholic social teaching.

The Ethics in Psychology Course at Santa Clara University

The purpose of this chapter is to discuss an Ethics in Psychology class taught at Santa Clara University, a Jesuit and Catholic university located in Silicon Valley near San Jose, California, that is an approved course for the applied ethics requirement of the core curriculum. This applied ethics requirement is mandated for all university students, regardless of their academic major or school (e.g., business, engineering, arts and sciences). The core applied ethics requirement can be fulfilled within numerous academic departments so that each student has the opportunity to select a class that interests them and that might be relevant to and consistent with their educational and career goals. Although many of these applied ethics classes are taught in the philosophy department, courses that meet this core requirement are also offered in the business and engineering schools, as well as in the departments of sociology, ethnic studies, psychology, child studies, communications, and many other fields within the arts, sciences, and humanities across campus. In this particular case, the Ethics in Psychology class typically attracts and enrolls not only psychology majors but also those students typically majoring in public health, child studies, and pre-med related majors such as biology. Many of the students who enroll in the course have interests in careers in the helping professions, such as clinical psychology, counseling, social work, medicine, nursing, occupational therapy, physical therapy, and various additional applied health professions. They often have interests in educational fields as well, such as primary or secondary school education. A multidisciplinary core curriculum committee must approve all of the applied ethics courses offered to fulfill the university-wide core curriculum requirement. The committee includes at least one philosophy professor who specializes in ethics and moral philosophy. All of these approved courses must spend at least several weeks of the academic term reviewing moral philosophy using philosophy department–approved readings.

In Ethics in Psychology, an overview of moral philosophy occurs during the first few weeks of the term, followed by the application of ethical principles to psychology and related fields (i.e., psychiatry, social work, counseling, education, public health, medicine). The integration of Catholic social teaching and popular Jesuit principles such as *cura personalis*, or finding God in all things, approaching conflict with others with accommodation, humility, and the expectation of goodness, reflection and discernment, and so forth are integrated into class readings and discussion.

Community-Based Learning Is Offered and Highlighted

The class typically includes a community-based learning requirement too. At Santa Clara University, all students, regardless of their academic major or school of study, must complete at least one class that is community-based, referred to as an experiential learning for social justice (ELSJ) course offered through our university's Arrupe Partnership program (named after Pedro Arrupe, SJ, former superior general of the Jesuits). The university's community-based partners include approximately fifty local nonprofit agencies (e.g., homeless shelters; food pantries; adult day care facilities; and centers that provide services to those experiencing autism spectrum disorders, Alzheimer's and other dementia disorders, stroke survivors, and developmental disabilities of various sorts). Students can "double dip" these requirements by taking a core applied ethics class that also offers the community-based learning element as well, thus fulfilling two university core requirements at once. After selecting a placement that interests them and participating in an onsite orientation session, students spend two hours each week during the academic term volunteering in the community placement. Issues and experiences from their community-based placements are then integrated into class topics and discussions. Students then write a reflection paper at the end of the term that speaks to their experiences at the community placement and how the placement illustrated themes presented and discussed in class and in their course readings.

Class Readings

The readings for the class include a basic text on moral philosophy, a text that discusses psychology ethics, a text that highlights college student ethical development, and a text that discusses everyday ethics.[2] After students are introduced to the major approaches to ethical decision-making informed by moral philosophy (e.g., virtue, justice, the common good, absolute moral rules, utilitarianism, egoism, social contracts), they then apply these approaches, among others, to ethical dilemmas in psychology and related fields. These include issues related to confidentiality, evaluating and treating patients against their will, dealing with patients who are a danger to self or others, and managing ethical conflicts in hospitals, clinics, and with colleagues. Common virtues in the field of mental health and health care such as competence, responsibility, integrity, compassion, and respect for others are highlighted, as well as ethical standards associated with assessment, treatment, consultation, teaching, supervision, and research within these fields. Students review the ethics code in psychology published by the American Psychological Association[3] that is discussed and unpacked in class. Students also review how ethical issues overlap or contradict legal guidelines; while the law typically provides a floor for expected professional behavior, ethics represents the ceiling or aspirational qualities.

2. Lewis Vaughn, *Beginning Ethics: An Introduction to Moral Philosophy* (New York: Norton, 2015); Samuel J. Knapp and Randy Fingerhut, *Practical Ethics for Psychologists: A Positive Approach* (Washington, DC: American Psychological Association, 2024); Thomas G. Plante, *Living Ethically in an Unethical World: Doing the Right Thing*, 2nd ed. (San Diego: Cognella, 2024); and Thomas G. Plante and Lori G. Plante, *Graduating with Honor: Best Practices to Promote Ethics Development in College Students* (London: Bloomsbury, 2017).

3. American Psychological Association, *Ethical Principles of Psychologists and Code of Conduct*, 2017, https://www.apa.org/ethics/code.

Making Ethics Personal

In order to personalize the course material and ethical principles, we begin each class session by asking what ethical dilemma students have personally experienced since the previous class session and what ethical principles they used to think through and attempt to solve these particular dilemmas. This acts as a warm-up exercise for the topics of the day. It is important to nurture an open, friendly, welcoming, and confidential environment in class for students to feel comfortable discussing personal ethical challenges that they face. We ask students to be mindful and respectful of one another and to hold in confidence information that students wish to keep within the confines of the class. We also highlight how egoism, or self-interest, is always considered when reflecting on ethical issues and that being open with each other about our self-interests is welcome.

At the beginning of the academic term, students generally have few dilemmas to discuss. They typically fail to see many ethical conflicts or dilemmas in their lives, nor do they think about their various life challenges in ethical terms. However, once they are sensitized to ethical issues and have a number of tools to identify and consider ethical challenges, they then tend to have plenty of examples to bring up and discuss in class. It is gratifying to see their transformation during the course. They are better able to see ethical nuances in their lives and filter their experiences through an ethics lens. This checking-in question and brief discussion at the start of each class session helps students to think more about ethics and ethical challenges that they and their peers face regularly. It also gets them engaged with helping their peers think through ethical problems and gives them a chance to offer their insights and suggestions to help others. The conversation about personal ethics gets their attention and puts them in the mood and spirit to tackle the scheduled academic topics discussed during the rest of the class session. It also provides students with an opportunity to apply their developing skills to practical issues and problems that they face and receive feedback and support from their peers.

The Catholic Angle

Although the Ethics in Psychology course could be offered at any university, including faith-based or secular private or public schools, the class lends itself nicely to discussions that infuse Catholic social teaching and Catholic principles for better living, both personally and professionally. Because Santa Clara is a Jesuit and Catholic university, the class can more seamlessly integrate Jesuit and Catholic principles, perspectives, and values that students tend to be at least somewhat familiar with after they arrive on campus. These principles include topics such as social justice, solidarity, and kinship, as well as *cura personalis* (i.e., care for the whole person), using reflection and discernment to make good decisions, and managing conflicts with accommodation, humility, and the expectation of goodness in mind.[4] Additionally, the university embraces and highlights moral virtues of what are referred to as the "Santa Clara three Cs," representing competence, conscience, and compassion. More on this topic will be offered at the end of the chapter, but for now, here are several class examples of ethical conflicts students often bring up for discussion and advice.

Three Examples of Student Ethical Dilemmas

Example 1: Campus protests

Several students in the Ethics in Psychology class were planning to protest an upcoming invited campus speaker who has conservative viewpoints and a history of statements that many women have found to be offensive. The students were planning various strategies and options for a protest during his speech. In class, we discussed the situation in terms of ethical principles that could be used to determine how best to protest in an ethical manner. Additionally, we discussed Catholic social teaching and paying attention to the rights and dignity of all people, including the invited speaker and the group that invited him to campus. The students ultimately stood silently at the entrance of the lecture venue, holding respectful signs about their concerns about the speaker. They were not disruptive to anyone, the speaker offered his perspectives, yet the students made their points known to people as they entered and exited the auditorium. Afterwards, the students felt that the protest was successful, and they reported having engaging conversations with some of those who passed by them.

4. Thomas G. Plante, *Living Better with Spirituality Based Strategies that Work: Workbook for Spiritually Informed Therapy* (San Diego: Cognella, 2024).

Example 2: The burrito bandit

A student in class mentioned that he orders a breakfast burrito each morning from the university's dining hall through an online app, but when he arrives to pick up his burrito, it has been taken by someone else. This had happened frequently enough to cause concern, and he wondered how he should handle the situation if he caught the "burrito bandit." Using various moral philosophy perspectives such as egoism, absolute moral rules, the social contract, and justice models, along with the university's professed virtues of competence, conscience, and compassion, the class helped him come up with a plan for intervention. The "burrito bandit" was finally caught, and the student offered him corrective feedback in a firm but respectful manner. The bandit explained why he stole the burritos, asked for forgiveness, and the student forgave him. They eventually became friends and later became roommates.

Example 3: Sexual misbehavior and infidelity

A student described the sexual misbehavior of friends attending another college several hours away from Santa Clara. She reported that she spends a good deal of time with these friends during weekends and holidays and recently found out that one of the students in a committed relationship was having sexual liaisons with someone else within the friend group, and that these liaisons were occurring in secret and in violation of the couple's relationship agreement. She wondered what, if anything, she should do about it. The class discussed her conflict and considered a variety of ethical approaches to help problem-solve the dilemma. These included concepts such as the social contract, egoism, utilitarianism, and absolute moral rules. The class also discussed Catholic social and ethical teachings. The student created a plan to discuss her concerns with the offending party and mapped out some ideas for resolution.

These examples offer the types of ethical dilemmas college students frequently confront and wish to receive feedback on and discuss. Students are offered informed consent about the limits of confidentiality in disclosing ethical issues in class. For example, disclosure regarding serious and immediate danger to self or others, as well as issues pertaining to child abuse or neglect, cannot be held in confidence according to state laws. As various ethical principles are used to help problem-solve these ethical issues and conflicts, they often all provide an energized way to introduce the academic topic of the day. Students typically enjoy using the tools of ethical decision-making to consider and then select an ethical course of action in their personal lives and the lives of their peers. Once they are comfortable in doing so, they feel better equipped to engage larger societal problems in an academic yet practical manner. These brief discussions at the beginning of class perhaps whet the whistles of students for further conversation about the assigned readings for the day and the topics that are featured each week.

Ethics through an Adaptable Catholic Lens

Catholic and Jesuit principles can easily be woven into any of these ethical decision-making discussions and topics. For example, strategies about dealing with conflict and disagreements through the lens of seeing God in all things and people, and treating each person with dignity and respect, are often integrated into class discussions. Managing interpersonal conflict with accommodation, humility, and the expectation of goodness also is helpful in discussing ethical challenges. The four Ds (discovery, detachment, discernment, and direction) model of reflection and discernment[5] is frequently used to structure our decision-making strategies for ethical resolutions. Catholic and Jesuit principles can also be used to further consider ethical challenges in psychology and related fields. For example, highlighting a respect for and the dignity of all people is highlighted in the American Psychological Association's Code of Ethics (Principle E) as well as within Catholic social teaching.

Although Santa Clara is a Catholic university, about half of the students enrolled are not Catholic, and the university works hard to be inclusive and embrace students from all faith traditions and those with no faith tradition. Therefore, while Catholic themes, principles, and strategies might be used in class, they are presented in a manner that strives to be inclusive and not off-putting to non-Catholics. Many of the Catholic themes and principles can easily be made to be more generalizable, inclusive, and even secular. For example, "seeing God in all things" could easily translate into "seeing the sacred in all things." The four Ds of decision-making can also be easily secularized to avoid references to God's will or calling. Thus, strategies that might originate in the Catholic sphere can be adapted

5. Thomas G. Plante, "The 4 Ds: Using Ignatian Spirituality in Secular Psychotherapy and Beyond," *Spirituality in Clinical Practice* 4, no. 1 (2017): 74.

and secularized to appeal to Catholics and non-Catholics alike. Similar to both mindfulness and yoga that originated within Eastern religious traditions, they can be adapted to appeal to everyone, regardless of their spiritual or religious interests and traditions.

Conclusion

The state of the world is troubled, and at the heart of all of our troubles are problems with ethical decision-making. The tension between acting for the common good versus our own selfish interests is a balancing act, but it seems that egoism often rules the day. College students, and everyone else, could likely benefit from training and reflection in ethical decision-making, seeking to develop thoughtful and tried-and-true tools for considering and acting on ethical challenges, both small and large. Catholic universities and other faith-based institution of higher learning can be at the forefront of offering quality ethics courses for all of their students. The Ethics in Psychology course at Santa Clara University is one of many and can be used as a template at other universities, religious or secular. Certainly, in our current cultural and societal climate, more training on ethics is better than less. The future of the planet may depend on it.

Acknowledging What Is While Moving Toward What Could Be in Teaching Perspectives on Social Justice

Anne Pitsch Santiago
University of Portland

I was born on Good Friday, raised Catholic, and educated in Catholic schools. Because of this, I playfully asserted that I was a Good Friday Catholic. Suffering was something that deeply resonated with me, and it led me to Catholic social teaching (CST). What I often struggled with in this world that bombards us with news of war, disaster, and disagreement was the resurrection, the hope, the Good News. I sensed the potential of humanity, but I was so often disappointed in how we treated one another. I remain disappointed, but I've come to understand that part of my faith journey has been to let go of my ego and realize that humans are much more complex than the simple good-bad dichotomy allows for. Wrestling with the messiness of the human condition is what attracted me to higher education as a student, and it continues to intrigue me as a professor of political science. My growth as a teacher has led to a change in attitude: from dwelling on the problems to teaching from a place of hope and possibility. One of my goals as a professor is to foster curiosity in my students. Curiosity leads to wonder and creates a space in which students can develop empathy and care for one another, even those they disagree with or who have different worldviews from their own. Curiosity allows for grace and hope, essential Catholic virtues necessary when exploring issues of social injustice.

Students need not be Catholic or religious to encounter grace and hope. As Fr. Michael J. Himes explains, "Catholic liturgy is a lifelong pedagogy to bring us to see what is there, to behold what is always present, in the conviction that if we truly see and fully appreciate what is there, whether we use the language or not, we will be encountering grace. We will see the love which undergirds all that exists."[1] Whether or not students have a faith community or profess a particular religion, they seek meaning in their lives. As educators in Catholic institutions, we help students discern meaning, and in teaching social justice, I must balance the prophetic and sacramental imaginations to explore both what is and to imagine what could be. This essay offers examples of specific assignments and pedagogy I employ in a course called "Perspectives on Social Justice" that lead to thinking rigorously and reflectively about issues that matter in our society. With some modification, these strategies are portable to any discipline that engages students with our complex world.

Teaching Social Justice

Catholic social teaching is a structured framework that provides guidance for Catholics on how to understand their role as Christians within a flawed society. I attended a Catholic college, where I learned a robust theology that explored CST. I also attended college during the waning years of the Cold War and started learning about the United States' less-than-ethical foreign policy. For example, our government overthrew several governments in Latin America (including Guatemala and Chile) and provided weapons to many more "anti-communist" regimes. The United States funded the Contras of Nicaragua and the El Salvadoran death squads who murdered many people, including four American nuns. The United States took a utilitarian approach to morality: justifying something terrible (invading, arming, and supporting "freedom fighters") by claiming a greater good (protecting citizens against the potential spread of communism) for a greater number: being the shining light of democracy to the world. CST rejects a utilitarian approach, instead

1. Michael J. Himes, "Finding God in All Things: A Sacramental Worldview and Its Effects," in *Becoming Beholders: Cultivating Sacramental Imagination and Actions in College Classrooms*, ed. Karen E. Eifler and Thomas M. Landy (Collegeville, MN: Liturgical Press, 2014), 14.

challenging its adherents, as individuals and collectively, to prioritize the most vulnerable within society.

Unfortunately, issues of social justice have become highly politicized. In this atmosphere, there is rarely the space to explore the "why" behind the "what" of people's beliefs. Partisans of every stripe too often resort to simple slogans and lack a willingness to have nuanced dialogue on critical topics or to compromise on policy. One way to overcome this and to unpack complexity is to present several frameworks for understanding injustice that explore underlying values and beliefs. All cultures and faith traditions have frameworks for understanding what is just and unjust. Giving students multiple lenses through which to explore issues helps them to discern not only their own underlying beliefs, values, and ideals, but also helps them to understand why some people may not see those issues in the same way.

One way of thinking in political science is through levels of analysis. I explicitly focus on the tension between policies and incentive structures for the individual and the society because it is from this tension that many of our disputes arise. What might be good for me at the individual level can be bad for the community in which I live and vice versa. It may be in my interest to pretend to be ill rather than attend a jury summons, but that is not good for the community that relies on a large pool of willing jurors to empanel a jury of one's peers to support fairness. Through this analytical framework, students begin to wrestle with their own beliefs, identities, and experiences, and to understand how these individual characteristics are influenced by community and societal dynamics, which in turn can lead to a better grasp of the complexity of addressing injustice. At the end of each semester, I ask students to anonymously create a diagram of what they learned in the course. One student detailed their major takeaways including "complexity and intersectionality of social justice issues" and "social justice is and will always be a work in progress, not a finished product." All of their diagrams are always insightful and help me continually improve the course.

Teaching the Prophetic and Sacramental Imaginations

The basic principles of CST are rooted in gospel values; among its pillars are human dignity, solidarity, and subsidiarity. There is an assumption of interconnectedness between the major CST themes: life and dignity of the human person; call to family, community and participation; rights and responsibilities; option for the poor and vulnerable; the dignity of work and the rights of workers; solidarity; and care for God's creation.[2] Individuals are social creatures who must shape their societies to allow individuals to live with dignity, uplifting the most vulnerable in society and encouraging solidarity with one another.

Theologian Matt Eggemeier posits Catholicism as an invitation to see reality in a particular way, through both prophetic and sacramental lenses.[3] The prophetic sees the suffering world and responds to it with outrage, anger, and protest. It criticizes what is, imagines what could be, and works for change.[4] The sacramental recognizes that beauty, grace, and wonder are always available to us in all aspects of life because God is present in all things.[5] Identifying what needs to change and the interconnectedness of all components of injustice is usually the easy part, but imagining a different future is taxing. Embracing both prophetic and sacramental lenses allows students to engage in an authentically Catholic way of understanding the world. I encourage students to acknowledge but not get stuck in despair, dualisms, and internalizing injustice. In embracing that "both/and" approach, we must call out injustice *and* work toward transformation to create better societies for all, while also remaining open to wonder, love, and hope because everything is graced. We receive grace even in our flawed actions. In this course, students work toward the sacramental from the despair of the prophetic through three assignments: a reflective essay on their beliefs, a book review, and a policy paper.

Assignment 1: How beliefs shape frameworks of social justice

After listening to lectures on CST, reviewing secular approaches to social justice,[6] hearing guest speakers illuminating Hindu and Jewish

2. The USCCB (https://www.usccb.org/beliefs-and-teachings/what-we-believe/catholic-social-teaching/seven-themes-of-catholic-social-teaching) offers these seven major themes, while other Catholic institutions, for example, the University of St. Michael's College at the University of Toronto (https://stmikes.utoronto.ca/wp-content/uploads/2020/07/180-Catholic-Teaching-v2.pdf), have other ways of organizing the same principles.

3. Matt Eggemeier, "Prophetic Imagination in a Suffering World," Plenary Presentation at Collegium (June 16–17, 2024).

4. Ibid.

5. Ibid.

6. Secular approaches are also rooted in beliefs. While these beliefs may have nothing to do with the religious or spiritual, secular approaches articulate faith in something, be

perspectives, and reading Buddhist and Islamic scholarly writings, students are asked to consider their own frameworks of social justice and to compare and contrast their own beliefs with other belief systems they encountered. The assignment reads:

> In a five- to seven-page paper, compare and contrast at least three different perspectives on social justice that were introduced in weeks 2 and 3 (Judaism, Hinduism, Islam, Catholicism, Buddhism, secularism). Think about the tensions between individuals and groups when it comes to these perspectives on justice/social justice and the ways that societies come to develop their conceptualizations of justice. Think about what influences how we know what is right and what is wrong.

I also provide students a grading rubric and guiding questions such as: What are the similarities and differences between the perspectives? How do they align with your own conceptualization of social justice?

Students begin to understand how people of different faith traditions view injustice while reflecting on what they value and believe. One student stated,

> To delve into my own personal social justice framework, it is crucial to highlight that my culture, upbringing, faith, and passions influence my framework. My background as a child of immigrants, an ex-Catholic, and an environmental and political scientist constantly informs my view of social justice. So, my social justice framework's golden rule states: act in equitable and compassionate ways that uplift, empower, protect, and foster a thriving community. While this is a boiled-down version of my social justice framework, expanding it would reveal five central values, which include generosity, accessibility, learning, solidarity, and compassion.

This assignment illuminates that many core values of social justice are found across faith traditions and that living these values is daunting. Another student wrote, "Religion and social justice often parallel and

---

it belief that humans have the capacity to change or that justice necessitates privileging the disenfranchised to restructure society.

perpetuate the same motives of diversity, inclusion, and the fight for the common good. Within Buddhism, Judaism, and Christianity, the most fundamental teachings align with the universal principles of social justice and encourage followers to live with compassion, love, and kindness. It is therefore not the difference in religious perspectives that combats justice but instead the exploitation of religious principles [by human actors]."

These essays demonstrate comprehension of how belief systems shape perceptions of social justice, including one's own. Students articulate ideals of belief systems, identify their similarities and differences, and recognize how humans who profess these ideals often fall short. Students are most sensitive and critical when it comes to the religion in which they were raised. Through focused comparisons, students identify elements of both the prophetic (recognizing injustice and its underlying causes) and sacramental (recognizing the grace and hope in the shared goals of different faith traditions), while also engaging in personal discernment. It is clear from the term-end diagram reflections that students appreciate and find meaningful the opportunity to explore similarities and differences in how justice is defined across religious traditions.

Assignment 2: Reflecting on the self and the other

Mark Yaconelli asserts that storytelling is the key to understanding "the other." He writes, "[T]he honest listening and telling of personal experiences naturally endears us to one another. The illusion of separateness dissipates, and we see ourselves in one another's story. When that happens, we are no longer able to demonize, ridicule, oppress, or neglect the other."[7] Early in the semester, students choose a memoir of any author who does not share their dominant identities and then write a reflective essay. Part of the assignment's prompt reads: "The purpose of the book review is to try to understand the experiences and ideas that shaped the author. Think about what the author has to say about issues of social justice within the context of their personal stories. How does their worldview align with or diverge from your own ideas?" This assignment seeks to cultivate understanding of "the other" and to recognize that humans are graced, even as we experience hardship and injustice.

7. Mark Yaconelli, *Between the Listening and the Telling: How Stories Can Save Us* (Minneapolis: Broadleaf Books, 2022), 10.

Before students choose their books, we view a TED talk by author Chimamanda Ngozi Adichie.[8] Adichie expertly relays that anytime we think we understand "the other" because we have read something by them, know something about their experiences or identities, or have a positive or negative encounter with them, we should step back and recognize that each individual is a complex, multifaceted person who is more than the sum of her parts. None of us is understood through a single story. In asking students to read and reflect on another's story, they must recognize that they are encountering a mere snippet of another person's life. Such an encounter demands humility.

Yaconelli's belief in the power of stories reflects the prophetic and sacramental imaginations. There is beauty and grace in vulnerably sharing stories of our struggles. Yaconelli asserts, "Every life holds beauty. Every life encounters suffering. Every life is a struggle to claim dignity and worth. And each of us has lived a story worth telling."[9] One student insightfully reflected, "In an academic setting, conversations based around theory can easily become speculatory and lack human grounding, especially when the topic is rooted in lived experiences that are inaccessible to those having the discussion." Through these encounters, we develop empathy and understanding.

After graduating, Rick, a former student in the Perspectives on Social Justice course, worked as a volunteer intake coordinator at Northwest Immigrant Rights Project in Wenatchee, Washington. In a newsletter article, Rick affirmed what Yaconelli and this volunteer assert: storytelling is important because it brings one into solidarity with others, stating,

> When I have a particularly sensitive intake, my heart both *shatters and repairs* [emphasis added] as the narrative explains the perilous journey all the way to my office in Wenatchee where we are trying to help the client move on from their persecution. . . . I see [this] nonprofit as in the business of creating. Creating security through one's immigration status, creating livelihood through work authorization, but most importantly, creating peace of mind for clients who

8. Chimamanda Ngozi Adichie, "The Danger of a Single Story," *TEDGlobal*, July 2009, video, 18:32, https://www.ted.com/talks/chimamanda_ngozi_adichie_the_danger_of_a_single_story.

9. Yaconelli, *Between the Listening*, 14.

> have the odds systematically stacked against them. We record the stories of those who need a voice, because the world can be extremely unfair, and we believe that everyone, especially the most vulnerable, should have the chance to live a secure and dignified life.[10]

Rick's description connected the course's dots, beautifully expressing the fundamental interconnectedness of the prophetic and the sacramental in social justice work. I hope that all my students, in whatever work they pursue, can reach the same level of sensitivity, grace, and solidarity as Rick has as an immigrant rights advocate.

Students experience the prophetic dimension through stories of those who have struggled because of their marginalized identities. This approach demands that students ponder their own place in the world and sit in solidarity with the storyteller. Yet, Yaconelli poignantly asserts, "Stories are designed to move us, to inspire us to act;"[11] this assignment propels students along the path of discernment about where and how to engage in creating a world that is more just. Stories are a powerful tool of encountering the sacramental while inspiring a prophetic call to action. Demonstrating the power of encountering another's story, one student wrote in their assignment, "This book has pushed me even further to get comfortable in the uncomfortable" while a second wrote, "This book was the pinnacle shift for me: 'we are more than the worst thing we have ever done' [quoting Bryan Stevenson, author of *Just Mercy*]." Students were truly transformed through story.

Assignment 3: Imagining solutions

As I argued previously, it is necessary to transition beyond the despair that comes from uncovering the layers and causes of injustice. The final assignment focuses on designing a policy proposal to address a specific injustice. While the policy paper assignment is important in demonstrating potential steps towards solutions, the key learning outcome is fulfilled through encounter. In spring 2024, I recruited seven alums who had taken this course and asked them to share their career journeys to inspire current students to imagine the possibilities of working for greater

10. *JVC Northwest Newsletter*, Spring 2019, 63, no. 1.

11. Yaconelli, *Between the Listening*, 104.

social justice after graduation. These professionals were working in environmental law, health and education policy development, activism in Guam's independence movement, civil rights lobbying, local public service, and legal activism. Each brought their own stories, frameworks of social justice, and perspectives on how college shaped their career paths. In the final course evaluation, many students were enthusiastic about these guest speakers. "I have gained a much broader understanding of social justice in the US and a variety of ways in which I can be an effective mode of change post-grad," and "It was really interesting to hear from people out in the real world (and they were in our positions just a few years ago)," represent the appreciation students had about encounters with graduates working in social justice arenas.

My former students bring sacramental grace, love, and hope to the classroom, even as they exercise their prophetic voices. Through these encounters, current students begin to see how their Catholic education helps to cultivate a commitment to the common good. The alums contributed a wide range of approaches to their work. Joshua, after working on social justice issues in Portland, moved home to dedicate his life to independence for Guam. He articulated the very values that the US espouses as the reasons Guam should be free, arguing especially that the US military presence has made Guam a target of power politics and put the island environmentally at risk because of warships, missiles, and US personnel. Lydia, an environmental lawyer, asserted that the Perspectives on Social Justice class allowed her to imagine herself doing social justice work. The willingness of these former students to return to their school is a testament to the education they received and the relationships they formed. This is the sacred work we do as an institution, and there is no greater reward than seeing former students succeeding. This encounter strategy of inviting alums into the classroom is portable to all our institutions.

Conclusion

My journey of transitioning to a more hopeful way of teaching social justice and creating varied pedagogical tools and assignments translates to many different disciplines. I intentionally combine the prophetic and sacramental imaginations in my pedagogy. Students are encouraged to be intentional in their choices of topics, to work in teams and network with those who are engaged in social justice work, and to ask questions and think creatively about solutions while taking care of themselves as social justice advocates. bell hooks describes maintaining hope while working towards greater justice: "When we turn our gaze away from all that has not happened, we can see more clearly the enormous changes individuals have made in just a short space of time, the movement from slavery to freedom, from sexism to feminism, from discrimination to greater openness. All these incredible movements for social justice succeeded when they evoked an ethic of love rooted in the embrace of the spirit. It is crucial for spiritual nourishment that we all attend to what works even as we understand the need to continue to resist."[12]

Catholic institutions must inspire our students to help create a better world. My former students demonstrate an ethos of hope through their social justice work. The authors that students read inspire thoughtful reflection. Engagement with multiple religious traditions helps transform binary thinking to embracing commonalities. Pope Francis, in his papal document *Spes Non Confundit* (Hope Does Not Disappoint) declares, "We need to recognize the immense goodness present in our world, lest we be tempted to think ourselves overwhelmed by evil and violence," while he also exhorts that "we are called to be tangible signs of hope for those of our brothers and sisters who experience hardship of any kind."[13] Our work is one of both/and: prophetically decrying injustice while also embracing the grace, hope, and love that come from sacramental encounters. Students are ready to embrace their own roles in creating a more just world, and our role as educators is to show them multiple pathways to a more hopeful future.

12. bell hooks, *Teaching Community: A Pedagogy of Hope* (New York: Routledge, 2003), 183.

13. Quoted in Gerard O'Connell, "Hope Is the Central Message of Pope Francis' Decree for Jubilee Year 2025," *America Magazine*, May 9, 2024, https://www.americamagazine.org/faith/2024/05/09/pope-francis-jubiliee-year-2025-247898.

Humanizing the Humanities

Bridging Curriculum and Community through Story Work

Deogratias Fikiri, SJ, and Sarah Wadsworth
Marquette University

Scene: Early September, a beautiful, late-summer afternoon. In a seminar room overlooking Lake Michigan, a mix of graduate students, advanced undergraduates, faculty, and leaders from an array of community organizations have gathered at the Center for Twenty-First Century Studies on the University of Wisconsin–Milwaukee (UWM) campus. With introductions accomplished, pairs consisting of a student and a mentor from one of the community organizations form to begin a yearlong journey to collaboratively produce a project that will share the story of the organization and the people it serves. The overarching goal is to retell the story of the city as a patchwork of community stories from the ground up. The atmosphere in the room is charged with excitement about this collective vision and sense of purpose.

The scene above refers to the orientation to the Story Experience Program, a joint endeavor between Marquette University and the University of Wisconsin–Milwaukee in which students and community partners collaborate to co-create the stories of their organizations. The program was the brainchild of Dr. Anne Basting (UWM), who has a distinguished history of developing innovative arts-based collaborations.[1] In recent years, Basting had introduced a Student Artists-in-Residence program, in which students used their training in the arts to tell community stories through creative forms of expression. To scale up this model to serve more organizations and students, Basting built on existing relationships with community partners while inviting students from all disciplines and joining forces with the Center for the Advancement of the Humanities at Marquette University. Now, as the program entered its second year, a further refinement, ignited by a cross-campus grant aimed at addressing poverty in Milwaukee, had drawn a cohort of students from both campuses. To kick off the orientation, faculty leading the program had brought the students and their mentors together to get better acquainted, participate in an "asset mapping" workshop, and begin to define common goals.

The Story Experience began at Marquette as a pair of independent studies, a format suitable for its pilot year. It became clear, however, that sustainability rested on situating the program within an approved course. The solution was to design a practice-based "shell," or practicum, in which experiential learners divided their time between "field work" and seminars organized around readings, guest speakers, and writing assignments. One key to success was gathering students whose internships, placements, and projects had a family resemblance to one another and then designing a unifying curriculum around common goals. In practical terms, this meant the class consisted of Story Experience students ("Story Fellows" for short), publishing interns, student editors of the campus literary magazine, and a collective of student writers producing an internal newsletter. In the second semester, two students took on the additional role of designing and producing an e-book documenting and reflecting on the story projects. What all these activities had in common could be conceived as bringing to light texts or "stories," whether poems, fiction, creative nonfiction, artwork, monographs, personal narratives, feature stories, interviews, or something else, and shepherding them through the stages leading toward some form of public release. This overarching purpose defined the arc of the two-semester sequence, which proceeded from introductions, asset mapping, and goal setting to entering a community with humility; listening and observing; seeking, inviting, and

1. See, for example, Anne Basting, Maureen Towey, and Ellie Rose, eds., *The Penelope Project: An Arts-Based Odyssey to Change Elder Care* (University of Iowa Press, 2016).

gathering; vetting and selecting; critiquing, offering feedback, and editing; designing, producing, and presenting; publicizing; and archiving.

In this chapter we evoke the transformative potential of the Ignatian pedagogical paradigm (IPP), encapsulated in the key words context, experience, reflection, action, and evaluation, to explore what happens when students and community members work together to create, celebrate, and preserve community stories. In the first section, we provide context for the program, focusing on the need to bridge the gap between traditional humanistic study and the application of skills and knowledge developed in humanities classrooms to the broader environments in which our universities exist. In the second section, narrated from a student perspective, we turn to the experience of the program to convey a sense of what it was like to take the course. The third section, presented from an instructor perspective, focuses on how the course integrated reflection, and the fourth section highlights action. Finally, we consider the challenges of establishing and sustaining such a program and evaluate its potential to help shift humanities education from detached observation and analysis in classrooms that function as "textual labs" to participation and partnership with diverse, underrepresented, and under-resourced communities beyond the university.

Context: The "Crisis in the Humanities" and the Crises in Our Communities

As the last twenty years have shown, the humanities are not immune to the doom that is part of the prophetic imagination. Under increasing institutional pressures, humanities requirements in core curricula have been reduced, programs phased out, majors eliminated, and entire departments shut down. The humanities are often overshadowed by STEM disciplines, undermined by technological innovations such as AI, and undercut by an increasing emphasis on specialized vocational training within four-year colleges and universities. At the same time, pressures on students send a strong message that their course of study should be instrumental and identifiable with a specific career.[2] Yet efforts to address

2. The Modern Language Association of America report of 2024 on "Career Preparation and Outcomes" challenges misconceptions and misleading assumptions about the employability of humanities majors in general. See also Kenneth L. Woodward, "The End of Joy in College Education," *America Magazine*, January 29, 2024, https://www.america

what is often perceived as a failure of the humanities to meet contemporary curricular and economic needs can coalesce meaningfully to address societal injustices. Programs like the Story Experience provide opportunities for students to develop and apply skills and knowledge cultivated in humanities classrooms, heightening their sense of who they are and how they can become catalysts for change.

From a student perspective, Ean Hill argues that although the humanities and liberal arts are central to American culture and democracy, their future is worrisome. Yet, Hill maintains, society cannot function by developing only technical skills at universities and colleges. Thus, higher education has the responsibility to maintain the liberal arts curriculum for the betterment of society while adopting necessary changes.[3] Danielle Zito states that the humanities are "shrinking but not dying" because students are still interested in the humanities; the problem is not in the liberal arts curriculum itself but rather in the "natural self-interest of individuals reaping the economic benefits of the new economy."[4] As Victor Hanson points out, if yesterday the debate was about the death of the humanities, today it is about "whether college itself is worth attending. Will earning a bachelor's degree ensure greater lifetime earnings than bypassing college altogether?"[5] Amid these debates, John Petillo, president of Sacred Heart University, articulates a vision that lies at the heart of the Story Experience when he says that the university should not "lose the richness of the liberal arts and humanities" even as they "prepare students for life out there."[6]

---

magazine.org/faith/2024/01/29/college-education-vocation-profession-247033, and "The Labor Market for Recent College Graduates," accessed February 8, 2024, https://www.newyorkfed.org/research/college-labor-market#--:explore:unemployment.

3. Ean Hill, "The Decline of the Liberal Arts," *Colgate Maroon-News*, December 8, 2023, https://thecolgatemaroonnews.com/46941/commentary/the-decline-of-the-liberal-arts/.

4. Danielle Zito, "The Decline of Liberal Arts and Humanities," *Wall Street Journal*, March 28, 2023, https://www.wsj.com/articles/the-decline-of-liberal-arts-and-humanities-western-philosophy-college-students-major-degrees-progressive-conservative-odysseus-6f327963.

5. Victor Davis Hanson, "The Death of the Humanities," *Hoover Institution*, January 28, 2014, https://www.hoover.org/research/death-humanities.

6. Quoted in Jon Marcus, "Beer Making for Credit: Liberal Arts Colleges Add Career Tech," *Hechinger Report*, March 19, 2021, https://hechingerreport.org/some-academic-focused-colleges-are-adding-career-and-technical-training/.

In this rapidly evolving higher-educational landscape, bridging the gap between academic study and practical application is critical. Strategies to bridge this divide include valuing theoretical and applied research, developing flexible funding models, promoting interdisciplinary education, engaging with stakeholders, and fostering collaborative partnerships between community administrators and academic staff.[7] Enhancing humanities curricula to develop practical skills through project-based learning, internships, and community-engaged courses while maintaining the integrity of deep learning in the humanities enables students to apply theoretical and practical knowledge to real-world problems.[8]

The Story Experience Program offers one approach to bridging this gap while "humanizing the humanities" through sustained public engagement. In doing so, it encapsulates the ideal of Catholic liberal arts education, which, in the words of John Freeh, aims to form "one's greater humanity, over and above any career one might choose, and the ability to enter into dialogue with the great thinkers of the past and speak, analyze, read or assess reality around us."[9] It is also about discerning the path of working within a community while gaining skills required for a career. The program combines theoretical foundations introduced through academic readings with practical applications and real-world experiences. Working within their communities, students gain deeper insights into human experiences as they co-create meaningful narratives of resilience and resistance.

7. Paul Reitter and Chad Wellman, *Permanent Crisis: The Humanities in a Disenchanted Age* (Chicago: University of Chicago Press, 2021).

8. Donald Levine highlights the crisis that liberal arts face in the modern world by elucidating the historical development of liberal education and the need for reinvention through curricular and teaching methodologies. Thus, although there is a decline in the number of students in the humanities, there is also the potential for revival by reinventing curriculum and programs effectively for modern times. See Donald Nathan Levine, *Powers of the Mind: The Reinvention of Liberal Learning in America* (Chicago: University of Chicago Press, 2006).

9. Quoted in Sara Weissman, "A Rise in Hyperspecialized Catholic Colleges and Trade Schools," *Inside Higher Ed*, February 8, 2024, https://www.insidehighered.com/news/institutions/religious-colleges/2024/02/08/new-catholic-colleges-and-trade-schools-emerge.

Experience: Collaborating with/as Community

While service learning has deep roots and a broad reach at Marquette, the Story Experience Program offers something different: a year-long collaboration between a nonprofit organization with stories to tell and a student embedded within it. Similar in some ways to a project model of service learning in which groups of students "collaborate with community members to devise and implement a project,"[10] the Story Experience differs from it in important ways. First, in the Story Experience, each organization is typically matched with one student at a time, and the student is thoroughly integrated into the community over the duration of the academic year. Second, the project undertaken by the student is co-created with the community partner, with the student actively working alongside community members to gather stories and shape them into the final form. Third, while project-based service learning often engages students from pre-professional programs such as Business, Computer Science, and Engineering in ways that allow them to apply specialized technical or vocational skills in real-world settings, the Story Experience offers students opportunities to bring open-ended, humanities-based skills to bear on complex real-world problems. This is especially valuable because students of the humanities often underestimate the extent to which abstract critical thinking, effective oral and written communication, knowledge of history and culture, and a broad perspective on human experience translate to the workplace.

The Story Experience Program emphasizes that co-creating an organization's narrative requires profound experiential knowledge built on humility, trust, and extended engagement. Rather than completing set tasks, students collaborate with the community to design expansive projects that amplify existing or emerging community stories through a gradual process marked by mutual respect and shared leadership. Beyond the final product, the program values the journey in partnership and solidarity, which integrates the student's vocational and academic goals with meaningful contributions to the community.

Partnering organizations included residences and support systems for elders, food pantries, and organizations supporting city parks and recrea-

10. "Service Learning Models," Marquette University, accessed December 10, 2024, https://www.marquette.edu/service-learning/service-learning-models.php.

tion, fair housing practices, and youth with disabilities. Other placements involved a grant-funded collaboration involving public high schools, a college, and the public library to foster and preserve the stories of girls and young women, and a historic organization dedicated to the advancement of social justice in Milwaukee. Students were expected to devote five to six hours per week working in or with the community, observing its operations, getting to know its constituency, and collaborating with staff to develop their project. The remainder of the time dedicated to the course was devoted to shared readings, seminar meetings, and writing.

The Story Experience seeks to challenge and revise incomplete, biased, or harmful narratives by uncovering and celebrating the authentic stories of individuals and organizations that shape the city's identity and potential. At the end of the academic year, these stories are preserved and honored, fostering a deeper understanding of the city and its people. This collaborative project unites vision and action, cultivating students' skills and insights within and beyond the community. The partnership with Milwaukee Turners, a historic advocate for social justice, exemplifies this transformative process and its impact on both the organization and the students involved.

A Student Perspective by Deogratias Fikiri, SJ

My educational background has been in the liberal arts, but at some point, I wanted to break into the intricate interplay between theory and lived experiences. I needed a program to move me into a realm where intellectual exploration transcends the theoretical confines of academia, manifesting as a force of tangible impact. The Story Experience fed that hunger while creating strong relationships and coupling academic frameworks with practical skills in listening and engaging with the community.

The program began with an extraordinary retreat that transformed a typical orientation into the foundation of a vibrant community. Unlike traditional academic beginnings, the retreat fostered reflection, connection, and collaboration. Despite arriving slightly late and feeling a familiar twinge of uncertainty, I was immediately welcomed into a circle of stories and laughter, where icebreakers sparked meaningful connections among strangers. By mid-morning, the energy and purpose in the room made it clear that this was more than an introduction—it was the start of an inspiring learning experience and transformative journey.

Each of the two days of retreat greeted us with a bright, clear sky, as if the world itself was rooting for our success. Those were radiant days of navigating unfamiliar streets in search of new beginnings. The labyrinth of new surroundings, the challenge of finding parking and the right building and room—it was all part of the adventure. As I ventured onto the UWM campus for the first time and approached the retreat venue, a mix of curiosity and nerves bubbled up inside me, and I remembered an old African proverb: One should only attend a party if they have a friend to meet. Would I see familiar faces? Fortunately, what started as a foreign experience ended up in meaningful and lasting friendship.

The retreat was a masterfully crafted introduction to the Story Experience, transcending logistics to focus on self-discovery and collective potential. What began in uncertainty among strangers evolved into a transformative experience of connection, shared values, and purposeful anticipation. Through reflective exercises, storytelling workshops, guest speakers, and guided discussions, every moment felt intentional and grounding. Mentors inspired new perspectives, and goal-setting expanded beyond academic boundaries to embrace a broader vision. By day's end, the mystery of the unknown gave way to a profound sense of belonging, marking the retreat as the catalyst for an extraordinary journey ahead.

My work experience with Milwaukee Turners provided the kind of integration of theoretical knowledge with practical skills I was looking for. Engaging in sessions organized for Milwaukee Public Schools fostered a sense of belonging and empowerment. For example, participating in a first-aid program equipped me with essential emergency response skills. I also took part in a workshop series on mental wellness practices for one of the local high schools that provided valuable insights into holistic community care. Through discussions and activities, I gained a deeper understanding of mental health challenges and learned practical strategies for promoting well-being within community settings. From stress management techniques to encouraging resilience and self-care, these workshops equipped me with tools that I could immediately apply to support individuals facing mental health issues in diverse communities. Upon evaluation, it proved that bringing the community of learners together was even more beneficial to mental wellness than the content alone. Amid escalating social isolation and increasing mental health challenges at the college level, this kind of integration between a supportive community and college students assumes heightened significance.[11] These workshops allowed me to apply humanities-based skills in real-life scenarios, such as facilitating group discussions, which reinforced my learning and enhanced my professional capabilities.

By shifting from classroom instruction to direct engagement with individuals and communities, my journey as a Story Fellow transformed theoretical concepts into catalysts for social change. Over nine months, this immersive experience expanded my personal growth, both academically and professionally, as each week contributed to an evolving narrative of exploration, collaboration, and friendship as personal encounters and shared stories deepened my understanding of human experiences through crafting meaningful narratives that reflect the diversity of human life. My exploration of personal narratives through Milwaukee Turners' oral history project unearthed a compelling theme—the conception of liberal arts as a space where theory transforms into tangible life experience with lasting impact and a call to move from detached observation to engaged participation.

Fundamental to Ignatian pedagogy is the practice of reflecting on experience as a step toward action. If a program like the Story Experience can be thought of as a bridge between the academy and surrounding communities, then we might conceive of experience as the roadway we journey across, action as the ramparts or towers anchoring the bridge, and reflection as a continuous series of suspension cables lifting and supporting the entire structure. Reflection is "baked into" the model, intentionally figuring into the course design in two main sites: written field notes and a biweekly seminar with readings and occasional guest speakers.

An Instructor Perspective by Sarah Wadsworth, PhD

The majority of students' time in the course was spent working at placement sites or with partnering organizations, which enabled them to learn and practice skills specific to their project from mentors, supervisors, and peers. Seminars balanced readings relevant to each stage of the semester's arc, with check-ins in which each student shared positive

11. Robert Coles argues that stories and community involvement have therapeutic qualities for both the sharers and listeners by fostering a sense of support, human connection, healing, and understanding of one's personality. See Robert Coles, *The Call of Stories: Teaching and the Moral Imagination* (Boston: Houghton Mifflin, 1989).

experiences, accomplishments, and victories (joys) along with difficulties, obstacles, puzzles, or setbacks (challenges), which often benefited from group feedback. Guest speakers included individuals involved in various professional publishing and public storytelling endeavors.

While the seminars provided opportunities to reflect on the work informally and make immediate connections to readings, field notes, submitted biweekly, formalized the practice of writing up experiences while they were fresh and reflecting on their significance and implications over time. Students received a template that asked that they document their time spent working in or with their communities, or doing work specifically related to their semester goal; describe the experience as objectively as possible, including descriptions of surroundings, interactions, and details of the work; and write an extended reflection on the activities they described. These field notes proved to be rewarding as they allowed students to slow down, survey and synthesize their progress, identify and acknowledge difficulties, anticipate next steps, and step back to see the bigger picture to which they were contributing. At the same time, they gave instructors a window into the remarkable work students were doing beyond the classroom.

Over the course of the academic year, students developed a sustained practice of listening and observing attentively in order to document and reflect on their experiences through writing. Ideally, with repetition, the practice becomes ingrained, habitual: a way of encountering an environment actively and reencountering it through deliberate recollection in the context of discussions, readings, and other experiences. For students, this reflective practice led to recognition of accomplishments, an overall sense of progress and purpose, awareness of work that remained to be completed, increased clarity about how to prioritize tasks, and heightened appreciation of and gratitude toward those they encountered along the way. Reflection also helped them keep their "eyes on the prize": the project all their efforts were building toward, often in ways difficult to discern in the moment.

Action: Bridging the Gap between Classroom and Community

The Story Experience Program emphasizes the importance of moving beyond written narratives, data collection, and library research to co-create narratives with communities beyond our campuses. It underscores the power of meeting real people, listening to diverse voices marginalized by dominant narratives, and honoring their stories. The premise of the program is that relying solely on mediated research can never fully encapsulate the richness of a community's actual successes and failures. Rather than studying about a community, the call is to learn with the community, ensuring a more profound and accurate understanding of who they are as individuals and as a group. This community-centric approach challenges conventional academic barriers, demonstrating that impactful research can emerge when scholars actively engage with their community. As Clarence Karier argues, hidden narratives are those experiences and voices within the community that are marginalized in mainstream discourse and that the humanities have failed to humanize.[12] These hidden narratives contain the power of the community to represent experiences seldom displayed or brought to light. These stories of resilience, resistance, and survival carry educational values that should inform, challenge, and enrich the curriculum by offering a nuanced understanding of the community, challenging dominant narratives, and presenting alternative perspectives for a more inclusive culture, society, and history.

Once student-mentor pairs had conceptualized a project, set an end goal, and established a series of intermediate goals to serve as checkpoints, the student was ready to begin working towards the goal in a step-by-step fashion. What this looked like in practice varied greatly from student to student and organization to organization. After a month spent getting to know the organization, its mission, and members, students typically began conducting interviews with organization leaders, founders, clients, volunteers, or others in the community. Story projects took the form of public-facing narratives in various media: podcasts, newsletter articles, informational and interpretative signs, even cookbooks. Each individual production helped articulate the community's sense of itself, while collectively they recast the narrative of who we are as a city. Students documented the entire experience by creating the Milwaukee Stories e-book, with each project represented in a chapter that gave an overview of the organization, a project

12. Clarence J. Karier, "Humanizing the Humanities: Some Reflections on George Steiner's 'Brutal Paradox,'" *Journal of Aesthetic Education* 24, no. 2 (1990): 49–63, https://doi.org/10.2307/3332784.

description, illustrations, and a final reflection.[13] The community stories thus become part of a living library that can be extended indefinitely. The process whereby the students became part of the collective "we" rather than outsiders or mere observers was no less transformative than the process of rewriting the narrative of the city from the bottom up and the center out.

Hidden and marginalized narratives hold transformative power, fostering empathy, cultural awareness, resilience, and social justice. In many cases, the community holds the materials for the revitalization of the humanities as it carries from generation to generation traditions, languages, knowledge, and wisdom that cannot necessarily be discovered through traditional academic research. By amplifying the voices of marginalized communities, universities and civic leaders can inspire societal shifts toward greater social mobility and cohesion. Introducing such stories into classrooms challenges dominant narratives, empowering communities, restoring pride, and recognizing their vital role in shaping society. When students and individuals encounter diverse experiences, they cultivate the capacity to build a more just, understanding, and compassionate world.[14]

Evaluation

Despite its successes, there are challenges in conducting a program like the Story Experience. The greatest challenges facing the instructor, apart from ensuring the course "counts," involve recruitment, discerning and supporting the overall trajectory of multiple projects, and coordinating occasional combined class meetings and special events across campuses. The section below provides a student's perspective on how the program tested his ability to pivot, think outside the box, and collaborate effectively under pressure. These challenges, while potential obstacles, provided invaluable lessons in adaptability, creative problem-solving, and resilience.

A Student's Perspective by Deogratias Fikiri, SJ

The Story Experience Program was a crucible of growth, where obstacles became agents of transformation. Technical glitches in transcrip-

13. *Milwaukee Stories* is available at https://mkestories.raynordslab.org/1/.

14. Robert I. Gannon, *The Poor Old Liberal Arts* (New York: Farrar, Straus and Cudahy, 1961).

tion, once frustrating, became lessons in patience and problem-solving, sharpening the art of remaining flexible in the face of setbacks. The relentless demands of coordinating a diverse team with conflicting schedules brought to mind a symphony seeking harmony and taught me to find rhythm through adaptability, strategic delegation, and effective communication. Collaborating with individuals of varied backgrounds and perspectives created a kaleidoscope of wisdom, proving that true community flourishes in the union of diverse viewpoints. Each challenge added a brushstroke to the canvas of cultural preservation, illuminating the power of merging the theoretical and tangible with empathy. A tapestry of community story work and personal and professional evolution, the program equips students with the skills and vision to lead with purpose and integrity. Its strengths can be summarized as follows.

1. Empowerment through Storytelling

The program is not merely about documentation but also about empowerment. Through collaborations with organizations in the city, students encounter narratives that not only preserve cultural heritage but also challenge dominant discourses and amplify marginalized voices to catalyze social change. Participating in the building of stories and storytelling allows communities to reclaim agency and assert their identities in a society often characterized by silence and exclusion.

2. Collaboration and Mutual Growth

Central to the program's success is its emphasis on collaboration, fostering relationships among students, academic institutions, and diverse community groups. Working with the community, students develop adaptability, humility, and a deeper appreciation for diverse perspectives. In addition, students gain practical skills directly applicable to future careers. These experiences enhance not only professional competence but also the capacity to engage thoughtfully and effectively with diverse communities.

3. Remedy for AI

The Story Experience Program offers an antidote to technological overload and isolation by grounding education in authentic human connections and creativity. Collaborative person-to-person storytelling demands emotional depth, relational engagement, and an appreciation of cultural nuance and human contact. It affirms that the most profound knowledge comes not from artificial systems but from human connections, where students become active participants in a living archive of stories, cultivating relationships that transcend time and place, and where their expertise and empathy transform stories into authentic, resonant narratives. This program proves that no matter how advanced technology becomes, the most powerful and meaningful stories will always require the heart, insight, and hands of a human being.

4. Transformative Pedagogy for a Just Society

The Story Experience Program embodies a shift toward participatory education that humanizes learning and fosters social responsibility. It challenges traditional academic boundaries, promoting a pedagogy where storytelling becomes a tool for cultural preservation, establishing empathy, and advancing social justice. By bridging academic theory and community action, it positions students as agents of change, ready to address contemporary social issues with sensitivity, resilience, and a deep sense of purpose.

Conclusion

Suzanne Toton writes, "If the church is to speak God's word today, it must be prepared to speak God's prophetic word, a word of contrast that brings the reign of God to bear on the reality of the present order." Drawing on the work of Ignacio Ellacuría, SJ, she explains,

> From the location of the poor and marginalized, the church must ask itself what is the life-giving word that must be spoken in this particular, concrete situation? What words are required to pry open this situation to God's saving action? In short, what word from the church is needed to produce greater justice, greater compassion, greater peace, and greater hope in this particular situation?

At the same time, she points out, words are not enough. Instead, actions are needed "to participate in God's salvific work of redeeming the structures and systems of society." Toton cautions, however, that "[s]ocial change . . . rarely comes through individuals acting alone." Rather, "It comes through counter institutions . . . which mobilize, organize, amass power, apply pressure, and negotiate." It is entering into relationships of solidarity with such counter institutions that is "the key to transforming our colleges and universities into more effective instruments for justice." The Story Experience is an example of a program that can facilitate such relationships between Catholic higher education and community organizations working for justice. It offers a pedagogical structure for what Toton, building on Ellacuría's work, describes as "keeping new company, the company of not only the poor, but the poor *with* spirit and in daring to build a different kind of relationship with them, a relationship of genuine solidarity."[15]

15. Suzanne C. Toton, *Justice Education: From Service to Solidarity* (Milwaukee, WI: Marquette University Press, 2006), 14, 16, 73, 74, 76.

"grammar of justice, / syntax of mutual aid"

Cross-Disciplinary Pedagogies of Hopeful Action

Cynthia R. Wallace
St. Thomas More College

Denise Levertov's poem "Making Peace" opens with a demand for poets to give the world "imagination of peace, to oust the intense, familiar / *imagination of disaster*."[1] But Levertov's poetic persona resists the demand, and the poem unfolds as an argument for another way: peace not as the blueprint of a solitary poet but as a communal project, composed through shared practice. Levertov employs an insistent plural *we* throughout the poem, constructing a sustained metaphor of living-toward-peace as a mode of poetic making: "grammar of justice, / syntax of mutual aid."[2]

I return to this poem often as I consider what it means to invite students into clear-eyed attention to the world's suffering as well as a hopeful imagination of the world we might build together. I want to teach my students not just a "grammar of justice" but also "mutual aid," especially across the many diversities that shape my classes at St. Thomas More College (STM), a small, Catholic liberal arts college federated with the University of Saskatchewan. The Canadian model of federation allows religiously affiliated colleges to be administratively distinct but academically integrated within the public university. While some of my students

1. Denise Levertov, *Collected Poems* (New York: New Directions, 2017), 757.
2. Levertov, *Collected Poems*, 757.

register intentionally for a Catholic college's courses, most consider them public university courses incidentally taught in the STM building. The institutional structure results in a wide range of student perspectives on religion, politics, and social justice in most of my classes. This is especially true of the courses I teach in the English department, focused on women writers and feminist theory, life writing, and decolonizing literatures and theories. But it's also true in the classes I teach in Catholic Studies and our minor in Social Justice and the Common Good.

These courses offer ample opportunity to prophetically examine the world's past and present injustices, including many in which the church is implicated. So what can good news look like? How do we, in Levertov's words, find a "cadence of peace" and justice without becoming immobilized by sorrow? How do we hold both the truth of what is wrong in the world and the hope for what good we might make together without losing sight of either? And how do we find common cause together in classes shaped by widely varied student experiences and perspectives, especially given our increasingly polarized public life?

In this chapter, I describe some of the ways I invite students into a community of clarity about injustice and practices of hopeful action. I begin with a framework that borrows from philosopher-mystic-activist Simone Weil and theologian Walter Brueggemann to conceptualize both ethical attention to the world and hopeful imagination for its future. I then move into a discussion of practical strategies I employ in my classes, including course structures, classroom experiences, and assessment models. My hope is that these practices will offer sparks of recognition and possibility to readers in the humanities, social sciences, and beyond.

Weil and Brueggemann: Clarity and Hope

I do not need to tell you—or my students—that we bear witness to violence and injustice at an unprecedented scale, thanks to rapidly developing information technologies. Philosophers and sociologists have penned convincing studies of these realities, popularized in books like Douglas Rushkoff's *Team Human*,[3] Nicholas Carr's *The Shallows*,[4] Casey

3. Douglas Rushkoff, *Team Human* (New York: W. W. Norton, 2019).

4. Nicholas Carr, *The Shallows: What the Internet Is Doing to Our Brains* (New York: W. W. Norton, 2010).

Schwartz's *Attention: A Love Story*,[5] and many others. Our brains don't fully distinguish between directly experienced, observed, and imagined threats, and so our nervous systems are chronically activated, and much talk in recent years has addressed the rise of anxiety in modern society, especially among young people.

It's no wonder we want to look away. In many ways, we *need* to look away. I was born in the last generation to experience adolescence without smartphones. By contrast, my students' entire social, emotional, and intellectual lives are bound up with their networked devices, and one outcome is overwhelm from constant connection. At the same time, many are also *disconnected* from current events, as well as longer historical understandings. They are less likely to read long-form journalism and more likely to bring up a stance they heard about on TikTok. Many admit to being checked out of the news altogether.

My task is to invite students into a steady practice of seeing and understanding injustice so that they can respond to it, and in this challenge I find the philosopher-mystic-activist Simone Weil enormously helpful. Although Weil's lifetime (1909–1943) predated most of our most pressing information technologies, she offers clarity on our fundamental struggle to pay attention to suffering. In her essay "Human Personality," Weil claims that paying attention to radical suffering is enormously difficult: "Thought revolts from contemplating affliction, to the same degree that living flesh recoils from death."[6] She argues that we resist acknowledging others' affliction because it confronts us with the truth that we are also radically vulnerable.[7] We prefer the illusion of control and security.

Yet attention to a suffering other is the foundation of Weil's ethics: we must see the world as it truly is, including both its extraordinary beauty and its extraordinary suffering, in order to respond appropriately to it. As Weil explains in *Waiting for God*, the primary ethical imperative is paying attention to an afflicted other, asking them, "What are you going through?" and truly listening, then responding to the utmost of our ca-

5. Casey Schwartz, *Attention: A Love Story* (New York: Pantheon, 2020).

6. Simone Weil, "Human Personality," in *Simone Weil: An Anthology*, ed. Sîan Miles (New York: Grove Press, 1986), 65.

7. Weil, "Human Personality," 70.

pacity.[8] At the personal level, she argues that we are obligated to feed anyone we encounter who is hungry. But Weil's call isn't just to an ethic of private charity; at the societal level, she argues that justice looks like structuring a society in which "no harm is done" and where everyone's basic needs are fully met.[9]

What I find compelling in Weil, and helpful in our twenty-first-century moment, is this insistence on seeing what is wrong and taking responsibility where we can, at both the micro and macro levels. Weil helps me think about the kinds of countercultural disciplines it takes to pay this kind of attention to the world, not in a frantic, passive intake of a 24/7 news cycle but in a careful and clear-headed engagement. In the words of Levertov's poem, I suspect we need to consider "restructur[ing] the sentence our lives are making," slowing down and inviting "long pauses . . ."

When we begin to slow down and truly attend to the world's suffering in a sustained practice, we often find ourselves needing to grieve. On the topic of grief and its surprising connection to hope, I find inspiration in theologian Walter Brueggemann's work on the prophetic imagination. Brueggemann famously argues that the biblical tradition anchors hope for the future in remembrance of the past: in a Jewish or Christian framework, this means remembrance of God's faithful action. In his book *Like Fire in the Bones: Listening for the Prophetic Word in Jeremiah*, Brueggemann echoes Weil in claiming that we can't access true hope for the future without telling the truth about the past and the present: we're frequently in deep denial of all that is wrong and prefer risk management and certitude to admitting the wild truth of everything that needs to change.[10] He writes, "Prophetic spirituality is preoccupied now with the question: Is there a future? Can we hope, and if so, on what grounds?"[11] The grounds he offers, against our control-oriented culture, which seeks efficiency and assured outcomes before any effort, are *risk* and *lament*. Brueggemann suggests that a hope-filled imagination—one he links to

8. Simone Weil, *Waiting for God*, trans. Emma Craufurd (New York: Harper and Row, 1951), 115.

9. Weil, "Human Personality," 73.

10. Walter Brueggemann, *Like Fire in the Bones: Listening for the Prophetic Word in Jeremiah* (Minneapolis: Fortress Press, 2006), 69.

11. Brueggemann, *Fire in the Bones*, 166.

poetry—requires that we tell the truth about everything that is wrong, robustly grieve it, and open ourselves up to possibilities that might utterly surprise us. We are afraid of the unknown, both the unknown of our sorrow and rage and the unknown of a way forward that might ask us to live in new and unexpected ways. Concretely, I think of the lifestyle changes climate change increasingly demands of North Americans if we want a livable planet; I think of the cost of reparations to those harmed by church-run residential schools; I think of farmers' complicated feelings around Indigenous land-back movements. These are not abstract concerns. All of them require dramatic and even sacrificial change, and yet all of them could lead to more goodness and beauty in the world.

Brueggemann roots his vision in a Christian imagination of death and resurrection and in a vision of the church as gathered community. However, his suggested approach—remembering past successes, telling the truth about past and current wrongs, and collective hope in the possibility of surprise on the other side of risky action—is resonant with other recent scholar-activists' approaches, detailed in books like Joanna Macy and Chris Johnstone's *Active Hope*, which draws on Buddhism,[12] and Valarie Kaur's *See No Stranger*, which is rooted in Sikhism.[13] It also translates into a nonreligious framework in the writing of Rebecca Solnit. I often assign my students to read her essay "Hope is an Embrace of the Unknown," in which she cites Brueggemann to argue that while optimism is a banal false assurance that everything will work out, hope is a commitment to the possibility of a better future, rooted in collective action and fueled by remembrance of past collective wins.[14] In much of her work, as in the book *Hope in the Dark*, Solnit bears witness to moments in history where people have come together to achieve shared justice and flourishing, often in the wake of serious disaster.[15] Her work opens

12. Joanna Macy and Chris Johnstone, *Active Hope* (Novato, CA: New World Library, 2012).

13. Valarie Kaur, *See No Stranger: A Memoir and Manifesto of Revolutionary Love* (New York: Random House, 2020).

14. Rebecca Solnit, "Hope Is an Embrace of the Unknown," *Guardian*, July 15, 2016, https://www.theguardian.com/books/2016/jul/15/rebecca-solnit-hope-in-the-dark-new-essay-embrace-unknown.

15. Rebecca Solnit, *Hope in the Dark: Untold Stories, Wild Possibilities* (Chicago: Haymarket Books, 2016).

up Brueggemann's to a wider swath of nonreligious students, while her citation of Brueggemann reminds religiously affiliated students that they can anchor their perspectives in their spirituality as well as in a secular public ethic of collaborative justice.

Structuring Courses

By their nature, many of the courses that I teach include representations of diversity: gender, race, class, (dis)ability, religion, region, and historical particularity. Yet I am committed to building intersecting modes of diversity into all of my courses—in Life Writing and Introduction to Catholic Studies just as much as in Decolonizing Literatures and Theories or in my seminar in Postcolonial Women Writers. I do this not just to stage encounters with difference in my classes and to broaden our imaginations of the literary canon or the Catholic tradition, but also to offer marginalized students the opportunity to recognize themselves in the curriculum. Over and over, I've had a student tell me that this was the first time they saw their experiences reflected in assigned reading.

In these representations of diversity, though, I'm careful to balance accounts of suffering with those of strength and even joy. In part, this practice resists what Chimamanda Adichie influentially calls the "danger of the single story" about oppressed peoples, but it also avoids pushing students into frozen overwhelm.[16] In Introduction to Feminist Theory and Women Writers, for example, I carefully counterbalance readings that explicate harms against women with readings that showcase women's dignity, persistence, and activist successes. We read both Ida B. Wells-Barnett's classic work on lynching, bearing witness with her to gross injustice, and also selections of poetry by Lucille Clifton, Audre Lorde, and Alice Walker that embody Black women's strength. We read Crystos's powerful poem "I Walk in the History of My People," which outlines harms against Indigenous women and children but ends on the gripping line, "see / How I Am Still Walking." We read Adrienne Rich's excoriations of structural and personal

16. Chimamanda Ngozi Adichie, "The Danger of a Single Story," *TedGlobal*, July 2009, video, 18:32, https://www.ted.com/talks/chimamanda_ngozi_adichie_the_danger_of_a_single_story.

violence against women but also her celebrations of female friendship.[17] With Weil and Brueggemann, we are seeing clearly what is wrong in the world while also anchoring a sense of hopeful possibility in past strength.

I approach the counterbalance not just within classes but in the broader scope of the full curriculum. In recent years, I've planned ENG 111, a composition course focused on reading poetry, around the theme of joy, inspired by the poet Christian Wiman's anthology *Joy: 100 Poems*[18] and the poet Ross Gay's magnificent essay collection *Inciting Joy*.[19] I teach *many* courses centered on suffering and injustice, and for my own sake as well as that of my students', it makes sense to spend a term exploring joy at its most fulsome, which is to say communal, rooted in communion. I'm convinced this focus on joy helps serve as a ballast to help us "stay with the trouble," in Donna Haraway's words,[20] as we attempt to truly attend to suffering in other contexts.

The joy-focused composition class participates in another strategy I've increasingly turned to over the last decade, which is slowing the pace of my courses to allow time to think, discuss, and integrate the material. A cynical reading of this practice traces it to decreasing attention spans and capacity for reading, and I'll admit that these are real struggles in our student population. However, assigning fewer texts is another counter-balancing structure in a culture of speed and surface-level interactions. There's relief in a sense of spaciousness as we approach our texts and topics together more slowly, and I believe it increases students' capacity to do the hard work of close reading, paying attention to suffering, and grappling with complexity.

To further help us in these tasks, I work very hard to structure my course syllabi with intentional scaffolding. For example, in Life Writing we practice reading and discussing lower-stakes texts—like social media and classic biographies—before we move into memoirs of racial injus-

17. Many of these readings appear in Susan Archer Mann and Ashly Suzanne Patterson, *Reading Feminist Theory: From Modernity to Postmodernity* (Oxford: Oxford University Press, 2015).

18. Christian Wiman, *Joy: 100 Poems* (New Haven: Yale University Press, 2017).

19. Ross Gay, *Inciting Joy: Essays* (Chapel Hill, NC: Algonquin Books, 2022).

20. Donna J. Haraway, *Staying with the Trouble: Making Kin in the Chthulucene* (Durham, NC: Duke University Press, 2016).

tice, and we read about such injustices in a more distant cultural setting before applying these lessons to our own tenuous local social location. In Introduction to Catholic Studies, we begin with a sweeping historical overview that is painstakingly balanced in its truth-telling about both triumphs and harms in church history before moving into case studies of developments, such as monasticism and the Second Vatican Council, that reformed or revivified the church. These first two units prepare us for the term's second half, in which we discuss more recent and current challenges in the institution and its role in the world, including the sex abuse scandal and the outrage of Canada's residential school system, which until as recently as 1996 removed Indigenous children from their communities and cultures to inculcate colonial norms through a partnership of church and state. Importantly, we end with these current scandals of conscience only after we've done the work of shaping our imaginations to both criticize well and imagine what repentance and repair might begin to look like. I do not think there is a way to teach such a class in this context without doing this fraught work in a steady and intentional way.

Classroom Experiences

The assigned readings and course structure give rise to classroom experiences which I both carefully plan and adjust in the moment. In general, I am a dialogic instructor, preferring to offer shorter scaffolding lectures paired with open conversation. I seek to build a classroom environment of trust. Due to their topics, most of my classes require a blanket trigger warning, and some students make the choice to drop the class when they realize they don't have the current capacity to take on the subjects in a sustained manner. But one of my goals as a trauma-informed educator is to try to empower students to regulate themselves in such a way that they can maintain engagement with the material in a way that is safe for them.

I begin with strategies that are very basic and probably obvious, but that I mention here to draw out their significance. I work to get to know students *and to help them get to know one another*. One of their first assignments is a brief self-introduction note in our online course management software, in which I ask them to let me know any concerns or accommodations I should be confidentially aware of, along with their motivations for taking the course. In the classroom setting, I have students use folded name tents at their desks so I can call on them by name, both so they feel known and so they get to know one another's names. I take time in class to encourage students to exchange contact information to share notes in case of illness. I use ridiculous icebreakers to help us humanize one another, which sounds silly but relies on neuroscientific research that imagining an other's favorite foods can shift us into a more open relation. In a setting of polarization and loneliness, these small and pragmatic practices can dramatically alter the classroom culture.

In Life Writing, the course content allows me to take this priority still further by assigning paired biographies. I pair up students to interview each other, and each person writes a biographical profile of their partner. I have heard more than once that this assignment—which students often resist at first—led partners to their first real university friendship, even after several years in school. I think some of the challenge here has to do with the COVID-19 pandemic's long shadow, but I don't think that's the only factor limiting their social connections. I'm amazed at how grateful many have been for my insistence that they get to know one another.

This foundation of shared humanness helps us build capacity to do the hard work of studying the world's pain and discussing contentious questions. I increasingly seek to incorporate other trauma-informed strategies into the classroom to help students regulate themselves to access resilience and stamina, rather than shutting down. One such strategy came to an interdisciplinary course I teach called Cultivating Humanity when my friend, Dr. Mark Bigland-Pritchard, came to guest-lecture about the science of climate change. Climate is contentious in the province of Saskatchewan, where economic prosperity relies heavily on resource extraction and large-scale farming, and the news on climate has also been deeply unsettling in recent years. Mark showed up with photocopies of a detailed feeling wheel for the students. Originated by Dr. Gloria Willcox, the wheel offers basic emotions in its center, with two additional concentric layers of increasingly descriptive feelings.[21] Mark invited my students (and their instructor!) to keep the wheel in front of them dur-

21. Gloria Willcox, "The Feeling Wheel: A Tool for Expanding Awareness of Emotions and Increasing Spontaneity and Intimacy," *Transactional Analysis Journal* 12, no. 4 (1982), https://doi.org/10.1177/036215378201200411.

ing his presentation on the science of climate catastrophe to facilitate our emotional processing during the experience of looking at information we tend to avoid. This is an evidence-based strategy for emotional regulation: naming our feelings helps us to walk with them rather than shutting down in overwhelm, an insight I first learned not as a teacher, but as a parent while reading Daniel Siegel and Tina Payne Bryson's *The Whole-Brain Child*.[22] I encouraged the students to continue to use the wheel throughout the term as we discussed other difficult topics, such as the justice system, immigration, racism, and war.

Cultivating Humanity takes a topical approach to justice challenges and lends itself to trauma-informed classroom practices, but I borrow many strategies for the course from my work in other classrooms. For example, at one point during the term when the classroom discussion was very painful, unearthing stories of significant loss, I had us pause for three minutes just to breathe. I invited the class to settle our feet on the floor and feel our bodies supported by the floor and our chairs, then led us in a pattern of slow breathing. I had done this exercise in a previous class when the news of a horrific local accident had shaken everyone, offering not only a moment of silent witness-bearing but also a container for coming back into our bodies in the present. I felt the need for this moment as much as my students did, and it grounded us to carry on.

Emotional self-regulation and social connection are increasingly important to my teaching practice in ways I never would have foreseen even five years ago, and I understand them as a foundation that helps empower students to engage in the hard work of addressing social wrongs. However, I also want to use classroom experiences to help students envision paths forward. To that end, I've also started in-class journaling exercises, in which I invite students to think and write for a few minutes about what their own personal responsibility might be in light of an injustice we have discussed. I invite them to think at the micro and macro levels, considering possible individual practices, community connections, and advocacy opportunities they could undertake. I then invite students to report back in small groups and to the larger class, sparking one another's imaginations. In many cases, at least one student in the room will be connected

22. Daniel Siegel and Tina Payne Bryson, *The Whole-Brain Child* (New York: Bantam Books, 2012).

to an organization or initiative that other students were not yet aware of, and so these mini-brainstorming sessions become a setting of mutual invitation to action to which I can also supplement my own network of on-the-ground initiatives. I invite my students to set an intention about taking on one of these practices.

The final classroom experience I will mention is actually an out-of-classroom curricular experience, and, unlike the others, it relies heavily on the support of my college's excellent Engaged Learning Office. Whenever possible, I offer students the opportunity to engage in community service learning. These opportunities are often but not always paired with our class themes—in Life Writing, for example, students often volunteer at an assisted living facility, where they interview residents and co-create memoirs with these individuals. In other classes, the community service is connection with incarcerated individuals or newly arrived immigrants. I adjust assignments for students who choose this stream so that they can integrate their co-curricular learning into the work of the class. I have never had a student who chose this opportunity tell me they regret it: the experience typically introduces them to a wider array of neighbors and possibilities for their future work. It gives them a taste of the energy that comes from *doing something* in the world, which can be a powerful antidote to frozen overwhelm. Students frequently continue their volunteering beyond the end of the term.

Assessment as Responsive Practice

The final category I'll discuss here is assessment, which is another arena that allows us to invite students into a more active response to the injustices we've studied, rejecting an attitude of passive hopelessness. For the Community Service Learning stream, my students typically incorporate reflections on this experience in a modified term paper or final exam essay. Indeed, modifying such summative assignments is one of my more common strategies for building empowerment into the course experience.

In Introduction to Catholic Studies, I have experimented with shifting a traditional term paper into a research inquiry assignment modeled on the classic I-Search essays I was first introduced to in the late 1990s by some extraordinary high school English teachers. Students choose a topic that genuinely interests them within the scope of the class, completing a project that documents their process of brainstorming questions, choosing one, and researching it thoroughly throughout the term. The end product is not a final essay but rather a portfolio documenting their process of inquiry, ending with a summary of what they have learned about their topic, the process of research, and themselves, as well as what they would like to continue to learn. My hope is that this paper encourages my students to shift from assignment-completers to intrinsically motivated lifelong learners, one of the core values of the Jesuit education that formed me in graduate school. In Introduction to Catholic Studies, the project also allows students to take on subjects that have intrigued or troubled them—I've had students research health care ethics, the death penalty, the Crusades, contemporary monasticism, and the church's role in colonization, among other topics. The opportunity to choose widely and research intensively gives students agency, but it also helps them to develop a much more integrated ethical response to these issues and histories.

One year, in an English course on Transnational Literatures, we took the idea of active response even further. Realizing how impassioned this cohort was about forced migrancy and global inequalities, I offered them the opportunity to skip one of the exam essays if they engaged in an act of public creative response to our course material. Many students took me up on the offer: one copied out quotations from one of our texts about migrant agricultural laborers and attached them to snacks she offered in a student study lounge. Another wrote a letter to the editor of her hometown newspaper, quoting one of our novels, and the letter was published. Another student made stickers about fair trade economic practices and affixed them to chocolate bars in a grocery store! We had to talk later about how this was probably illegal, but it was wonderful to see students' energy poured into creative awareness-raising and advocacy actions.

In a senior seminar focused on women writers and activism, we discussed the benefits and risks of offering land acknowledgments at events, on syllabi, and in classrooms. Fourteen percent of our university's undergraduates self-declare as Indigenous, and we are shaped by the ongoing realities of Canada as a settler-colonial society with varying commitments to decolonization. One Cree student challenged the common practice of copying a single-sentence rote land acknowledgment used by the university: she noted that the most meaningful acknowledgments are personally crafted by individuals and smaller communities, locating ourselves in relation to the land we come from and currently inhabit and the First Peoples of those places. In response, I chose to include a question on our untimed, take-home final examination that invited students to craft a carefully considered personal land acknowledgment. This assessment—which I graded pass/fail for completion—arose at the intersections of our course content, our classroom community, and our situatedness in this particular place and time. It led to an actual change in the practices of many in class, including the land acknowledgments I use on my syllabi and in my email signature.

These integrative moments don't happen all the time, but when they do, it feels, to borrow again from Levertov, like a "vibration of light": a certain energy wells up in the space we co-create and *has somewhere to go*. So often, the structures of our educational institutions generate that energy and then abandon it in the dusty corners of our classrooms. My hope is always to cultivate an environment in which students can build the stamina and moral courage it takes to look at what is really happening in the world and seek to understand it, then to respond *together, in community*, making something out of the learning we are doing together.

Of course, the temptation is always business-as-usual—distraction, numbness, despair. At times it feels as though educators are up against nothing less than the entire structure of society, not just in its injustices but also in the habitual ways of being that disempower real engagement. It's no wonder the apostle Paul wrote about struggling not against flesh and blood but against "powers and principalities" (see Eph 6:12). But, with Weil and Levertov, I try to slow down and see not just the world's suffering but also its beauty; with Brueggemann and Solnit, I try to anchor my future hope in remembrance of these past classroom moments, sparkling with life and change. I remind myself, again and again, of Toni Morrison's insistence in the essay "No Place for Self-Pity, No Room for Fear," that eras of heightened injustice leave "no time for despair": "I know the world is bruised and bleeding, and though it is important not to ignore its pain, it is also critical to refuse to succumb to its malevolence."[23]

So I take a deep breath and plot out another syllabus. I pick up my purple grading pen and invite clearer communication and nuance with

23. Toni Morrison, "No Place for Self-Pity, No Room for Fear," *The Nation*, March 23, 2015, https://www.thenation.com/article/archive/no-place-self-pity-no-room-fear/.

as much tenderness as I can gather. I walk to the front of a new class, a little trembly with caffeine and first-day nerves, and as I look out into a sea of new faces, I try to really *see* them, to wonder what they are going through. I muster all the hope and courage I can find. We humans have built goodness together before; we're doing it all over the world, every day. And this is my prayer for each class I teach: Let us make goodness together, again.

List of Contributors

Rebecca Berrú Davis is assistant professor of theology at St. Catherine University in St. Paul, Minnesota. She graduated from the Graduate Theological Union in Berkeley, California, and she is interested in the intersections of art, faith, and justice to better understand the spiritual and religious expressions and lived faith practices of those located on the margins.

Elizabeth Boquet is professor of English and director of the Writing Center at Fairfield University in Fairfield, Connecticut. Her scholarly writing and creative nonfiction routinely engage her interests in life-writing and in the health humanities.

Jonathan M. Bowman is professor of communication and director of the Honors Program at the University of San Diego. He teaches about and conducts experimental research on human communication processes across a variety of interpersonal relationship contexts.

Susanna L. Cantu Gregory serves as an associate professor of religious studies at Clarke University and a spiritual director in Dubuque, Iowa.

Michael R. Carey is associate professor in the School of Leadership Studies at Gonzaga University. He has fifty years of teaching experience in Catholic schools on the elementary, secondary, undergraduate, and graduate levels of education.

T. M. Vanessa Chan-Devaere is assistant teaching professor in the Department of Psychology at the University of Notre Dame and a core contributor to the Neuroscience and Behavior major. She completed her PhD in psychology at the University of Toronto in 2020.

Christopher J. Cobb teaches English and environmental studies at Saint Mary's College in Notre Dame, Indiana, where he also directs the college's sustainable farm.

Ana Fonseca Conboy is associate professor of French at the College of Saint Benedict and Saint John's University in Minnesota. Her research interests include intercultural communicative competency and contemplative pedagogy, and she has successfully integrated mindfulness into curricula in study abroad programs and her courses.

Kimberly Rae Connor is faculty emerita at the University of San Francisco School of Management. She writes on religion and literature and Ignatian spirituality and is a spiritual director in the Ignatian tradition.

Jessika Crockett-Murphy is a Stonehill College alumna currently pursuing a master's in ministry and theology and a certificate in higher education at Villanova University. She wants to work in collegiate ministry and student leadership development, with a focus on queer students, women in ministry, and faith formation.

Esteban del Río is professor of communication and serves as director of the Frances G. Harpst Center for Catholic Thought and Culture at the University of San Diego.

Karen E. Eifler is director of Collegium, the national colloquy of faith and intellectual life, and professor emerita of education at the University of Portland. She co-edited this book's companion volume, *Becoming Beholders: Cultivating Sacramental Imagination and Actions in College Classrooms.*

Deogratias Fikiri, SJ, is a Jesuit priest from Congo-Kinshasa and a PhD student at Marquette University focusing on leadership and policy. All of his background and education have been in the liberal arts.

Kathleen M. Gallagher-Brau is a social anthropologist, former associate professor of graduate international relations (St. Mary's University, San Antonio), and Collegium mentor. Her work in Nepal focuses on marginalized communities and a desire to provide visibility and voice to people, stories, and struggles that might otherwise go unseen or unheard.

Hans Gustafson directs the Jay Phillips Center for Interreligious Studies in the College of Arts and Sciences at the University of St. Thomas (Minnesota), where he teaches courses in (inter)religious studies, theology, dialogue, and leadership. Recent books include *Everyday Wisdom: Interreligious Studies in a Pluralistic World* (Fortress, 2023) and *Everyday Encounters: Humanizing Dialogue in Theory and Practice* (Fortress, 2025).

Sandra L. Guzman-Foster is associate professor and director at the University of the Incarnate Word's Center for Teaching and Learning. Her expertise lies in technology's role in education, curriculum innovation, equity in education, inclusive excellence, and critical pedagogy. Her broad teaching experience underpins her commitment to inclusive, equitable education and transformative teaching methods.

Elizabeth Keenan teaches in the Social Work program at Southern Connecticut State University in New Haven. Her service and scholarship focus on infusing social justice across curriculum and social work practice. She is one of the founding leaders of CONECT: Congregations Organized for a New Connecticut and is an oblate (lay affiliate) with the sisters at St. Benedict's Monastery in St. Joseph, Minnesota.

Thomas Knestrict is professor of education at Xavier University in Cincinnati, Ohio. His research deals with using critical theory to deconstruct unjust systems in education. His latest book is entitled *Controlling Our Children*, available from Peter Lang Publishing.

Anna Lännström is professor of philosophy at Stonehill College, and her background is in ancient Greek philosophy. Her current research and teaching explore ways we can broaden philosophy to include insights from other traditions and disciplines and use philosophical reflection to help us live better lives.

Kala Mayer, PhD, MPH, RN, CNE, MCHES, NBC-HWC, is associate professor at the University of Portland School of Nursing, where she teaches courses in health promotion, nutrition, and population health. Her research focuses on community-driven participatory action, student-faculty collaboration, and advancing health equity through innovative nursing education and community-academic partnerships.

William (Bill) McDonough is professor emeritus of theology at St. Catherine University in Minnesota. He coordinates the university's *Initiative for Contemplative Discipleship*, in which trained spiritual directors teach contemplative practices in Christian congregations throughout the Twin Cities.

Nancy A. Michael earned her doctorate in neuroscience from the University of Minnesota in 2012. She joined the faculty at the University of Notre Dame in 2015 and currently serves as the co-director and director of education for the Neuroscience and Behavior major.

Rodger Narloch is professor of psychology and director of the Benedictine Institute at the College of Saint Benedict and Saint John's University. He is also an oblate with the Order of St. Benedict in Collegeville, Minnesota.

Thomas G. Plante is the Augustin Cardinal Bea, SJ, University Professor of Psychology, and, by courtesy, of religious studies at the Jesuit School of Theology at Santa Clara University. He directs the Applied Spirituality Institute and is a scholar-in-residence at the Markkula Center for Applied Ethics. An emeritus adjunct professor of psychiatry and behavioral sciences at the Stanford University School of Medicine, he maintains a private clinical practice as a licensed psychologist in Menlo Park, California.

Mary M. Doyle Roche is professor of religious studies at the College of the Holy Cross, where she teaches courses in Christian ethics, health and medical ethics, and the ethics of work and family life.

Anne Pitsch Santiago is associate professor of political science and global affairs and the Dundon-Berchtold Faculty Fellow for Constructive Dialogue at the University of Portland. A cradle Catholic, she has been teaching for twenty years, with a passion for Catholic social teaching and dialogue.

Richard W. Stackman is professor of organizational behavior and change and serves as the associate dean for graduate programs in the Masagung Graduate School of Management at the University of San Francisco. He is also the co-editor-in-chief for the *Journal of Management Inquiry*.

Dũng Q. Trần is associate professor in the School of Leadership Studies and an adjunct faculty member for both the PhD program in Leadership Studies as well as the MA program in Theology and Leadership at Gonzaga University. He had the privilege of co-editing *Servant-Leadership and Forgiveness: How Leaders Help Heal the Heart of the World* (SUNY Press).

Aaron Van Dyke is associate professor of chemistry and a spiritual director at Fairfield University in Connecticut. His undergraduate-driven research lab uses the tools of organic chemistry to study ribonucleic acid (RNA).

Sarah Wadsworth is professor of English at Marquette University, where she also serves as director of Marquette University Press.

Cynthia R. Wallace is associate professor of English and director of the Irene and Doug Schmeiser Centre for Faith, Reason, Peace, and Justice at St. Thomas More College, University of Saskatchewan, Canada. She is also the author of the books *Of Women Borne: A Literary Ethics of Suffering* (Columbia University Press, 2016) and *The Literary Afterlives of Simone Weil: Feminism, Justice, and the Challenge of Religion* (Columbia University Press, 2024).

Rachel Wheeler is associate professor at the University of Portland and secretary of the Society for the Study of Christian Spirituality. Her most recent book is *Radical Kinship: A Christian Ecospirituality* (Fortress Press).